STUDY GUIDE

Diana Denton
Ryerson Polytechnic University

Whitney Hoth
Ryerson Polytechnic University

Interpersonal Communications
Relating to Others

Second Canadian Edition

Steven A. Beebe
Susan J. Beebe
Mark V. Redmond
Terri M. Geerinck
Carol Milstone

Allyn and Bacon Canada
Scarborough, Ontario

Allyn and Bacon, Inc., Needham Heights, Massachusetts
Prentice-Hall, Inc., Upper Saddle River, New Jersey
Prentice-Hall International (UK) Limited, London
Prentice-Hall of Australia, Pty. Limited, Sydney
Prentice-Hall Hispanoamericana, S.A., Mexico City
Prentice-Hall of India Private Limited, New Delhi
Prentice-Hall of Japan, Inc., Tokyo
Simon & Schuster Southeast Asia Private Limited, Singapore
Editora Prentice-Hall do Brasil, Ltda., Rio de Janeiro

ISBN 0-205-31410-4

Acquisitions Editor: Dawn Lee
Developmental Editor: Karen Elliott
Production Editor: Sarah Dann
Production Coordinator: Wendy Moran

1 2 3 4 5 04 03 02 01 00

Printed and bound in Canada

Visit the Prentice Hall Canada Web site! Send us your comments, browse our catalogues, and more.
www.phcanada.com Or reach us through e-mail at **phcinfo_pubcanada@prenhall.com**

Table of Contents

Preface

Dear Student,
This Study Guide is designed to reinforce your understanding of concepts presented in the Canadian edition of *Interpersonal Communication: Relating to Others*. Each chapter of the Study Guide corresponds to a chapter in your text. Many of your Study Guide activities and exercises are designed to strengthen memory and improve your recall of important terms and ideas (the sort of thing useful for test taking), but other exercises and activities seek to deepen your understanding of important terms and ideas by challenging you to apply them in both hypothetical and real-life situations. In general, the heading "Activities" in the Study Guide designates tasks requiring analytical thinking; the heading "Exercises" designates basic chapter review. As the authors of your text tell you, communication is something we all do all the time – it is a part of our lives. Working through the Study Guide exercises should help improve your classroom performance and also provide you with useful skills applicable in all your activities, both personal and professional. Interpersonal communication is about being human, and we hope the exercises in this guide will be immediately helpful to you in your classroom work and may also prove beneficial and even entertaining in your ongoing experience with communication.

Each chapter opens with an outline and summary of the corresponding textbook chapter. These outlines and summaries are designed to compress the information of each textbook chapter into as small a unit as possible for quick review and memorization. We recommend that you review these outlines and summaries frequently to freshen your knowledge as you advance from chapter to chapter in your text and study guide. Each outline and summary is followed by numbered activities and exercises. An answer key for exercise questions is included at the end of each chapter for self-correction. Study Guide activities and exercise questions can be completed conveniently with nothing more than a pencil and your textbook, although they may sometimes involve reflection on real-life behaviours.

In the first chapter of *Interpersonal Communication: Relating to Others*, the authors emphasize the importance of motivation. Yes, this is most important. The Study Guide seeks to provide you with direction and support in your encounter with the principles and practices of communication, but it depends on you to bring the process to life. We wish you success in your attempt, and we believe you will find useful tools and resources in your Study Guide. Your instructor may give you special guidance about how he or she wants you to use the Study Guide, but it is geared to the individual student working alone and is self-explanatory throughout.

Chapter 1

Introduction to Interpersonal Communication

CHAPTER OUTLINE

I. What Is Interpersonal Communication?

- **A.** Communication
  1. Human communication is a subset of communication
     a. Interpersonal communication has two dominant characteristics
        (1) Simultaneous interaction
        (2) Mutual influence

II. Evolving Model for Human and Interpersonal Communication

- **A.** Communication as Action: Message Transfer
  1. Source and Transmitter
     a. Encoding
     b. Decoding
  2. Receiver
  3. Channel
     a. Auditory
     b. Visual
     c. Olfactory
     d. Tactile
  4. Noise
     a. External
     b. Psychological
- **B.** Communication as Interaction: Message Exchange
  1. Feedback
     a. Intentional
     b. Unintentional
  2. Context
     a. Physical environment
     b. Psychological environment
- **C.** Communication as Transaction: Message Creation
  1. Episodes

III. Interpersonal Communication's New Frontier

- **A.** Technological advances
  1. Fax
  2. Telephone
  3. Computer Terminals

4. Video Exchanges - E-mail

IV. Four Principles of Interpersonal Communication

A. Inescapable
B. Irreversible
C. Complicated
1. Six "people" are involved whenever we communicate
    a. Who you think you are
    b. Who you think the other person is
    c. Who you think the other person thinks you are
    d. Who the other person thinks he or she is
    e. Who the other person thinks you are
    f. Who the other person thinks you think he or she is
2. Symbols
    a. Language and its complexities

D. Contextual
1. Psychological
2. Relational
3. Situational
4. Environmental
5. Cultural

V. Three Goals for Interpersonal Communication

A. Message is understood
1. Words
2. Symbols

B. Message has effect intended
1. Purpose
    a. Share information
    b. Persuade
    c. Solve a problem
    d. Establish trust
    e. Entertain
    f. Converse for fun

C. Message is ethical
1. Consider needs and rights of communication partner
    a. Allow freedom of choice
    b. Maintain honesty
    c. Keep confidences

VI. Why Study Interpersonal Communications?

A. Improve relationships with family
B. Improve relationships with friends

C. Improve relationships with colleagues
D. Improve your physical and emotional health

VII. How Do We Characterize Interpersonal Relationships?

A. Impersonal to intimate
   1. Cultural (least intimate)
   2. Sociological
   3. Psychological (most intimate)
B. Content and emotions
   1. What you say
   2. How you say it
      a. Tone of voice
      b. Eye contact
      c. Facial expression
      d. Posture
C. Patterns of interaction
   1. Complementary relationships involve partners who do different things
   2. Symmetrical relationships involve partners who do the same things
      a. Competitive symmetrical relationships involve aggressive contests
      b. Submissive symmetrical relationships involve passive avoidance
   3. Parallel relationships involve shared and alternating bchaviours
D. Governed by rules
   1. Explicit rules
   2. Implicit rules
E. Evolve in stages
   1. Development
      a. Testing
      b. Experimenting
      c. Exploring
      d. Intimacy
      e. Sharing
      f. Bonding
   2. Deterioration
F. Range from self-oriented to other-oriented

VIII. How Can You Improve Your Own Interpersonal Communication?

A. Knowledge
   1. Components
   2. Principles
   3. Rules
   4. Concepts
   5. Theories

B. Skill
   1. Practice
      a. Hear it
      b. See it
      c. Do it
      d. Correct it
   2. Feedback

C. Motivation

D. Flexibility

E. Other-orientation
   1. Decentring
   2. Empathizing

CHAPTER REVIEW: SECTION BY SECTION SUMMARY

I. What Is Interpersonal Communication?

All living beings communicate, including animals. Human communication is a subset of communication and involves our human effort to make sense of the world and share that sense with others. Interpersonal communication occurs when we interact with another person and mutually influence each other. The key aspects of interpersonal communication are *simultaneous* and *mutual* influence.

II. An Evolving Model for Human Communication

Theoretical models of human communication have evolved in three significant stages: (1) **action or message transfer**, (2) **transaction or message exchange**, (3) **interaction or message creation**. The dominant components of (1) **action/transfer** include: **source**, **receiver**, **message**, **channel** and **noise**. (2) **Transaction/exchange** adds the component of **feedback** and **context**. (3) **Interaction/creation** adds the idea of continuous and immediate feedback in communication periods called **episodes**. The three models are progressively dynamic, and the most recent model of (3) **interaction/creation** includes eight major components: source, receiver, message, channel, noise, feedback, context, and episode.

All thoughts and feelings have to be put in a **code** to function as a message. Putting thoughts and feelings into code is called **encoding**. Deciphering encoded messages is called **decoding**. Language itself is a code. When we converse with others, we are involved in a continuous process of encoding and decoding. **Feedback** can be either intentional (e.g., an answer to a question) or unintentional (e.g., yawning while someone is talking). **Channel** corresponds to the sense medium of communication: sound, sight, smell, and touch. **Noise** interferes with message communication and can be either physical (e.g., a noisy lawnmower) or psychological (e.g., a feeling of anger or fear).

III. Interpersonal Communication's New Frontier

Electronic media – faxes, telephones, e-mail, video tape – have revolutionized communication. It is important to remember that the same basic components of communication – source, receiver, message, channel, noise, feedback, context, and episode – are also involved in electronic communication. Unlike face-to-face dialogue, electronic communication is mediated communication – communication through some *medium* or *means* other than the immediate living presence of individuals. Consequently, electronic communication often involves limits to communication (lack of visual or physical contact, delay in transmission and receipt of messages).

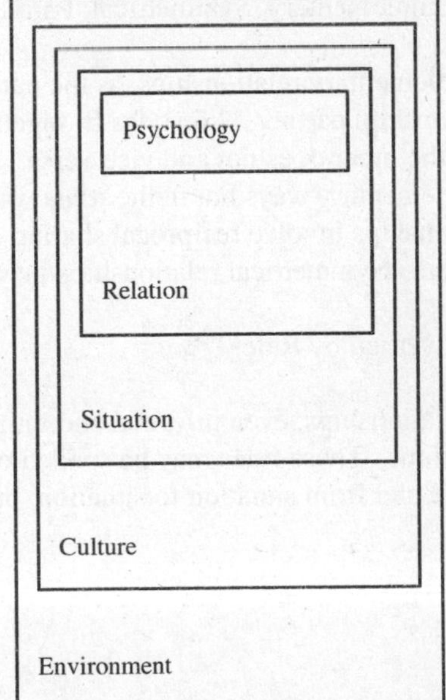

IV. Four Principles of Interpersonal Communication

1. Interpersonal Communication is Inescapable
2. Interpersonal Communication is Irreversible
3. Interpersonal Communication is Complicated
4. Interpersonal Communication is Contextual

We all have to communicate to live (**inescapable**), and once we communicate any message, that message cannot be recalled (**irreversible**) but becomes part of other messages in an on-going process of message generation and exchange between people who may or may not understand one another due to many factors (**complicated**). All messages are generated and exchanged in some time/space situation (**contextual**) which involves psychological, relational, situational, environmental and cultural contexts. We might view these various contexts as a series of Chinese boxes, one enclosing the other.

V. Three Goals for Interpersonal Communication

1. Message Understood
2. Message Has Intended Effect
3. Message Is Ethical

(1) A message must be understood. It must be in a code (language/symbol-system) the intended receiver can understand, and it must be as free as possible from ambiguities. Sending a message requires awareness and control of all the factors (tones/gestures) involved in its reception. (2) One must be aware of one's purpose in sending a message and be sure that the message meets the purpose. (3) Ethical messages respect the freedom of receivers by conveying information honestly and without gratuitous insult.

VI. Why Study Interpersonal Communication?

1. Improve relationships with (1) family (2) friends (3) and colleagues.
2. Improve one's own physical and mental health.

VII. How Do We Characterize Interpersonal Relationships?

1. Range from Impersonal to Intimate

Everyone is a member of some larger group such as a culture, a church, or a profession, but everyone is also a unique individual. When we deal with people as members of groups, our relationships with them tend to be impersonal, but when we deal with them as unique individuals our relationships become more intimate.

2. Content and Emotions

A neutral message, such as "close the door," can have very different meanings depending on how it is spoken or expressed. It can be a simple request or an angry command depending on the intent, gestures, tone of voice, and facial expressions of its speaker. What we say and how we say it are two aspects of every message.

3. Complementary, Symmetrical, Parallel

Complementary relationships, as the name implies, involve the idea of "completion." In a complementary relationship, partners' lifestyles fit together in a compatible way because one partner predominantly does what the other does not and vice versa. In symmetrical relationships, partners do not behave in complementary ways but in the *same* way, whether that way is competitive or submissive. Parallel relationships involve reciprocal sharing and alteration of functions, responsibilities, and privileges between partners. Symmetrical relationships may involve high levels of conflict.

4. Governed by Rules

All relationships, even informal and intimate ones, are governed by rules of appropriate and inappropriate behaviour. These rules may be spelled out explicitly or understood implicitly. Rules vary from culture to culture and from situation to situation, but they are always present in any interpersonal relationship.

5. Evolve in Stages

Relationships, like living things, grow and develop over time. While there is nothing automatic about human relationships, they do tend to progress through a series of recognizable stages – from a period of testing and exploration to greater intimacy and bonding.

6. Self-Oriented to Other-Oriented

In our relationships we either direct our energy and interest towards others or towards ourselves.

VIII. How Can You Improve Your Own Interpersonal Communication?

1. Knowledge – Learn the basic principles of communication theory.

2. Skill – Put what you know into practice and get feedback from others.

3. Motivation – Just do it! Seize opportunities to communicate.

4. Flexibility – Be sensitive and open to the needs of each emergent situation. Communication situations are complicated and various. Be ready to try new combinations and methods for new situations.

5. Other-Orientation – Step out of yourself. Walk in someone else's shoes.

TERMS TO LEARN

Communication
Human Communication
Interpersonal Communication
Information Source
Source
Receiver
Encode
Decode
Symbol
Message
Channel
Noise
Feedback
Context
Psychological Context
Relational Context
Situational Context
Environmental Context
Cultural Context
Cultural Information
Sociological Information
Psychological Information
Interpersonal Relationship
Complementary Relationship
Symmetrical Relationship (Competitive)

Symmetrical Relationship (Submissive)
Parallel Relationship
Testing
Bonding
Decentring
Other-Orientation
Empathizing

Activity 1.1: Assessing Your Communications Skills

Objectives:
6. To help you identify your strengths and weaknesses as a communicator.
7. To help you formulate learning objectives for yourself in the course.

Instructions:
1. The following exercise is designed to help you assess your interpersonal communication skills.
   Answer the questions as honestly as you can. As much as possible try to answer YES or NO rather than SOMETIMES.
2. At the end of the exercise complete the scoring section. Once you have finished scoring you can begin to identify your strengths and weaknesses as a communicator. Answers for a particular question which differ from the preferred answer may suggest a weakness in that area.

Listening

	Yes	No	Sometimes
1. Do you interrupt others when they are speaking?	___	___	___
2. Do you check with the speaker to ensure you have understood her/his message before making your own point?	___	___	___
3. Do you find your mind wandering from the speaker's ideas to your own while she/he is speaking?	___	___	___
4. When others are speaking do you appear to be listening when you are not?	___	___	___
5. When listening to a speaker are you easily distracted by your own thoughts (i.e., daydreams)?	___	___	___
6. Do you listen to the feeling in a speaker's message as well as the words?	___	___	___
7. Are you aware of a speaker's nonverbal messages?	___	___	___

Feedback and Self-Disclosure

1. Are you comfortable receiving positive feedback from others?	___	___	___

2. Are you able to give constructive criticism to others? ___ ___ ___

3. Do you become defensive when receiving constructive criticism about your own behaviour? ___ ___ ___

4. Do you have difficulty praising others? ___ ___ ___

5. Are you comfortable disclosing your feelings to others? ___ ___ ___

6. Do you encourage others to share their feelings with you? ___ ___ ___

Communicating Clearly

1. Are you able to communicate your thoughts clearly to others? ___ ___ ___

2. When you are uncertain about the meaning of another's message do you ask for clarification? ___ ___ ___

3. Are you aware of how your nonverbal communication (including tone of voice, gestures, facial expressions, posture, eye contact, etc.) may affect others? ___ ___ ___

4. When in a group setting are you able to communicate your ideas effectively? ___ ___ ___

5. Are others attentive to you when you speak? ___ ___ ___

6. When speaking are you conscious of how others are responding to your message? ___ ___ ___

7. Are you able to make your message relevant to the other person by using that person's language and terms? ___ ___ ___

8. In group settings (e.g., meetings) are you able to help the group stay focussed? ___ ___ ___

9. Are you able to get the knowledge and information that you need from others? ___ ___ ___

Managing Conflict

1. Are you satisfied with the way you resolve conflict situations? ___ ___ ___

2. When a conflict arises are you able to discuss your differences without getting angry? ___ ___ ___

3. Do you avoid conflict with others because you fear they may get angry? ___ ___ ___

4. When there is a disagreement between you and another person do you sacrifice your own concerns to appease her/him, i.e., do you tend to give in to the other person? ___ ___ ___

5. Do you try to satisfy your own needs at the expense of others? ___ ___ ___

6. When a difference of opinion arises between you and another are you able to put yourself in the other person's place and see things from her/his perspective? ___ ___ ___

7. When involved in a disagreement do you try to satisfy both parties' concerns? ___ ___ ___

8. Do you jump to conclusions or make assumptions about another's meaning before clarifying your understanding of her/his message? ___ ___ ___

9. Are you able to confront and challenge others? ___ ___ ___

10. Do you aggressively try to win at any cost? ___ ___ ___

Self-Concept and Awareness

1. Are you comfortable trusting others? ___ ___ ___

2. Are you comfortable expressing your ideas even when they differ from those of others? ___ ___ ___

3. Are you able to communicate your needs effectively to others? ___ ___ ___

4. Are you condescending or sarcastic towards others when they disagree with you? ___ ___ ___

5. When in discussion do you encourage others to voice differences of opinion? ___ ___ ___

6. Are you conscious of how your behaviour affects others? ___ ___ ___

Scoring Instructions:

Score your answers according to the following score key. Then circle all of the questions where your answer differed from the ones in the score key. These may indicate areas where you are weak as a communicator. Identifying these may offer opportunities to improve communication skills. While this exercise provides a general guide to effective communication skills it is also important to remember that communication is situational. Behaviour that might be appropriate in one situation may be less so in another. Each section listed below includes text chapters in brackets which contain information about relevant communication skills.

Listening (Chapters 4, 5)
1. No
2. Yes
3. No
4. No
5. No
6. Yes
7. Yes

Feedback and Self-Disclosure (Chapters 6, 8)

1. Yes
2. Yes
3. No
4. No
5. Yes
6. Yes

Communicating Clearly (Chapters 4, 6, 11, 14)

1. Yes
2. Yes
3. Yes
4. Yes
5. Yes
6. Yes
7. Yes
8. Yes
9. Yes

Managing Conflict (Chapters 3,10, 11)

1. Yes
2. Yes
3. No
4. No
5. No
6. Yes
7. Yes
8. No
9. Yes

Self-Concept and Awareness (Chapters 2, 11)

1. Yes
2. Yes
3. Yes
4. No
5. Yes
6. Yes

<u>Areas of Weakness as a Communicator:</u>

<u>Areas of Strength as a Communicator:</u>

Activity 1.2: Learning Effective Communication

Objectives:

1. To increase your awareness of effective communication behaviours and your skill at performing them.
2. To help you recognize and overcome barriers to effective communication.

Instructions:

1. Think of people you know who communicate effectively. List the behaviours that make them effective.
2. In the following exercise apply these behaviours to situations in your own life.
3. Review the following example before you do your own.

Option:

Roleplay one of your situations with another classmate. Have a third classmate act as an observer during the roleplay and give you feedback on your behaviour.

Example:

1. Situation in which you would have liked to communicate more effectively:
   recent job interview

2. What was ineffective about your behaviour:
   I interrupted the interviewer several times. I was nervous and got confused with my answers to her questions. I began to slump in the chair. I did most of the talking and in the end was not really sure what kind of person they were looking for to fill this position.

3. What behaviours would help you communicate more effectively:
   listen, ask questions, relax

4. How could you practice these behaviours:
   I could have a positive attitude and relax in the interview. I could feed back what I am hearing. I could pause and allow myself to reflect on my answers before responding to her. I could sit tall. I could ask her questions about the position.

Example 1

1) Situation in which you would have liked to communicate more effectively:

____

____

____

2) What was ineffective about your behaviour?

3) What behaviours would help you communicate more effectively?

4) How could you practise these behaviours?

Example 2

1) Situation in which you would have liked to communicate more effectively:

2) What was ineffective about your behaviour?

3) What behaviours would help you communicate more effectively?

4) How could you practise these behaviours?

Example 3

1) Situation in which you would have liked to communicate more effectively:

2) What was ineffective about your behaviour?

3) What behaviours would help you communicate more effectively?

4) How could you practise these behaviours?

Activity 1.3: Goals for Communication

Objectives:
1. To understand the three goals of communication and be able to apply them to real-life situations.
2. To recognize when communication goals are not met.

The text identifies three goals for communication:
1. Make sure your message is understood.
2. Make sure your message has the effect you intended.
3. Make sure your message is ethical.

Part 1

Instructions:
1. In the following examples identify what communication goals were not achieved.

Situations:

1. Your friend John asks you to go to the movies on Friday night. You do not want to hurt John's feelings but you would rather spend the evening with your friend Jason. You tell John that you are busy on Friday evening because you have to work.

   Goal Not Achieved:

   ____

2. Your history teacher returns your recent essay with a grade of "D." You are extremely upset and would like to get further feedback as to why you have received such a poor mark and about what you can do to improve it. You discover that several classmates have received an "A" on their papers. You confront your teacher after class and accuse her of showing favouritism.

   Goal Not Achieved:

   ____

3. You decide to ask a classmate for help on an essay you are writing. You approach her after class. As you begin to speak with her she seems uncomfortable with your attention and blurts out, "I already have a boyfriend!"

   Goal Not Achieved:

   ____

4. A doctor about to perform an unavoidably painful procedure on a nervous patient says, " Now this won't hurt a bit."

   Goal Not Achieved:

   ____

5. At a recent performance review you congratulate an employee that you supervise on his performance. You say, "Your efforts will not go unrewarded." As he leaves you think about your intentions to recommend him for a promotion. Three weeks later he appears in your office very angry and demanding,"Where is my raise?"

   Goal Not Achieved:

   ____

6. Your girlfriend calls you long-distance. You are attending universities in different cities and have not seen each other in a month. You are eager to talk with her but your father is expecting an important business call. As she begins to speak you abruptly interrupt her and tell her you will call her back later. Before you have a chance to explain the situation with your father she slams down the phone in a huff.

   Goal Not Achieved:

   ____

7. A sales manager is attending an out-of-town business conference. She tells her husband she will call home in the evening. When she calls at 11:30 p.m. her husband is upset and says, "You promised to call in the evening not 11:30 at *night*!"

   Goal Not Achieved:

   ____

8. A customer goes into a store and demands a refund on a purchase. The manager says, "I am sorry you are dissatisfied but all we can do is commiserate." The customer responds, "That's great. I was worried you wouldn't give me my money back."

   Goal Not Achieved:

   ____

9. A new restaurant opens called *Your 2nd Choice*. The owners intend to imply that the 1st choice is your own kitchen at home. The food and service are excellent but business fares poorly. A survey reveals customers are deterred by the name.

   Goal Not Achieved:

   ____

10. Along with several others in your department, you and a friend are both up for promotion. Your friend anxiously asks you if you have heard anything about the decision. Although you have learned just that morning that you were the only one promoted, you tell your friend you have still heard nothing.

Goal Not Achieved: ______________________________

Part 2

Instructions: In the space provided list 3 examples in your own experience where these goals were not achieved. Explain why.

1. Situation:

____

Goal Not Achieved:

____

2. Situation:

____

Goal Not Achieved:

____

3. Situation:

____

Goal Not Achieved:

____

Activity 1.4: Characterizing Interpersonal Relationships

Objectives:

1. To help you identify the characteristics of interpersonal relationships
2. To help you analyze a relationship in your life by applying these characteristics

Instructions:

1. Think of a significant relationship in your life. Analyze it according to the following characteristics: Impersonal to Intimate; Content and Emotions; Complementary, Symmetrical or Parallel; Rules Governing the Relationship; Stages of the Relationship; Self-Oriented to Other-Oriented.

Example:

Relationship:

I have completed my internship and become a staff physician at a hospital where my medical school professor and chief mentor now works. She is always asking me to assist her in various minor capacities just as I did when I was a student. She is an excellent diagnostician, and I have always been skillful in patient relations, but that kind of divided relationship will not work any longer and she has to realize things have changed. We both have to take full responsibility for all aspects of practice now. I cannot just be working here for her. When she asks me to do something, she needs to address me by my professional title and behave as she does towards other professionals.

Characteristics:

Impersonal to Intimate:

Very close though perhaps not intimate.

Content and Emotions:

Although most of our interaction is about standard professional matters, my mentor's tone and manner is inappropriately casual, even condescending.

Complementary, Symmetrical, or Parallel:

Our relationship was complementary when I was a student, but now that I am a colleague, it has become symmetrical competitive.

Rules Governing the Relationship:

The professional courtesies and decorum suitable between two fully accredited colleagues in a professional environment should apply, but unfortunately, my old mentor assumes that the old, informal classroom rules of teacher/pupil still apply.

Stages of the Relationship:

I am not a student anymore but a doctor in my own right. Despite the difference in our ages and experience it is time to work together as equal partners on the staff. The old bonds are coming apart and we are entering a new beginning period of boundary testing and definition. Perhaps we could restore the old professional intimacy on a new basis.

Self-Oriented to Other-Oriented:

My colleague needs to think about my career requirements and needs as an independent professional. I owe her a great deal and I still feel a real willingness to assist her in every professional capacity.

Relationship:

Characteristics:

Impersonal to Intimate:

Content and Emotions:

Complementary, Symmetrical or Parallel:

Rules Governing the Relationship:

Stages of the Relationship:

Self-Oriented to Other-Oriented:

Activity 1.5: Looking at Communication Context

Objectives:

1. To help you recognize communication contexts and how they affect interpersonal communication.

Instructions:

1. Identify what contexts, psychological, relational, situational, environmental, and cultural, are involved in each of the following examples.

1. You and your boss meet unexpectedly at a party and you find it difficult to think of anything to say.

   Contexts:____

2. You and a colleague are interviewing an applicant whom you know to be a friend of your colleague's for a position in your department at work.

   Contexts:____

3. You are in a 9:00 a.m. class at school. Your instructor is moving into the second hour of a two hour lecture on Canadian history. You were awake all night finishing an assignment for this course and did not have time to eat breakfast.

   Contexts:____

4. You are picking your car up from a routine servicing at the local garage. When you arrive you are dismayed to discover you have a bill of $800.00 for a new carburetor. You wonder why you were not informed of this earlier. As you try to discuss this with the service manager, you are surrounded by the noises of revving engines. You can hardly hear each other and you both start losing your tempers.

   Contexts:____

5. You meet your doctor at the gym as you are both running on the track. You strike up a conversation but your doctor seems reserved.

   Contexts:____

   ____

6. You have recently moved to Canada from Singapore. You are used to a more formal relationship between teachers and students in the classroom. In your course on Interpersonal Communications at the local university you are surprised to hear your classmates address the professor by his first name.

   Contexts:____

   ____

7. You have learned unofficially from the office secretary that a junior colleague in your department has received promotion before you. Later that day you see him in the hall, and he says, "Good morning, pleasant day isn't it?" You respond, "I don't need your sarcasm!" He is taken aback and bewildered by your response.

   Contexts:____

   ____

DIFFICULT POSITION 1

You have recently started a new job. During your third week at work a co-worker tells you a racist joke. You know others are uncomfortable about this remark.

INSTRUCTIONS

1. Answer the following questions and discuss your responses with your classmates.

What are the issues involved here?

____

____

How would you feel?

____

____

How would you respond?

____

____

If you say nothing what might that communicate?

____

____

Option:

1. Roleplay this situation with another student. Have classmates participate as observers during the roleplay and give feedback on your communication behaviours.

Exercise 1.1: Learning Objective: Develop Understanding of Components of Human Communication Process

Instructions: There are at least seven possible components of every communication situation: source, receiver, message, channel, noise, context, and feedback. In the following communication situations identify and number as many components as you can.

Situation:	Components:
An officer gives a soldier an order to stand at attention. The soldier salutes and shouts, "Yes, sir."	
Situation:	**Components:**
A wife calls to her husband to turn down the television so the baby can sleep. The husband calls back, "What?"	
Situation:	**Components:**
A bartender tells a patron he's been cut off for drinking too much. The patron throws a beer in the bartender's face.	
Situation:	**Components:**
An airline pilot radios air traffic control about an equipment malfunction and requests clearance for a forced landing. Over the static of the radio and the roar of a malfunctioning engine, the traffic controller can barely be heard asking for the pilot's current position. The pilot shouts his answer. The co-pilot grips the pilot's shoulder firmly, looks him straight in the eye, and says, "You can do it."	

Situation:	Components:
A coach is reprimanding one of his players for using unnecessary roughness and earning a foul. While the coach is talking, the player keeps thinking the coach looks just like his father when he's angry, and he hardly hears a word. When the player stares blankly at the coach, the coach thinks, "He's ignoring me on purpose!"	

Exercise 1.2: Learning Objective: Mastering Vocabulary

Instructions: Place the appropriate word or words from column A in the blanks in paragraph B.

A	B
communication source encode decode receiver message channel noise context feedback episode symbol complementary (relationship) symmetrical (relationship) competitive symmetrical (relationship) submissive symmetrical (relationship) parallel (relationship) bonding decentring empathy	No matter how hard he tried, Tom could not understand Mary's unhappiness. He was, unfortunately, incapable of ________ himself and feeling ________ for her situation. He would often talk to her for hours, but perhaps a gentle touch would have been a better ________ to convey his ________ that he did still loved her. Mary could not ________ Tom's meaning from what he said because her own emotional ________ prevented her from hearing him accurately and objectively. She often felt hopeless and offered almost no ________ to what he said but only stared vacantly. They seemed to have lost hope of any meaningful ________. Once, after Tom talked for almost two hours and Mary still said almost nothing, he felt he was locked in the role of the ________ and Mary into the role of ________. Tom thought it would be best if they shared privileges and responsibilities in a ________ relationship, but Mary would have preferred a ________ relationship in which Tom would happily do all the talking while she listened. Instead, neither was happy and each tried to avoid accepting responsibility and was just as reluctant to claim privileges. When Tom talked and Mary was silent, they were both trying in their own way to avoid taking responsibility and making decisions. Their marriage was basically a ________ relationship. Finally, after months of fruitless talk, Mary pointed out to Tom how their friends, Lisa and Roger, were always trying to control each other and were always claiming responsibility and power in their ________ relationship, but even so, they seemed to spend all of their time going in circles, too. Tom laughed at that and so did Mary. In fact, Mary's observation seemed suddenly to break a spell and that day their conversation became a time of real ________ for the couple. Afterwards, whenever Tom and Mary found themselves in a dead-end situation, they only had to say "Lisa and Roger" to each other to realize how foolish it all was. The name of their friends had become for them a ________ of fruitless misunderstanding, and Tom and Mary agreed to ________ their private understanding in these two names.

Exercise 1.3: Learning Objective: The Four Principles of Interpersonal Communication.

Instructions: Which of the four principles of interpersonal communication do the following situations *best* describe? Write (1) **inescapable** (2) **irreversible** (3) **complicated** or (4) **contextual** in the blank space following.

I was just accusing my younger brother of stealing some money off my dresser when I suddenly realized it was in my pocket.________________.
Mary thought her friend Cheryl liked her, but she wasn't sure, and if she really didn't like her, then she wouldn't really want to help her with her work, so Mary said, "I need your help, but you probably have something else to do." Cheryl thought Mary really didn't want her to help or she wouldn't have asked like that, so she said, "I guess I do have something else to do after all." ______________.
The representatives of management and the union tried to resolve their differences that summer, but meetings in the rooms of the old union hall were so hot and stifling that everyone just seemed short-tempered and anxious to get away.____________.
Phillip does not like to talk to people when he's working out at the gym, but the man standing next to him at the squat stand doesn't have collars on his barbell and one of the weight plates is about to fall off near where Phillip is standing. ______________.
I knew what I wanted to say, but the moment I walked into the courtroom and saw all those people staring at me, I forgot everything and could only mumble.__________.
Jacques spoke some English and William spoke some French, but that only made their situation worse because they both used words the other could understand but without the proper meanings. Instead of just being unable to understand each other, they wound up insulting each other!____________.
I was angry when I said I'd never take a job at any company he worked for. Now I either have to swallow my words or lose this opportunity.____________.
I don't want to offend my hosts, but it's against the laws of my religion to eat certain foods. Unfortunately, just the ones they most like! I'd rather just go quietly about my business without raising the issue, but my dietary laws are very strict, and I have always observed them. ______________________________

Exercise 1.4: Learning Objective: Identifying the Five Types of Context

Instructions: In the following paragraph (A) identify the various types of communication context involved: (1) **psychological** (2) **relational** (3) **situational** (4) **environmental** or (5) **cultural**. Write a brief summary (B) of the communication context in the space following the paragraph.

(A) Patricia MaGee was often uncomfortable dealing with her mother-in-law because of her devout Catholicism. Before marrying her husband and moving to Toronto, Patricia had grown up a Protestant in Northern Ireland, and when she was young, her brother had been killed in a riot between Protestants and Catholics in Belfast. Even though her mother-in-law was the gentlest person in the world and treated Patricia with kindness, Patricia would always feel uncomfortable when she talked about religion. Once when Patricia and her husband were alone on a vacation in the mountains, where they had always been very happy, she finally told him about her brother's death and how she sometimes resented his mother for talking about religion. She had never told anyone before about her brother's death. Her husband said he understood, but he hoped she would learn to like his mother. Only a few months later, Patricia's mother-in-law lost her other son in a traffic accident. When Patricia had to stay alone with her while the funeral arrangements were being made, she told her all about her brother's death in Ireland. Somehow she was suddenly able to talk to her mother-in-law without resentment, and she wanted to comfort her for what she also had suffered by sharing her own experience of loss.

(B)____

Exercise 1.5: Learning Objective: General Review (**TRUE/FALSE**)

Instructions: Identify the following statements as either true or false.

1. Empathy is a means to shut out the disturbances of the environment so we can concentrate on our innermost thoughts and feelings. ( )

2. Friends often have practical roles to play in our lives as well as being our companions. ( )

3. Any means of communication is ethical, if it achieves a good purpose. ( )

4. Relational context concerns the attitudes and beliefs of different nationalities in interpersonal communication. ( )

5. Because the spoken word has no concrete form, a spoken message, unlike a letter, can be easily retracted, almost as if it never existed. ( )

6. Unlike highly formal business relationships, relationships between friends are without rules of any kind, which is why they are so enjoyable. ( )

7. Even the most loving relationships begin with at least some period of testing. ( )

8. Prior awareness of a goal in communication is often necessary to achieving it. ( )

9. The currently dominant model of interpersonal communication emphasizes one-way transactions within fixed time periods. ( )

10. E-mail messages are a form of unmediated electronic communication. ( )

11. A *channel* in communication theory corresponds to the different physical senses by which and through which we might convey a message. ( )

12. A symmetrical relationship always involves equal sharing of power and responsibility. ( )

13. Loneliness is painful but not physically damaging. ( )

14. If I respond to someone's comments with absolute silence, I deprive him or her of any feedback. ( )

15. The basic skills of communication are so firmly established that, once you master them, they can be applied in the same few ways in all situations. ( )

Exercise 1.6: Learning Objective: General Review **(FILL-IN-THE-BLANKS)**

Instructions: Fill in the blanks using the appropriate term or terms from the following list.

source	context	empathy
encode	feedback	orientation
decode	episode	impersonal
receiver message	symbol	intimate
channel	bonding	testing
noise	decentring	

1. Choosing between French and English to send a message in would be a decision about how to________________________.

2. ___________ involves the ability to feel and understand another person's experiences.

3. Shrugging your shoulders in response to a question is minimal________________.

4. When a police officer gives a speeder a ticket, their relationship is______________.

5. When the coach hit his player, it was the wrong_______ to use for his____________.

6. ______________ includes all the physical and psychological factors affecting communication.

7. A red octagonal sign at the intersection of North American roadways is a conventional_________ which means "stop."

8. Common membership on a sports team is often considered a good environment for ________________.

9. A man or woman who never thinks of anyone but himself or herself has an________________ which would prevent getting to know others from within.

10. Sometimes ten minutes, sometimes two hours, can be an adequate _________ for real communication to take place.

11. _________________ is a process by which people slowly get to know each other.

12. Trying to interpret the meaning of someone's gesture is an effort to______________.

13. If someone is going to function as a reliable______________of important information, they must be keep all ____________to a minimum, whether physical or psychological.

14. When two lovers at a marriage altar exchange vows, it is simultaneously an_____________and an____________moment, both private and public.

15. __________ might require a special and painful effort to step outside oneself.

Exercise 1.7: Learning Objective: General Review **(MULTIPLE CHOICE)**

Instructions: Choose the best answer for each question below.

1. Jack and Jill fight constantly about who will carry the pail of water up the hill and about everything else they have to do. The relationship of these siblings is best described as being

   a. parallel
   b. complementary
   c. symmetrical
   d. decentred

2. In some cultures, burping after a meal is a polite act expressing enjoyment. If someone accustomed to this practice burped loudly after a meal in most North American settings, he or she would probably be experiencing confusion about

   a. relational context
   b. physical context
   c. emotional context
   d. cultural context

3. If we know that someone is a member and supporter of a labour union, our knowledge about this person would best be described as

   a. sociological information
   b. psychological information
   c. cultural information
   d. relational information

4. Becoming strongly attached to another person is a process known as

   a. relational closure
   b. empathy
   c. bonding
   d. testing

5. Any reaction of one speaker to another is

   a. decentring
   b. feedback
   c. noise
   d. empathy

6. Interpersonal relationships can be characterized as ranging from

   a. encoded to decoded
   b. contextual to environmental
   c. ethical to opportunistic
   d. impersonal to intimate

7. All of the following statements are true except

   a. communication is so essential that solitary confinement has been used as a form of punishment
   b. loneliness can be a contributing factor in illness and death
   c. the emotional tone of a message is often as important as its content
   d. new technologies always enhance interpersonal communication

8. All of the following statements are true except

   a. an ethical message never offends its receiver
   b. an ethical message respects the receiver's freedom of choice
   c. an ethical message is honest
   d. an ethical message does not betray confidences

9. All of the following are necessary to improve interpersonal communication except

   a. financial security
   b. flexibility
   c. motivation
   d. other-orientation

10. All of the following statements are true about relationships except

   a. they evolve in stages
   b. they all enter a phase of irreversible decline
   c. they are governed by explicit and/or implicit rules
   d. they can range from self-oriented to other-oriented

11. All of the following statements about feedback are true except

   a. any response constitutes feedback, even silence
   b. all feedback is a source of potential information
   c. feedback can sometimes be unintentional
   d. useful feedback is always positive

Answers

CHAPTER 1

Exercise 1.1

(Answers to this exercise might reasonably vary, but we list here some of the more obvious components.)

1. Officer (source), Order (message), Soldier (receiver), "Yes, sir" (feedback).
2. Wife (source), "turn down television . . ." (message), Television (noise), Husband (receiver), "What?" (feedback).
3. Bartender (source), ". . . been cutoff" (message), Patron (receiver), ". . . beer in face" (feedback) (tactile-channel).
4. Pilot (source), ". . . malfunction" (message), Static (noise), Traffic controller (receiver/source), ". . . asking for position" (message/feedback), ". . . pilot answers" (receiver/source/feedback/message), Co- pilot (source), ". . . grips shoulder" (message/tactile-channel), ". . . you can do it" (message/auditory-channel).
5. Coach (source), Reprimand (message), Player (receiver), " . . . player keeps thinking the coach looks just like his father" (noise/psychological), ". . . player stares blankly" (feedback).

Exercise 1.2

(1) decentring (2) empathy (3) channel (4) message (5) decode (6) noise (7) feedback (8) communication (9) source (10) receiver (11) parallel (12) complementary (13) submissive-symmetrical (14) competitive symmetrical (15) bonding (16) symbol (17) encode.

Exercise 1.3

(1) irreversible (2) complicated (3) contextual (4) inescapable (5) contextual (6) complicated (7) irreversible (8) unavoidable.

Exercise 1.4

(This exercise calls for interpretation and answers might reasonably vary. We list here some of the more obvious contexts.)

Mary's experiences as a child in Ireland are part of both her **psychological** and her **cultural** communication context.

The talk between husband and wife in the mountains involves **relational** and **environmental** contexts.

Mary's talk with her mother-in-law before the funeral is primarily an instance of **situational** context.

Exercise 1.5

1. (F)
2. (T)
3. (F)[ethical messages must be honest]
4. (F)[national differences are cultural context]
5. (F)[all communication is irreversible]
6. (F)[all relationships have some rules]
7. (T)
8. (T)
9. (F)
10. (F)
11. (T)
12. (F)
13. (F)[loneliness can kill]
14. (F)[all reactions (even silence) are feedback]
15. (F)[flexibility is essential]

Exercise 1.6

1. Encode
2. Empathy
3. Feedback
4. Impersonal
5. Channel/message
6. Context
7. Symbol
8. Bonding
9. Orientation
10. Episode
11. Testing
12. Decode
13. Source/noise
14. Impersonal/intimate (or) intimate/impersonal
15. Decentring

Exercise 1.7

1. c
2. d
3. a
4. c
5. b
6. e
7. d
8. a
9. a
10. b
11. d

Chapter 2

Communication and Self

CHAPTER OUTLINE

I. Self-Concept: Who Are You?

A. Self-concept involves self-description in three major areas

1. Attitudes
   a. Preferences or likes and dislikes
2. Beliefs
   a. Ideas about what is true or false
3. Values
   a. Convictions about what is right and wrong

II. One or Many Selves?

A. Material Self

1. Physical aspects of self (possessions)
   a. Body
   b. Home
   c. Car
   d. Clothes

B. Social Self

1. Public or interactive aspects of self with others (roles)
   a. Formal interaction with others
      (1) Colleagues
      (2) Teachers
      (3) Government and law enforcement officials
   b. Informal interaction with others
      (1) Family members
      (2) Friends
      (3) Acquaintances

C. Spiritual Self

1. Introspective convictions concerning ultimate issues
   a. Values
   b. Morals
   c. Beliefs
      (1) Existence or non-existence of a deity

III. How Your Self-Concept Develops

A. Interaction with individuals

1. "Looking glass" relations: we see ourselves in the responses of others

2. Three conditions govern our acceptance of the comments of others
    a. The comment of another repeats what we have heard before
    b. The comment comes from someone in whom we have confidence
    c. The comment is consistent with our own experience

B. Association with groups

1. Membership in various types of groups contributes to our identity
    a. Religious
    b. Political
    c. Ethnic
    d. Social
    e. Occupational
    f. Professional
2. Group membership can be determined by birth or by choice
3. Group membership involves mutual influence and restraint (peer pressure)

C. Roles we assume

1. Gender roles
    a. Masculine
    b. Feminine
    c. Androgynous
2. Parental roles
    a. Father
    b. Mother
3. Marital roles
    a. Husband
    b. Wife
4. Traditional requirements of cultural roles may influence behaviours
    a. Men may be praised for behaviours criticized in women and vice versa

D. Self-labels

1. Descriptions and assessments of our selves based on self-reflexiveness
    a. Real self
    b. Ideal self

IV. Understanding Shyness

A. Shyness is discomfort or inhibition in interpersonal situations

1. Roots in childhood
2. Negative biases in self-concept
3. Social situations difficult
4. Less verbally and nonverbally expressive
5. Less interest in others
6. High levels of self-consciousness
7. Negative thoughts about self and others in social situations
8. Remember negative feedback
9. Remember negative self-descriptions

10. View self as physically unattractive
11. Passive behaviours
12. Stuttering or other speech impediments

B. Extreme shyness termed social phobia

C. Shyness treatable

1. Gradual exposure to feared situations
2. Visualization
3. Positive self-talk
4. Anxiety management
5. Medication
   a. May create dependence
   b. Does not solve underlying problem

V. Self-Esteem: Your Self-Worth

A. Self-esteem involves evaluation of self in comparison with others

1. The concept of "life position" describes our overall sense of self-esteem
   a. "I'm OK, you're OK," or positive regard for self and others
   b. "I'm OK, you're not OK," or positive regard for self and low regard for others
   c. "I'm not OK, you're OK," or low self-esteem and positive regard for others
   d. "I'm not OK, you're not OK," or low regard for both self and others

VI. Self-Esteem and Self-Concept Affect Interpersonal Communication and Relationships

A. Self-esteem and self-concept act as filters in our communication with others

1. To know others, we must decentre. To decentre, we must know ourselves
   a. We may use knowledge of ourselves as a frame for understanding others
   b. We may use a **specific-other perspective** to understand others
      (1) Information derived from observation of particular individuals
   c. We may use a **generalized-other perspective** to understand others
      (1) Theoretical information about people in general or specific subgroups

B. Self-fulfilling prophecy: what we believe about ourselves often determines the outcome of our actions and interpretations

1. What we expect to happen often does
2. We sometimes hear only what we expect to hear
3. Expectations can even affect our health

C. Self and interpretation of messages

1. Persons of low self-esteem tend to be intensely sensitive to criticism
2. Persons of high self-esteem tend to accept praise gracefully
3. Interpretation of messages is affected by the principle of **selective exposure**
   a. We often place ourselves in situations consistent with who we think we are and where we are likely to hear what we already know and approve

D. Self and communication style

1. We all tend to develop a "style profile": habitual mode of communication on a continuum between polar extremes
2. Researcher Robert Norton identifies nine distinctive styles
   a. Dominant
   b. Dramatic
   c. Contentious
   d. Animated
   e. Impression-leaving
   f. Relaxed
   g. Attentive
   h. Open
   i. Friendly
3. The Wilson Learning Corporation identifies four styles representing combinations of two dominant modes
   a. Assertive -- (Task-Centred)
      (1) A communication style emphasizing control and command
   b. Responsive -- (People-Centred)
      (1) A communication style emphasizing empathy and emotional openness
   c. Combined assertive/responsive communication styles
      (1) Drivers -- very high assertive
      (2) Analyticals -- high assertive
      (3) Expressives -- both assertive and responsive
      (4) Amiables -- high responsive and low assertive
   d. Backup communication style
      (1) Most communicators have a primary and secondary communication style used in differing situations

VII. Improving Your Self-Esteem

A. Improvement of self-esteem can be promoted in seven distinct ways

1. Self-talk or intrapersonal communication
   a. Positive but objective evaluation and reinforcement: "I think I can"
2. Visualization
   a. Promoting positive outcomes by envisioning them: "seeing success"
3. Avoiding comparisons
   a. Accepting ourselves and our abilities as unique and incommensurate
4. Reframing
   a. Seeing things from a different perspective: "taking the long view"
5. Developing honest relationships
   a. Fostering relationships of trust with colleagues, clergy, and friends
   b. Avoiding self-pity
6. Letting go of the past

   a. Not dwelling on negative experiences of the past
   b. Being mindful of the possibilities always inherent in change
7. Seeking support
   a. In the case of serious difficulties being open to professional help

CHAPTER REVIEW: SECTION BY SECTION SUMMARY

I. Self-Concept: Who Are You?

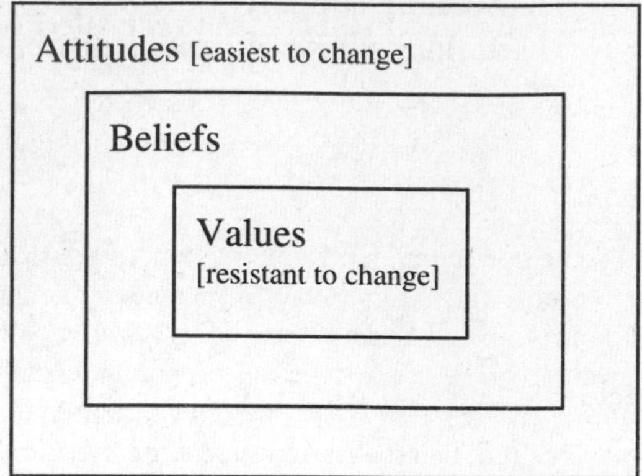

Our self-concept is a subjective *description* of who we think we are. Components of self-concept include

(1) **attitudes** (likes and dislikes)
(2) **beliefs** (judgements about what is true and false)
(3) **values** (convictions about what is good and bad)

Values are central to our concept of self; beliefs and attitudes derive from values. Values are often spoken of as being a part of our "core self."

II. One or Many Selves?

Some theorists, such as the American Philosopher and Psychologist William James (1842-1910), consider the self a composite of three components:

(1) **material self** -- all the physical elements that reflect who you are -- (body, clothes, car, home)
(2) **social self** -- the various selves reflected in interactions with others -- (formal and informal social roles)
(3) **spiritual self** -- introspections about values, morals, and beliefs -- (religious convictions)

III. How Your Self-Concept Develops

Psychologists and sociologists have identified four basic means of developing self-concept:

(1) **interaction with others** -- we see ourselves through the eyes of others -- **[the looking glass self]**
(2) **association with groups --** membership in political, ethnic, religious, occupational, and social groups
(3) **roles we assume** -- gender, paternal, and professional roles
(4) **self-labels** -- self-descriptions derived from our capacity for self-reflexiveness

III. Understanding Shyness: A Special Problem for Self-Concept and Self-Esteem

Shyness can be defined as discomfort or inhibition in interpersonal situations. Extreme shyness is labelled **social phobia**. Perhaps as many as 40 percent of North Americans suffer from shyness and 3 to 12 percent from social phobia. Shyness involves a variety of troubling behavioural, physiological, cognitive and affective symptoms ranging from slight nervousness to panic, from mild embarrassment to severe depression. Shyness can be treated by gradual exposure to feared situations, visualization, self-talk, anxiety management, and medication.

IV. Self-Esteem: Your Self-Worth

Our self-esteem is a subjective *evaluation* of who we think we are derived from comparing ourselves with others. The psychologist Eric Berne developed the four-part concept of **life position** to describe our overall sense of self-worth and the worth of others.

(1) **"I'm OK, you're OK"** -- positive regard for self and others
(2) **"I'm OK, you're not OK"** -- positive regard for self but low regard for others

(3) **"I'm not OK, you're OK"** -- low self-regard but positive regard for others
(4) **"I'm not OK, you're not OK"** -- low regard for both self and others

V. How Self-Concept and Self-Esteem Affect Interpersonal Communication and Relationships

Our self-concept and self-esteem act as filters in our interactions with others. These filters influence (1) our ability to be sensitive to others, (2) our expectations, (3) our interpretation of messages and (4) our communication of messages.

(1) To be open to understanding others (other-orientation), we must be able to decentre ourselves. To do this we must know ourselves and be able to distinguish between our own perception of ourselves ("I") and the perceptions others may have of us ("Me"). We must be aware that our "self" is different from others. In trying to understand others we do not know well, we may use ourselves and are own feelings and attitudes as a *frame of reference*. Because individuals can be very different, this method is very imperfect. What is natural and good for you may be unnatural and bad for another. If we have some specific information about an individual, we may use this knowledge as a *specific-other perspective* to predict or understand his or her actions. If we lack such information, we may use a *general-other perspective* which is based on general knowledge about human nature or the preferences and attitudes of specific social groups. If we know that person A tends to be very independent and controlling, we might assume that he or she would prefer to do the driving on a trip rather than being driven (specific-other). If we know that all members of profession A pride themselves on their objectivity, we may assume individual profession member B would be pleased to act as judge in a contest (general-other).

(2) Our expectations about situations and events often influence their outcome. What we believe will happen often does, in part because our belief has influenced our receptivity and responses beforehand. If I imagine I am very ill, I may begin to behave in ways that will make me very ill even if I am not or more so if I am. A pre-determining expectation or belief is termed **self-fulfilling prophecy**.

(3) Our self-esteem and self concept can colour how we hear and interpret the messages and actions of others. A person with very low self-esteem might interpret mild criticism as a personal attack because he or she is predisposed to be especially sensitive and responsive to the negative. Conversely, a person with very high self-esteem might be impervious to even very negative criticism because he or she is predisposed to be sensitive and responsive only to whatever is affirmative and reinforcing in messages. Our predisposition or openness to receive certain kinds of messages may also be expressed in the form of **selective exposure**, which can be defined as our tendency to place ourselves only in contexts consistent with our self-concept. In other words, we tend to seek out situations and contexts which conform to our preferences and avoid those which do not. An opera buff is not likely to attend a rap concert. Rappers rarely visit the opera. Conservative ministers are seldom speakers at union gatherings. Liberal ministers are not often the first choice of most business owners.

(4) All individuals tend to develop a primary communication style which characterizes their interactions with others. Researcher Robert Norton identifies nine distinctive styles: (1) dominant, (2) dramatic, (3) contentious, (4) animated, (5) impression-leaving, (6) relaxed, (7) attentive, (8) open, (9) friendly. The Wilson Learning Corporation identifies four distinctive communication styles ranging between extremes of **assertiveness** and **responsiveness**: (1) drivers, (2) analyticals, (3) expressives, (4) amiables. High assertive communicators are *task-oriented*. High responsive communicators are *people-oriented*. These various styles are also distinguished by their preference for either *telling* or *asking* in communication situations. In addition to each individual's primary communication style, there is commonly a **backup communication style** used as an alternative in situations where the primary style proves ineffective.

VI. Improving Your Self-Esteem

Self-esteem is vital to both the health of individuals and to the health of the society in which they are members. There is no royal road to self-esteem, but your text lists seven techniques for strengthening and reinforcing it:

(1) **Self-Talk** involves our ability to communicate objectively but positively with ourselves in an act of **intrapersonal communication.** Talking to ourselves, our internal conversation about our actions, abilities, and efforts, is a source of strength. Sometimes we admonish ourselves to "get up and get going!" Sometimes we affirm ourselves for "a job well done." Sometimes we even register disapproval of ourselves for "not doing what we should." We act as our own cheerleader and censor. Self-talk is beneficial if it is objective and constructive.

(2) **Visualization** involves picturing to ourselves outcomes we desire, a way of seeing ourselves getting to where we want to go. Visualization resembles a positive form of self-fulfilling prophecy. Visualization differs from fantasy and day-dreaming in being focussed on specific outcomes and in being linked with concrete practical efforts.

(3) **Avoiding Comparisons**. We all compare ourselves with others. In the words of William Shakespeare, we often "desire this man's gift and that man's scope," but we should always remember that we are all unique and incommensurate. Objective comparison of ourselves with others may sometimes be useful but should never degenerate into self-defeating envy. Look to see what you can do yourself before you judge and measure what others are doing. We cannot all excel but each is free to do his or her best.

(4) **Reframing** involves seeing things, people, and situations from a different, usually a broader, perspective. If we hold a coin immediately before our eyes, it will block out the sun itself. Standing back physically and emotionally from a situation may sometimes give us a clearer view of our surroundings.

(5) **Developing Honest Relationships**. Look to people you have learned to trust for objective and honest assessments. Sometimes we need the eyes of another to see more clearly with our own, and the eyes of a friend or colleague may not see or may see around an obstacle or problem that looms large for us.

(6) **Letting Go of the Past**. An old saying tells us: "What cannot be changed should not be lamented." We have wronged others and others have wronged us. When things can be put right between people, they should be, but often time moves on and nothing can be done. Without forgetting past hurt or unhappiness, which is often impossible, we should nonetheless learn to set them aside and move on.

(7) **Seeking Support.** When problems of self-esteem become severe seek help without shame. Various counselling services are available to those who need help. Here in Canada, these services are readily available to average citizens.

TERMS TO LEARN

Self
Self-Concept
Self-Esteem (Self-Worth)
Material Self
Social Self
Spiritual Self
Looking-Glass Self
Self-Reflexiveness
Attitudes
Beliefs
Values
Shyness
Social Phobia
Androgynous Role
Life Position
Specific-Other Perspective
General-Other Perspective
Self-Fulfilling Prophecy
Selective Exposure

Activity 2.1: Who Am I? Assessing Self-Concept

Objectives:
1. To help you reflect on your own self concept.
2. To give you insight into how others perceive you.

Part 1

Instructions:
1. For each category below list words or phrases that describe you most effectively.

Material Self

Possessions:____

Body:____

Home:____

Social Self

Friends:____

Family:____

Work:____

School:____

Spiritual Self

Values:____

Morals:____

Beliefs:____

Part 2

Instructions:

1. Write a summary paragraph describing yourself in terms of these three categories.

Part 3

Instructions:
1. Ask two other people in your life to describe you in terms of these categories.

PERSON (A)

Material Self

Possessions:____

Body:____

Home:____

Social Self

Friends:____

Family:____

Work:____

School:____

Spiritual Self

Values:____

Morals:____

Beliefs:____

PERSON (B)

Material Self

Possessions:____________________________________

Body:____

Home:____

Social Self

Friends:

Family:

Work:

School:

Spiritual Self

Values:

Morals:

Beliefs:

Activity 2.2: Self-Collage

Objective:
1. To provide an opportunity for further reflection on your sense of self.

Instructions:
1. Create a collage that represents who you are using the form on the next page. You can use pictures, clippings from magazines and newspapers, photographs, or any other materials or graphics that help to convey an image of who you are. These images might convey something of what you do or believe in, your special interests, talents, favourite places, food, people, personal tastes, your personality, or anything else that is significant in terms of who you are.

2. Share your collage in a small group in class. Invite others in your group to try to guess what you intended to convey about yourself. Discuss your collage with your group members. Have others share their collage with you.

3. When you have completed the exercise answer the following questions.

1. What was the most interesting thing I learned about myself in this process?

____

____

____

____

____

2. How did others perceive me?

____

____

____

____

____

3. Were there gaps between what others thought I was communicating about myself and what my intention was? If so, why?

____

____

____

____

____

COLLAGE

Activity 2.3: Self-Concept Development

Objective:

1. To help you reflect on how your self concept has developed.

Instructions:

1. Answer the question "How has my self-concept developed?" in relation to the categories below.
2. Give specific examples of experience or significant relationships that have been influential in your life.
3. Identify how these experiences or relationships influenced you either positively or negatively.

Example:

Interactions with others: *From the time I was six my grandmother began taking me to the opera.*

Influence: *This has been a positive influence giving me a love of classical music and influencing my decision to study music.*

Association with groups: *Bruce Trail Hiking Association*

Influence: *gave me a new appreciation for outdoors*

Roles I have assumed: *mother of two children*

Influence: *helped me appreciate the wonder of life, to take responsibility*

My own labels: *independent*

Influence: *helped me overcome opposition and work well even when there was no active support*

Interactions with Others
Example:
Influence:
Example:
Influence:
Association with Groups
Example:
Influence:
Example:
Influence:
Roles I Have Assumed
Example:
Influence:
Example:

Influence:
My Own Labels
Example:
Influence:
Example:
Influence:

Activity 2.4: Self-Talk

Objective:
1. To identify how self-talk influences our interactions with others.

Instructions:
1. In the following situations provide examples of negative self-talk and positive self-talk.

2. Give two examples from your own experience identifying the self talk that influenced your behaviour.

Example:
You passed your first two math tests but have failed the last three this term. Your final exam is next week. You need to pass this to achieve a passing grade in the course. The material on this upcoming test will be extremely difficult.

Negative Self-Talk: *The material is too difficult. I'll never understand it. Even if I studied day and night it is too much for me. I might as well give up now. I'm a math idiot anyway.*

Positive Self-Talk: *I passed the first two tests. I can pass this one. I just need to study more than I did last time. My friend Julie is doing well in math. I will ask her to explain the more difficult concepts to me. If I buckle down in the next week I'll make it through this.*

1. You have recently met a woman through a friend of yours. You are interested in asking her out for a date. You are uncertain about doing this, however, because you have heard through your friend that the last two men who asked her out were turned down.

Negative Self-Talk:
____
____
____
____

Positive Self-Talk:
____
____
____
____

2. You have just finished a major project at work that has succeeded in helping your company get three new major clients. You have not had a raise in two years and would like to take this opportunity to approach your manager on this subject. The last time you asked her for a raise, six months ago, she said, "Definitely not."

Negative Self-Talk:

Positive Self-Talk:

3. You are beginning a new job. You have been working in sales in the computer industry for five years. You are now assuming a sales position with a large pharmaceutical company. You are an excellent salesperson but know very little about the pharmaceutical business.

Negative Self-Talk:

Positive Self-Talk:

4. You are running your first marathon. You have been in training for the last three months. As you begin the race, you are overwhelmed by how quickly others in the race begin to pull ahead of you.

Negative Self-Talk:

Positive Self-Talk:

5. You have recently been let go from your previous job because of downsizing. You worked for that firm for seven years. You have strong references. You have heard that it will be difficult to find a new position because the market is flooded with people with your skills. You have your first job interview this afternoon.

Negative Self-Talk:

Positive Self-Talk:

6. Personal example:

Negative Self-Talk:

Positive Self-Talk:

7. Personal example:

Negative Self-Talk:

Positive Self-Talk:

8. Personal example:

Negative Self-Talk:

Positive Self-Talk:

Activity 2.5: Identifying Wilson Learning Corporation Communication Styles

Objective:
1. To develop an understanding of the four different communication styles.

Part 1
Instructions:
1. In the following situations identify how individuals using the four different communication styles (Analytical, Driver, Expressive, Amiable) might respond.

Example:

You and your husband are well educated. You have always expected that your son would go to university. His marks are excellent. He is in the beginning of his final year of high school when he informs you that he plans to drop out of school to work in a local factory where he can make a great deal of money. You want to convince him to stay in school.

Analytical Response:

"Well, you might make a great deal of money in the short run, but the loss of immediate income would be offset in the long run by the higher salary you would secure with a university degree. So, your education would be a long-term investment."

Driver Response:

"The idea is ridiculous. I will not hear of it. You will go to university as planned and fulfill your potential. I cannot allow myself to let you make such a damaging choice."

Expressive Response:

"How can you suggest such a thing? I could never forgive myself if I let you do that. It would break my heart to see you throw away so promising a future."

Amiable Response:

"Oh, yes, I can understand the temptation. I felt the same way when I was your age. Sometimes even now I wish I had simpler work. What gave you the idea? Aren't you happy in school? Whatever decision you make we will still love you, but I hope you'll think about it carefully because there is a lot at stake. How would you like to order a pizza tonight?"

1. Now imagine you are the president of a small land development firm with 20 employees. Recently the property manager appeared in your office and complained about his lack of autonomy in the running of his department. He felt you were interfering by speaking directly to his staff rather than coming to speak with him first.

Analytical Response:
Driver Response:
Expressive Response:
Amiable Response:

2. Imagine you are a social worker who counsels single mothers. A client of yours, Susan, has missed her last two appointments. This inconveniences you but also other needy clients who are on a waiting list for your services. When she arrives for her appointment today she is full of excuses for her previous absences saying that she forgot the first one and slept through the second because she had a cold.

Analytical Response:
Driver Response:
Expressive Response:

Amiable Response:

3. Imagine you are a management student in a fourth-year management course where 20 percent of your mark is based on your participation in a business computer simulation. You have been assigned to a group and each member is responsible for bringing their individual decision to your weekly group meetings. Once you input individual decisions you are able to arrive at a group decision. One group member, Chris, is consistently late for meetings and unprepared. This slows down your group and increases everyone's efforts. You approach Chris with your concerns.

Analytical Response:
Driver Response:
Expressive Response:
Amiable Response:

4. Imagine you are a new car salesperson. You have not met the expected quotas for sales in the last two months. You are eager to improve your record. A prospective customer has returned three times in the last week to look at a particular car. You know he is interested but deterred by the price. He says, "I don't know, it is a great car, but a bit pricey."

Analytical Response:
Driver Response:
Expressive Response:
Amiable Response:

Part 2

Instructions:

1. Think of a real-life situation and analyze how individuals using the four different communication styles might respond.

Situation:

Analytical Response:
Driver Response:

Expressive Response:

Amiable Response:

DIFFICULT POSITION 2

Tom's mother and father died in a car accident when he was only four years old, and he was raised by his paternal grandfather, a widower and farmer from New Brunswick. Tom worked side-by-side with his grandfather almost every day for twenty years, but they rarely talked. Tom's grandfather often said he had no patience for pain or complaint in a man. He himself did whatever work needed doing no matter how he felt about it, and he expected the same of Tom.

After his grandfather died and the farm was sold, Tom completed a teaching degree and took a job teaching high school math in Halifax. Tom couldn't understand his students. They seemed lazy and childish, and the girls especially complained about his harshness. Tom meant well, he knew that, but he wasn't getting the job done, and that made him feel ashamed. He had learned to do things the way his grandfather had done them, but it wasn't working now.

INSTRUCTIONS

1. Tom is experiencing a crisis of self. His self-concept and the communication style he derives from it are failing him. Imagine that Tom has asked you for advice and feedback about his situation. What could you recommend based on your knowledge of self, communication styles, reframing, and gender roles?

2. Discuss your recommendations in small groups and record your discussion.

Option:

1. Choose someone in your group to roleplay Tom. Whoever plays Tom should try to understand empathically what he might think and feel hearing about concepts like androgynous roles and backup communication. As a test of empathic understanding, Tom might be played by a female.

Exercise 2.1: Learning Objective: Identifying Wilson Learning Corporation Communication Styles

Instructions: In the following communication situation, identify the statements made by the various participants as instances of the four communication styles defined by the Wilson Learning Corporation: Driver, Analytical, Expressive, Amiable.

Chairman of the Board, Hiram Harrumph, arrives at the annual managers' meeting, sits at the head of the table under the corporate logo of a soaring eagle, and announces, "Things had better change around here or heads will roll!"_________ Dr. Occam Razor of Research and Development suggests that a new time and motion study be undertaken to assess management efficiency and observes, "If we divide tasks between those present, we should be able to complete the project within fourteen working days."__________ Peter Pathos of the Press Department interrupts at this point and almost shouts, "Do you have any idea of the stress the whole staff has been under these last few months?"___________ During all of this, Personnel Manager Grace Pleesing nods and smiles at everyone in turn and frequently repeats, "I quite understand what you mean."___________

Exercise 2.2: Learning Objective: Learning Terms and Definitions of Robert Norton's Nine Communication Styles

Instructions: Place the number of the term beside its appropriate definition.

(1) Dominant	( ) Says things in a memorable way. Uses words effectively.
(2) Dramatic	( ) Uses a variety of facial expressions when talking. Uses many gestures. Emotionally expressive, particularly around eyes and face.
(3) Contentious	( ) Easily expresses emotions and shares personal information with others.
(4) Animated	( ) Argues with others. Likes to debate. Demands evidence from others to support their arguments. Tenacious when arguing a point; difficult to turn off.
(5) Impression-leaving	( ) Talks a lot. Takes charge. Comes on strong. Controls conversation.
(6) Relaxed	( ) Listens well. Maintains eye contact and body posture that communicates interest in what others are saying. Good at paraphrasing what others have said.
(7) Attentive	( ) Often provides compliments, encouragement, and support to others. Helps others feel valued and affirmed.
(8) Open	( ) Seems cool, calm, centred, collected when talking with others even when under stress. Not easily affected by anxiety-producing situations.
(9) Friendly	( ) Tells stories and jokes. Often exaggerates. Acts out illustrations for comic effect.

Exercise 2.3: Learning Objective: General Review (**TRUE/FALSE**)

Instructions: Identify the following statements as either true or false.

1. Reframing is a defining characteristic of an assertive communication style. ( )

2. Our self-concept is fixed and inalterable after the period of infancy. ( )

3. In Western societies, possessions often influence assessment of self-worth. ( )

4. The most change-resistant aspect of our self-concept is our attitudes. ( )

5. A combination of traditional masculine and feminine roles in the behaviour of an individual is an instance of behavioural androgyny. ( )

6. A generalized-other perspective is a negative filter we impose on others due to our own expectations and prejudices. ( )

7. All individuals tend to develop a single characteristic communication style which they apply invariably in all circumstances. ( )

8. The four communication styles identified by the Wilson Learning Corporation – (drivers, analyticals, expressives, amiables) – are instances of intrapersonal communication. ( )

9. A hockey fan who goes to the ballet to please his girlfriend is a good example of selective exposure. ( )

10. We have as many social selves as we have social situations. ( )

11. The process of visualization is an attempt to make positive use of the power of self-fulfilling prophecy. ( )

12. Our sense of self-esteem is entirely dependent on the opinions of others. ( )

13. Our self-worth is our subjective description of who we are, and our self-concept is an objective evaluation of who we are. ( )

14. A predominance of assertiveness in a communication style is a sign of maladjustment requiring therapeutic correction. ( )

15. Our inner values and beliefs are contained within our looking-glass self. ( )

Exercise 2.4: Learning Objective: General Review (**FILL-IN-THE-BLANKS**)

Instructions: Fill in the blanks using the appropriate term or terms from the following list.

self	material self	self-reflexiveness	generalized-other perspective
self-concept	social self	self-esteem	
attitudes	spiritual self	specific-other perspective	self-fulfilling prophecy
beliefs	looking-glass self		selective exposure
values	androgynous role	life position	visualization
			reframing

1. When I started to learn my multiplication tables in grade school, my mother told me how hard it was for her to learn them at my age, and she said I would probably be just like her. I was scared, and I did have problems, but I suspect now it was just an example of ______________________.

2. _____________ involves seeing a thing or situation from a different perspective.

3. Refusing to even hear a political speaker because you belong to the opposite party is a good example of ____________________.

4. When someone's response to us confirms what we learned to think of ourselves from our own experience, his or her response is an instance of the__________________.

5. When the impoverished holy man remained happy despite want and even hunger, he demonstrated the power of his ________________ over his ________________.

6. ________________ involves our evaluation of self or our subjective assessment of our worth as an individual.

7. I knew Mary like to watch westerns, so I bought her a book about the Wild West for her birthday. She loved it. Everyone else bought her dolls and dresses. She liked the other gifts but not as much as mine. When it came to Mary, I had a ________________ and the rest had only a ____________________. In some things, Mary's preferences suit a more ______________________ that her older relatives don't understand.

8. Preferring vanilla ice cream or chocolate is a matter of _____________; considering sweets bad for one's health reflects one's____________; but judging people who eat sweets to be undisciplined and childish is an expression of ____________.

9. In the midst of the race, Tom pictured himself breaking through the tape at the finish line, and it was this powerful_____________________ which helped him to win.

10. The guys on the team told me I was no good, but when I thought about how many goals I had scored that season, I knew better. I used my capacity for __________ to correct the negative feedback I got from by peers.

11. When the waiter laughed at the customers' jokes, he sometimes felt strange. Often the jokes weren't even funny. He realized when this happened that he was acting a role prescribed by his ________________ which was only one part of the ________. He began to think about all the components of his personality because he wanted to develop a clear _______________________.

12. Yukio is always telling me how great I am and what a mess he is. I'm OK in his book, but he's definitely not OK in his own eyes. His ______________ is pretty sad.

Exercise 2.5: Learning Objective: General Review (**MULTIPLE CHOICE**)

Instructions: Choose the best answer for each question below.

1. Some theorists believe that the self is a composite of various elements, such as attitudes, beliefs, and values. Of these three which is the most resistant to change?

   a. attitudes
   b. beliefs
   c. values
   d. all three are equally resistant

2. Self-fulfilling prophecy can be either positive or negative. A positive instance would most probably be an example of what self-esteem boosting practice?

   a. reframing
   b. avoiding comparisons
   c. visualization
   d. letting go of the past

3. If you live in Vancouver and you learn that your new neighbour is from Quebec, you might greet him in French. If you did, what would be influencing your choice?

   a. selective exposure
   b. generalized-other perspective
   c. self-fulfilling prophecy
   d. specific-other perspective

4. A physician who never uses a patient's name, but who always gives an exhaustive account of symptoms and their causes with a carefully systematized treatment plan, might be best described as having which communication style?

   a. amiable
   b. driver
   c. analytical
   d. expressive

5. Our ideas about ultimate reality or truth are a part of what aspect of ourselves?

   a. material self
   b. social self
   c. spiritual self
   d. looking-glass self

6. Communication styles can best be characterized as ranging from

   a. specific-other to generalized-other
   b. masculine to feminine
   c. assertive to responsive
   d. amiable to friendly

7. All of the following statements are true except

   a. androgynous gender roles are an alternative to traditional masculine/feminine roles
   b. assessing our performance in a given action involves self-reflexiveness
   c. self-talk always consists of flattering and positive statements about ourselves
   d. persons of low self-esteem are more likely than others to be wounded by criticism

8. All of the following statements are true except

   a. visualization can assist us in our endeavours but is no guarantee of success
   b. we do not always give equal weight to comments of others concerning ourselves
   c. amiable communicators are always more effective than drivers
   d. communicators who use a driver style may sometimes appear harsh and unfriendly

9. All of the following are communication styles identified by Robert Norton except

   a. contentious
   b. attentive
   c. impression-leaving
   d. relentless

10. All of the following statements about the self are true except

    a. the self can be considered a composite of various elements
    b. our concept of self remains fixed from an early age
    c. self-esteem is vital to the health of individuals and entire societies
    d. our self-image is influenced by the comments and responses of others

11. All of the following statements about communication styles are true except

    a. individuals tend to develop a primary communication style
    b. most individuals are capable of using a backup or alternate communication style
    c. communication can be graphed as ranging between extremes of assertiveness and responsiveness
    d. responsive communication is always more effective than assertive

Answers

CHAPTER 2

Exercise 2.1

1. Driver
2. Analytical
3. Expressive
4. Amiable

Exercise 2.2

The correct sequence is: 5, 4, 8, 3, 1, 7, 9, 6, 2.

Exercise 2.3

1. (F)
2. (F)
3. (T)
4. (F)
5. (T)
6. (F)
7. (F)
8. (F)
9. (F)
10. (T)
11. (T)
12. (F)
13. (F)
14. (F)
15. (F)

Exercise 2.4

1. Self-fulfilling prophecy
2. Reframing
3. Selective exposure
4. Looking-glass self
5. Spiritual self/material self
6. Self-esteem
7. Specific-other perspective/ general-other perspective/ androgynous role
8. Attitudes/beliefs/values
9. Visualization
10. Self-reflexiveness
11. Social self/self/self-concept
12. Life position

Exercise 2.5

1. c
2. c
3. b
4. c
5. c
6. c
7. c
8. c
9. d
10. b
11. d

Chapter 3

Interpersonal Communication and Perception

CHAPTER OUTLINE

I. Understanding the Interpersonal Perception Process

A. Perception
1. Arousal of senses is the prior condition of perception
2. Organization and interpretation of sense information follows sense arousal

B. Interpersonal perception
1. Stage One (Selection)
   a. Selecting
      (1) The number of sensations we can attend to at once is limited
   b. Simplifying
      (1) Threshold arousal – many sensations are below threshold of arousal
      (2) Selective perception – we restrict attention to selected stimuli
   c. Categorizing
      (1) Prototypes – ideal models
      (2) Stereotypes – rigid categories disregarding individual differences
      (3) Those we like and those we dislike
         (a) Halo effect – (those we like do everything right)
         (b) Horn effect – (those we dislike do everything wrong)
2. Stage Two (Organization)
   a. Patterning – we organize or impose patterns upon sense information
   b. Punctuating – perception involves timing and rhythm
   c. Superimposing – we complete patterns we perceive as incomplete
      (1) Closure
3. Stage Three (Interpretation)
   a. Attribution of meaning – we ascribe meaning to the behaviours we see

II. Perception and Interpersonal Communication

A. Passive perception

B. Active perception

C. Six aspects of the interpersonal communication process
1. Impression formation
   a. First impressions (**primacy effect**)
   b. Last impressions (**recency effect**)
2. Implicit personality theory
   a. Beliefs and hypotheses about what people are like
3. Scripts
   a. Sequence of events that we expect in our interaction with others

4. Mental constructs
    a. Bipolar in their dimensions (good and bad, beautiful and ugly, etc.)
5. Cognitive complexity
6. Attribution theory
    a. Correspondent inference theory places emphasis on human motive
    b. Causal attribution considers circumstances
    c. Attributional biases
        (1) Self-serving bias ("I owe my present success to myself")
        (2) Self-handicapping bias ("I owe my future failure to someone else")

III. Ten Barriers to Accurate Perceptions

A. Ignoring detail
1. Undue weight given to obvious and superficial information
2. Overattribution

B. Overgeneralizing
1. Generalizing from small and inadequate data sample

C. Holding on to preconceptions
1. Distorting information to suit preconceptions
2. Ignoring information that does not suit preconceptions

D. Imposing consistency
1. Overestimating consistency and constancy of behaviour

E. Preconnecting causes and effects
1. Preexisting ideas about underlying causes and what we observe

F. Simplifying
1. Preferring simple explanations to complex

G. Ignoring circumstances
1. Attributing our own negative behaviour to circumstance
2. Disregarding circumstance in the negative behaviour of others

H. Crediting irrelevant information
1. Irrelevant information treated as relevant

I. Focussing on the negative
1. Giving undue weight to negative over positive information

J. Seeing good and bad
1. Distorting perception to favour those we like
2. Distorting perception to disfavour those we dislike

IV. Seven Ways to Improve Your Perception Skills

A. Increase understanding of perception process
1. Study text chapter
2. Question and analyze perceptions

B. Increase observation acuity
1. Increase active perception over passive

C. Recognize perception elements to which you attribute meaning

1. Become aware of stimuli to which you attribute meaning
    a. Eye contact
    b. Gestures
    c. Facial expressions
    d. Clothing
    e. Accents
    f. Vocal intonations

D. Check perceptions
1. Indirect perception checking
2. Direct perception checking

E. Increase awareness of and compensate for perception inaccuracies

F. Increase awareness of others' perceptions of you and seek honest feedback

G. Develop decentring, empathy, and other orientation
1. Gather knowledge about circumstances affecting other person
2. Gather knowledge about the person himself or herself
3. Gather knowledge about people in general

CHAPTER REVIEW: SECTION BY SECTION SUMMARY

I. Understanding the Interpersonal Perception Process

Perception involves the arousal of our various physical senses and the organization and interpretation of information we derive from them. Interpersonal perception is a subset of perception and involves judgements and inferences about the personality and motives of others based upon our perceptions of their behaviours, actions, and statements. There are three distinct stages in our processing of sense data relative to interpersonal perception: (1) **selection**, (2) **organization**, (3) **interpretation**.

Selection involves a necessary reduction in the amount and variety of stimuli to which we are exposed. The number of sensations to which we can attend at any given moment is limited. Many stimuli do not even register as a part of our conscious awareness unless they pass a *threshold of arousal.* For instance, we tend to be unaware of the feel of our clothing unless it is in some way uncomfortable. The process of selection involves simplifying perceptions by excluding some at the expense of others. If we are listening intently to a piece of music, we may be much less attentive to other ambient sights and sounds. Attending to selected perceptions and ignoring others is called **selective perception.** Another means of simplification involves **categorizing**. Three common categories for organizing and limiting our perception are (1) **prototypes,** (2) **stereotypes**, and (3) grouping people according to **those we like and those we dislike**.

A prototype is an ideal model for all similar instances of a given type. For instance, you may have an image in your mind of the ideal athlete (perhaps a real individual), and you might tend to use this image or ideal prototype as a measure of all other athletes, assimilating the characteristics of many others to your prototype.

A stereotype is a kind of negative prototype and involves the creation of a group type to which individuals are assimilated despite their own individual characteristics. Racial and gender stereotypes are common and often the cause of miscommunication and misunderstanding. Generalizations about groups are not always inaccurate or inappropriate, but a stereotype is a generalization which usually refuses to accept counterevidence and sets itself up as irrefutable.

In our perception of others we tend to see whatever favours those we like and whatever disfavours those we dislike. Seeing those we like as angels is an example of the **halo effect**, and making devils of those we dislike is an example of the **horn effect**.

Organization involves the arrangement of our perceptions by means of (1) **patterning**, (2) **punctuating**, and (3) **superimposing**

Whenever we are confronted with multiple and similar stimuli, we strive to discover the pattern of their relationship, and sometimes we create a pattern which may or may not reflect real connections existing among the perceived stimuli.

Just as grammatical punctuation regulates the rhythm and order of sentences and phrases, relational or behavioural punctuation regulates the rhythm and order of our perceptions and our responses to perceptions. In the perceptual interchange of a conversation, two people may have a different sense of the overall rhythm and order of their communication and may give emphasis or closure to different conversation elements at different times and in different ways. These differences in "relational punctuation" may cause mutual confusion.

Superimposing involves our tendency to complete any pattern presented to us as incomplete. If there is one word missing in a sentence, we are likely to provide one by guessing what it would be from context. It may be, however, that the omitted word was quite different from our guess. We often do this with people, fitting them to a pattern or type to which we feel they partially conform. We "fill in the blanks" in our desire to achieve **closure**.

Attribution involves the irrepressible human need to give meaning to things, especially to the behaviour and action of others. When someone does or says something, we are always asking ourselves what it means. Sometimes we are aware of this, sometimes we are not. In the behaviour of others we try to discover motives and intentions, significance, and implications. We hope we are accurate in our inferences based upon our perceptions, but accurate or not, we cannot avoid imposing meaning on what we observe. Where the meaning of a behaviour or an action is not obvious or manifest, we *attribute* a meaning to the best of our ability based on our perceptions.

II. Perception and Interpersonal Communication

Our perceptions of others affects the ways in which we communicate with them, and their perceptions of us affect the way they communicate with us. We are always involved in the ongoing process of perception, but often we are not explicitly aware of this. Such essentially automatic perception is called **passive perception**. It is in our power to become actively aware of our involvement in the perception process. Such active involvement is called **active perception**. Active perception is in our interest because it allows us to improve our power to control and predict the world around us to accomplish our personal goals, which always requires accurate and complete information for developing goal-oriented plans and strategies.

The collection, organization and interpretation of information in the process of interpersonal perception involves six distinct aspects: (1) **Impression Formation**, (2) **Implicit Personality Theory**, (3) **Scripts**, (4) **Constructs**, (5) **Cognitive Complexity**, (6) **Attribution Theory**.

Impression Formation involves our perceptions of physical qualities, behaviours, self-disclosures, and third-party information about others, which we collect and unify as overall impressions. Our first and last impressions in any encounter are likely to be the most influential. This disproportionate significance of first and last impressions is known as the **primacy effect** and the **recency effect**.

Implicit Personality Theory. We all tend to have some general assumptions about human nature. The French philosopher Jean Jacques Rousseau believed that human beings were good by nature. Protestant theologians like John Calvin believed that human beings were inherently sinful and wicked. Our implicit personality theory influences our perception of others.

Scripts. Actors need a script to know what their lines are. Once they memorize the script, their actions and statements are set. There are scripts offstage too. Many situations in daily life are like one-act plays in which we function very much like actors who have memorized a script. We know what's expected in the situation and we act accordingly. We follow the script and play our part. Shakespeare said "all the world's a stage," and sometimes it may seem that way to us as we move from one scripted situation to another. Communication scripts like theatrical scripts keep the action moving.

Constructs are bipolar systems of categorizing human behaviours and qualities: friendly or unfriendly, intelligent or unintelligent, graceful or clumsy, extrovert or introvert, funny or serious, conservative or liberal, overachiever or underachiever, playful or studious.

Cognitive Complexity. The number and subtlety of the constructs we develop and use to organize and interpret stimuli is a measure of cognitive complexity.

Attribution Theory. As mentioned earlier, we all attribute specific motives and causes to the behaviours we observe. Developing the most credible explanation for the behaviour of others is the goal of the **attribution process**. Your text mentions two dominant attribution theories and two forms of attribution bias: (1) **Correspondent Inference Theory**, (2) **Causal Attribution Theory**, (3) **self-serving bias**, (4) **self-handicapping strategy**.

Correspondent Inference Theory involves our attempt to uncover the intentionality of a person causing an action. This theory assumes that an individual's action reflects individual choice and purpose.

Causal Attribution Theory identifies three potential causes for any person's action: (1) circumstances, (2) stimulus, or (3) the person her- or himself.

Circumstantial attribution concerns the external forces which may sometimes compel an action. A person responding to pressure of circumstance has diminished or no responsibility for his or her action. Swerving to avoid an oncoming car and striking another is an action governed by circumstance.

Stimulus attribution concerns external causes which are activating but not compulsory. If someone insults you, and you strike out at him, you are certainly responding to stimuli, but your reaction is not compulsory, not like the instinctive flinching which causes us to turn away from an oncoming automobile. Responsibility may be diminished but still exists.

Person attribution assumes free and deliberate action for which the agent is fully responsible.

Self-serving bias is a way to have things both ways: if we succeed, we credit our free action and abilities; if we fail, we blame circumstances or the actions of others. **Self-handicapping strategy** attempts to compensate for possible failure by excusing it in advance as inevitable given adverse circumstances.

Our ability to make accurate attributions concerning the behaviour of others depends on (1) our ability to make effective and complete observations, (2) the degree to which we are able to directly observe the cause and the effect, (3) the completeness of our information, (4) our level of self-interest, and (5) our ability to rule out other causes.

III. Barriers to Accurate Communication

There are ten main barriers to accurate communication:

Ignoring Details – *giving too much weight to information that is obvious and superficial.* Stereotypes are an instance of this barrier since they disregard all the details of an individual's identity and focus only on such obvious group characteristics as race, ethnicity, and gender.

Overgeneralizing – *treating small amounts of information as if they were highly representative.* If we visited a strange city and had a traffic accident, we might judge that the citizens there were bad drivers. This would be an overgeneralization based on inadequate data.

Holding on to Preconceptions – *distorting or ignoring information that violates our expectations and preconceptions.* Once we make up our minds about someone, we are often reluctant to make changes, even when we have evidence that our conceptions are mistaken. The halo and horn effect are instances of this barrier.

Imposing Consistency – *overestimating the consistency and constancy of others' behaviours.* We usually reserve to ourselves the right to change whenever we wish, and we are often generous with friends when they are having a bad day or are just in a sour mood. However, when it comes to people we do not know well, we seem to think they should always be the same and are surprised when they are not. We require and strive to enforce a higher degree of consistency in the behaviour of others than we require of ourselves or our friends.

Preconnecting Causes and Effects – *relying on preexisting ideas about underlying causes and what we observe.* If we have often observed that a given effect is produced by a given cause, we may assume that all instances of that effect are always produced by the same cause. If you are running with a friend and he slows to a walk, you might assume that he is just not pushing himself enough. That's often the case with runners, and they sometimes benefit from friendly encouragement "to get going." However, it is also possible that your friend is suffering from asthma or a heart problem. Assumptions about cause and effect relationships in human behaviour are often reasonable but can seldom be certainties.

Simplifying – *preferring simple explanations to complex ones.* We often lack patience for lengthy explanations of behaviour and prefer those which are "short and sweet."

Ignoring Circumstances – *diminishing the effect of circumstances on another's behaviour.* When it comes to our own behaviour, we want others to understand all the obstacles and limitations which may have contributed to our failures, but with the behaviour of others, we tend to assume their actions are always freely chosen, unlimited by circumstance, and deliberate. Everyone has personal responsibility. Everyone also has limiting circumstances. Neither should be exaggerated in judging behaviours, our own and others.

Crediting Irrelevant Information – *treating irrelevant information as if it were relevant.* We sometimes interpret another's behaviour as if it were relevant to ourselves when it is not. If we ask a question of a teacher, and he or she winces, we might reasonably assume that we had said something stupid or insulting, but it is quite possible that the behaviour had some other cause entirely, maybe a tight shoe. In the absence of other confirming evidence, it is often unwise to attribute too much significance to any one minor action of another. One of the most difficult things to realize and remember is how little other people's behaviour has to do with us, how often it is irrelevant to us and our concerns.

Focussing on the Negative – *giving more weight to negative information than to positive information.* Shakespeare famously said, "the evil that men do lives after them, the good is oft interred with their bones," meaning we often tend to remember and emphasize the bad things in our experience over the good. Why is this so? Perhaps in the biological and cultural development of the human species fear and pain played a disproportionate part, and we are now "hardwired" to register this intensely. However, with conscious effort we can be aware of the real balance of good and bad in our experience and weigh them more accurately and justly.

Seeing Good and Bad – *distorting our attributions to match our like or dislike of someone.* Often enough, those we like can do no evil in our eyes, and those we dislike can do no good. We give the benefit of the doubt to our friends when their actions are sometimes less than perfect. We tend to distrust and discredit even the good actions of those we dislike.

IV. Improving Your Perceptual Skills

To improve perceptual skills, one must be willing to do three things: (1) grow as experience expands, (2) communicate perceptions with others, and (3) seek out and consider others' perceptions. There are seven specific strategies to achieve these goals:

Increase Your Understanding of the Perceptual Process. Read your text. Analyze your perceptions.

Increase Your Observational Acuity. Practise active perception over passive.

Recognize the Elements to Which You Attribute Meaning. Become aware of the stimuli to which you attend when attributing meaning to behaviours, such as eye contact, gestures, facial expressions, clothing, accents, vocal intonations.

Check Your Perceptions. Check your perceptions of the behaviour of others either **indirectly** by acquiring more information or **directly** by asking for confirmation from the people themselves. Direct perception checking may involve risks which should be pondered and assessed beforehand.

Increase Your Awareness of Perceptual Inaccuracies and Compensate for Them. If you recognize among the various barriers to communication listed above one or two to which you are especially susceptible, be aware of them and strive to overcome them.

Increase Your Awareness of Others' Perceptions of You and Seek Honest and Constructive Feedback. Try to imagine how others see your behaviours and welcome opportunities to hear what they think and feel about it.

Develop Decentring, Empathy, and Other Orientation. To improve your ability to decentre, strive for three key goals: (1) gather as much knowledge about the circumstances that are affecting the other person as possible, (2) gather as much knowledge about the other person as possible, and (3) gather as much knowledge as possible about understanding people in general.

TERMS TO LEARN

Perception
Interpersonal Perception
Selective Perception
Prototypes
Stereotypes
Halo Effect
Horn Effect
Closure
Passive Perception
Active Perception
Impression Formation
First Impression
Primacy Effect
Recency Effect
Implicit Personality Theory
Scripts
Personal Constructs
Cognitive Complexity
Attributions
Correspondent Inference Theory
Causal Attribution Theory
Self-Serving Bias
Self-Handicapping Strategy
Indirect Perception Checking
Direct Perception Checking

Activity 3.1: Perception Diary

Objectives:
1. To improve your observational skills.
2. To explore how your perceptions are similar or different from the actual intentions of others.
3. To explore how accurate the meanings we attribute to others' behaviour are.

Instructions:
1. For the next several days choose two people to observe. Record your observations and interpretations of their behaviour in the following chart.
2. At the end of your observation period check with these individuals to see if your perceptions of their behaviour were accurate.
3. Answer the questions following the exercise.

Name	Observations	My Interpretation	Actual Intent

Name	Observations	My Interpretation	Actual Intent

1. How were your interpretations similar or different from what you discovered when you questioned the individuals you observed?

2. If there was a difference, to what do you attribute the difference?

3. What did you learn from this experience?

Activity 3.2: First Impressions

Objectives:

1. To explore the forming of first impressions.
2. To identify the effects of forming first impressions.
3. To receive feedback about yourself.

Part 1

Instructions:

1. List at least 6 adjectives that you would use to describe yourself in column one. Join two others in your class group, preferably people you do not know very well. Ask these two individuals to provide you with adjectives that they would use to describe you based on their first impressions of you in class. Record these adjectives in column two.

2. Answer the questions at the end of Part 1.

Option 2:

1. Approach two people you have met recently in a context outside of class. Complete the exercise with them.

Column One	**Column Two**	**Column Three**
Self-Description	***Others' First Impressions***	***Revisiting Impressions***

1. How were the two lists in column one and column two similar or different?

2. If there were differences to what do you attribute this?

Part 2

Instructions:

1. Several weeks after your first discussion ask the same two people to provide you with adjectives as to how they would describe you now that they know you better. Record these in column three of the chart in Part 1.

2. Answer the following questions.

A. What differences do you notice between column two and three?

B. If there are differences to what do you attribute this?

Activity 3.3: Barriers to Accurate Perception

Objectives:
1. To identify barriers to accurate perception.
2. To improve your perceptual skills.

Instructions:
1. In the following examples identify barriers to perception.
2. Identify how these barriers could be prevented.

Example: *An employee has refused to work overtime on a project. His manager says, "Young people are so lazy!"*

Barrier: *Ignoring details or overgeneralizing*

How this could be prevented: *Explore with the employee why he will not work overtime on the project. Ask questions. Get more specific information.*

1. A professor who taught you an experiential course in interpersonal skills last term is now assigned to teach you a course on business concepts. In the first course she was dynamic, knowledgeable, and enthusiastic. You did well in the course and thoroughly enjoyed it. Your teacher is unaccustomed to delivering a three-hour lecture and the content in this business course is new to her. Her classes this term tend to be boring and disorganized. She reads extensively from her notes. When a classmate complains to you about your professor you retort with, "Hey, she's a great teacher!"

Barrier:

How this could be prevented:

2. Your wife was under tremendous pressure at work last week. Being overworked she tended to be short with you and ill-tempered. This week when she arrives home from work and goes upstairs to change you call up to her to see if she would like to go out for dinner. She doesn't respond. You assume she is angry when in fact she simply does not hear you.

Barrier:

How this could be prevented:

3. You are late to work this morning because of an accident on the freeway. When you arrive at your office you are confronted by your boss. He is angry and pontificates, "You can't ever trust a woman to be on time or to act responsibly on the job. Women should stay at home."

Barrier:

How this could be prevented:

4. You provide computer support to various clients. Just as you are about to leave work to meet a friend for dinner an important client calls with a problem that needs to be resolved immediately. You are half an hour late for your dinner engagement. Your friend refuses to listen to your explanations and assumes your lateness is an indication that you do not value the friendship.

Barrier:

How this could be prevented:

5. You are an instructor and have requested verbal feedback from your students as to how the course is going. The feedback is overwhelmingly positive; however, one student complains that you don't bring much enthusiasm to the course and that your lectures are repetitive of the text. This student's comments keep you awake all night.

Barrier:

How this could be prevented:

6. A speeder is stopped and issued a ticket. As he drives away he turns to his wife and says, "I'm not surprised he refused to give me just a warning. Law enforcement appeals to authoritarian personalities."

Barrier:

How this could be prevented:

7. The president of your college has decided to give the faculty a 3 percent raise. You are quite impressed with his decision because you know that he had to advocate a local tax increase to get the raise and that is never popular. You tell one of your colleagues the president made the right decision, and she says, "He only did it

because he'll get a raise himself. As far as I am concerned that guy never does anything right."

Barrier:

How this could be prevented:

8. A customer comes into a bakery and says, "I'm sorry, Ms. Wilson, but your husband is so rude. Whenever I come into the store he stares right at me, and even if I look back, he goes right on staring. I don't like being ogled like that." You respond, "Oh, I am sorry, dear, but Mr. Wilson thinks he doesn't have to wear his glasses at work. I very much doubt he can see to the end of his own nose, and I know for a fact that you are nothing but a pink blur."

Barrier:

How this could be prevented:

Part 2: Give three examples from your own life and identify the barriers.

Example:
Barrier:
Example:
Barrier:
Example:
Barrier:

Activity 3.4: Perception Checks

Objective:

1. To give you practice in checking your perceptions of observed behaviour.

Part 1

Instructions:

1. For the following examples write perception checking statements. Each statement should describe the observed behaviour, offer at least one interpretation, and check for understanding.

Example:

You and a co-worker from another department are working on a project together. In order to meet deadlines you need his report by the 25th of each month. You have agreed on this time frame together. He has been a week late in submitting this to you for two months in a row now.

Perception Check:

A few months ago we agreed that you would have your report to me by the 25th of the month. You have been a week late in submitting your report to me for the last two months. Are you finding the project too cumbersome to meet the deadline or have you been busy with other work? What's up?

1. You and a roommate have agreed to share household chores. It is her week to do the dishes. For four days now the dishes have been piling up in the sink.

Perception Check:____

____

____

____

2. Your sixteen year old daughter is out on a date. You have told her to be home by midnight. At 2:30 a.m. her boyfriend drops her off at the front door.

Perception Check:____

____

____

____

3. You are on your way out to a party. You can't find your new jeans. Later that evening you return home to find them lying on your sister's bed.

Perception Check:____

4. You have arranged to meet a friend at the movies at 7:00 p.m. The show starts at 7:20. Your friend does not arrive until 8:00 p.m.

Perception Check:____

5. Three weeks ago you left a voice mail message for your professor regarding your final mark in his course. You indicated that you would like to find out what you scored on your final exam so you can understand why your grade is so low. He has still not returned your call.

Perception Check:____

6. You have been meeting with your work team for an hour and you notice a group member has not spoken once during this time. You know she has good ideas to contribute and information necessary to the completion of your project.

Perception Check:____

7. You and your girlfriend are spending the evening at home eating pizza and watching a movie. In the middle of a suspenseful scene she jumps up and says she has to go out for awhile.

Perception Check:____

Part 2

Instructions:

1. Give three real-life situations.
2. Write a perception check for each of these examples.

Situation:
Perception Check:
Situation:
Perception Check:
Situation:
Perception Check:

DIFFICULT POSITION 3

At a family gathering, your uncle starts talking about welfare reform, his favourite topic. "They're all a bunch of bums," he declares. "They don't work because they don't want to work. All they want is to have kids and make us pay for them." Your uncle doesn't know that you, his niece, were on welfare once for a year when you were out of work in Vancouver after the birth of your first child. You have a good job now, but welfare got you through a hard time long ago.

INSTRUCTIONS

1. Without revealing anything about her own background, how might the niece use what she knows about communication concepts such as ignoring circumstances, stereotypes, and preconnecting causes and effects to help her uncle to a new perspective?

2. If you were the niece, would you reveal your background as a welfare recipient? If so, why? If not, why not? Do you think such self-disclosure would make your message more or less effective?

3. Discuss in small groups and appoint a secretary to take notes and write a brief summary.

Exercise 3.1: Learning Objective: General Review (**TRUE/FALSE**)

Instructions: Identify the following statements as either true or false.

1. Our ability to attend to sensory stimuli is unlimited. ( )

2. A self-handicapping strategy is a kind of stereotype. ( )

3. First and last impressions often have greater impact than those in between. ( )

4. Prototypes and stereotypes are members of a bipolar mental construct. ( )

5. Correspondent Inference Theory bases attributions on the assumption of free choice and intention in the action of individuals. ( )

6. Predicting failure in an upcoming contest due to the bias of unfair judges might be described as an instance of self-serving bias. ( )

7. By superimposing we complete patterns presented to us as incomplete. ( )

8. A script is a distortion we impose to explain the actions of those we dislike. ( )

9. All judgements about the behaviour of others based on race, ethnicity, and gender are inaccurate generalizations. ( )

10. Causal Attribution Theory seeks to explain our inability to overcome selective perception. ( )

11. Our Implicit Personality Theories are subject to change over time. ( )

12. Active perception tends to create the halo effect and passive perception tends to create the horn effect. ( )

13. Attribution Theory argues that attributing meaning to human behaviours based on observation is a barrier to accurate communication. ( )

14. One way to check the accuracy of a perception is to directly ask the person you are observing if your perception is, in fact, accurate. ( )

15. Decentring cannot help to improve the accuracy of our perceptions. ( )

16. Failure to consider the circumstances of someone's behaviour may lead to our making an inaccurate attribution of intention. ( )

Exercise 3.2: Learning Objective: General Review (**FILL-IN-THE-BLANKS**)

Instructions: Fill in the blanks using the appropriate term or terms from the following list.

perception	horn effect	first impression	correspondent inference theory	cognitive complexity
interpersonal perception	closure	primacy effect	self-serving bias	direct perception checking
selective perception	passive perception	recency effect	self-handicapping strategy	stereotype
prototype	attributions	indirect perception checking	causal attribution theory	
scripts	active perception	personal constructs	halo effect	
naive psychologists	impression formation	implicit personality theory		

1. In examining the murderer's behaviour, the criminal psychologist considered the combination of circumstances and stimuli involved, as well as the intentionality of the killer. Only after considering all three did he attribute a motive to his actions. The psychologist's approach resembled the threefold structure of ______________.

2. Tom believes all human beings are motivated primarily by greed, so when his employees claimed to be dissatisfied with working conditions, he assumed they were simply trying to get more money. His assumptions derive from his own ________.

3. When the head of the daycare facility refused to consider a male applicant for the position because she was convinced men were incapable of nurturing care, she was using a __________ in making her decision.

4. Mary had been dating Tom for three weeks, and she was convinced he was perfect. Beth, one of her classmates, told her Tom was seeing someone else on the sly, but Mary refused to believe it. She knew Tom would never do anything selfish or mean, and she was sure her classmate was lying to spite her. Beth never said or did anything Mary approved of anyway. Mary's attitude toward Tom demonstrates the_________ and her attitude toward Beth the__________.

5. We can't help searching for and speculating about the meaning of others' behaviours. When it comes to human beings and what they do, we are all________________.

6. _____________ involves an effort to anticipate and excuse possible failure in a way that shifts responsibility from ourselves to outside circumstances.

7. I realized I had seen the conductor's peculiar gestures before, but it was only ___________________ then, of which I was hardly aware. Now I trained my attention on his strange mannerism in a real effort of _______________________.

8. I was afraid to risk _______________________ by asking him outright if I was correct, so instead, I resorted to _____________________________ and continued to watch him carefully for days to see if my _________________________ was the right one.

9. The ingestion of hallucinogenic drugs by the writer Aldous Huxley was an effort, he claimed, to expand and alter ____________________.

10. To categorize adequately a personality of his type requires a broad range of ___________________only available to someone of considerable __________________.

11. The moment she first walked into the room, the process of ___________________ began. Her first appearance was so dramatic and captivating that for many years afterwards it still influenced my view of her. A grand entrance like that has a ________________ not easily forgotten. Sadly, the _______________ of her cruelty and vulgarity at the party yesterday dims her image considerably.

12. My appointment with the dentist did not seem like a rich opportunity to experience the full range of________________. An appointment is just a matter of everyone following their_____________. Everything is so obvious that ________________ about intentions and motivations are almost certain to be accurate and can be made effortlessly.

13. In the case of a woman who is financially secure, in good mental health, and fiercely independent, it is reasonable to assume her actions derive from unhindered intentionality. I therefore applied the _______________ in attempting to account for them.

14. At the health club, I realize I block out almost everything around me. I guess I have to practise _____________________ to maintain any concentration. I admit, health clubs are not my __________________ of a pleasant environment. I always say "you're welcome" when I let people work in, even though they almost never say "thank you." I can't help providing that _____________ required by courtesy.

15. _____________ is a way of taking credit for what we do right and shifting blame for what we do wrong.

Exercise 3.3: Learning Objective: General Review (**MULTIPLE CHOICE**)

Instructions: Choose the best answer for each question below:

1. The theory which emphasizes intentionality in the interpretation of human behaviour is known as

   a. Impression Formation
   b. Cognitive Complexity
   c. Implicit Personality Theory
   d. Correspondent Inference Theory

2. Bipolar categorization of human behaviours is an aspect of our

   a. Scripts
   b. Personal constructs
   c. Active perception
   d. Self-serving bias

3. Giving balanced consideration to circumstances, stimuli, and intention in interpreting human behaviour is most characteristic of

   a. Correspondent Inference Theory
   b. Causal Attribution Theory
   c. Implicit Personality Theory
   d. Cognitive complexity

4. The urge and tendency to provide the missing element or elements in an incomplete pattern is known as

   a. selective perception
   b. punctuating
   c. superimposing
   d. imposing consistency

5. Predicting one's defeat in a forthcoming contest due to the favouritism of the judges is an instance of

   a. self-serving bias
   b. self-handicapping strategy
   c. stereotyping
   d. superimposing

6. The ordinary reception of most incoming stimuli is characteristic of

   a. active perception
   b. patterning
   c. categorizing
   d. passive perception

7. All of the following statements are true except

   a. prototypes are generalizations about people based on their group membership
   b. first and last impressions are often most influential in forming a total impression
   c. perception involves the arousal of our senses and the organization of sense data
   d. numerous personal constructs is a sign of cognitive complexity

8. All of the following statements are true except

   a. direct perception checking is always the best method for checking our perceptions
   b. indirect perception checking is likely to require more time than direct perception checking
   c. a self-serving bias seeks to claim credit for success and shift blame for failure
   d. attribution of meaning to behaviour is a natural aspect of human perception

9. All of the following are aspects of impression formation except

   a. primacy effect
   b. recency effect
   c. prototypes
   d. self-handicapping strategy

10. All of the following statements about perception are true except

    a. perception is always selective
    b. most ordinary perception is passive
    c. the halo effect may distort our perceptions of our friends' behaviours
    d. the horn effect leads us to attribute the behaviour of people we dislike to scripts

11. All of the following about attribution are true except

    a. attributions about human behaviour based on stereotypes are always inaccurate
    b. attributions about human behaviour based on prototypes involve categorization
    c. attributions which diminish the circumstances influencing the behaviour of others are more commonly made of strangers than friends
    d. attributions are often influenced by superficial and irrelevant information

Answers

CHAPTER 3

Exercise 3.1

1. (F)
2. (F)
3. (T)
4. (F)
5. (T)
6. (F)
7. (T)
8. (F)
9. (F)
10. (F)
11. (T)
12. (F)
13. (F)
14. (T)
15. (F)
16. (T)

Exercise 3.2

1. Causal Attribution Theory
2. Implicit Personality Theory
3. Stereotype
4. Halo effect/Horn effect
5. Naive psychologists
6. Self-serving strategy
7. Passive perception/ Active perception
8. Direct perception checking/ Indirect perception checking/ First Impression
9. Perception
10. Personal constructs/Cognitive Complexity
11. Impression formation/ Primacy effect/Recency effect
12. Interpersonal perception/ Scripts/attributions
13. Correspondent Inference Theory
14. Selective perception/ Prototype/closure
15. Self-serving bias

Exercise 3.3

1. d
2. b
3. b
4. c
5. b
6. d
7. a
8. a
9. d
10. d
11. a

Chapter 4

Listening and Responding

CHAPTER OUTLINE

I. Listening Defined

- **A.** Hearing -- the physiological process of decoding sounds
- **B.** Listening -- the process we use to make sense of what we hear
  1. Selecting -- focussing on a sound among sounds competing for attention
  2. Attending -- focussing attention on a selected sound
     a. Some things tend to intensify attention more than others
        (1) Conflict
        (2) New ideas
        (3) Concrete things
        (4) An invitation to participate or respond
  3. Understanding -- the process of assigning meaning to selected sounds
     a. Understanding is aided by relating new things to what we already know
        (1) Analogy
        (2) Comparison
        (3) Shared cultural background
     b. Learning by experiencing is an aid to understanding
  4. Remembering -- information recall
     a. Short-term memory -- limited storage
     b. Long-term memory -- storage of significant information
        (1) Dramatic and vital information
        (2) Details associated with dramatic and vital information
  5. Responding -- interactive communication
     a. Verbal responses
     b. Nonverbal responses

II. Why You Listen

- **A.** Listening to enjoy
  1. Entertainers
  2. Television
  3. Musicians
  4. Storytelling of friends
- **B.** Listening to learn
  1. The more motivated you are the more you are likely to listen
  2. Learning takes place outside classrooms
     a. Media news
     b. Everyday information

            c. Daily activities of others

C. Listening to evaluate

1. Critical decisions and judgements
   a. Job interviewer
   b. Job applicant
2. Using critical thinking skills to evaluate
   a. Separating facts from inferences
   b. Identifying fallacies in reasoning
   c. Analyzing evidence

D. Listening to empathize

   a. Empathy -- to feel what someone else feels
   b. Sympathy -- to think about or acknowledge feelings

III. Seven Listening Barriers

A. Men and women may communicate differently

1. Men listen to solve a problem and are instrumental and task-oriented
   a. Focus on main ideas
2. Women listen to seek information to enhance understanding
   b. Attend to details

B. Focussing on personal agenda -- waiting our turn in a conversation

1. Focus on our own internal message can keep us from attending

C. Emotional noise -- emotional arousal interferes with communication

1. Fighting words -- obscene or provocative language
2. Emotional state of speaker

D. Criticizing the speaker -- being critical may distract us from message

1. Appearances
   a. Clothing
   b. Body size and shape
   c. Age
   d. Ethnicity

E. Speech rate versus thought rate -- we listen faster than we talk

1. Speech rate = approximately 125 words a minute
2. Thought rate = 600 to 800 words a minute

F. Information overload – bombardment by multiple auditory stimuli

1. Computers
2. Fax machines
3. Car phones

G. External noise

1. Literal noise
   a. Television
   b. Computer games
   c. Music
2. Distractor noise

a. Desire to attend to other stimuli than the ones before you

IV. Improving Your Listening Skills

A. Stop – make conscious effort to stop internal running commentary
1. Skill acquisition gradual
    a. Abraham Maslow's four stages of skill acquisition
        (1) Unconscious incompetence
        (2) Conscious incompetence
        (3) Conscious competence
        (4) Unconscious competence

B. Look – attending to nonverbal messages
1. Primary means of communicating feelings, emotions and attitudes
    a. Facial expressions, vocal cues, eye contact, posture, gesture
2. When nonverbal message contradicts verbal, nonverbal is believed

C. Listen – concentrated effort to stop internal dialogue and to see nonverbal cues
1. Mentally summarize details of message
2. Mentally weave summaries into focussed major points or ideas

V. Transform Listening Barriers into Listening Goals

A. Avoid focus on personal agenda
1. Use self-talk to manage emotional noise
2. Set a goal not to criticize Speaker
3. Make summaries that capitalize on different speech and thought rate
4. Choose communication environment free of distractions

B. Listen to challenging materials
1. Documentaries
2. Debates

C. Determine your listening goals
1. Learn
2. Enjoy
3. Evaluate
4. Support

VI. Responding with Empathy

A. Good listening is active not passive
1. Responses measure how accurately you understand message
2. Responses indicate agreement or disagreement with comments others make
3. Responses tell speakers how they are affecting others

B. Understanding your partner's feelings
1. Imagine how you would feel under same circumstances

C. Ask questions
1. Ask questions to identify sequence of events ("what happened first?")
2. Ask for definitions of terms ("what does that word mean?")

3. Ask for an example
4. Ask how they are feeling

D. Reflect content by paraphrasing
1. Restate elements of message received in your own words and phrases
   a. Events
   b. Key points
2. Use responsive phrases
   a. "Are you saying . . .?"
   b. "You seem to be describing . . . ."
   c. "So the point you are making seems to be . . . ."
   d. "Here is what I understand you to mean . . . ."
   e. "So here is what seemed to happen . . . ."

E. Reflect feelings by paraphrasing
1. Be an active listener
   a. Avoid unsolicited advice
2. Use responsive phrases
   a. "So, you are feeling . . . ."
   b. "You must feel . . . ."
   c. "So, now you feel . . . ."
   d. "Emotionally, you must be feeling . . . ."

F. Reflect both content and feelings through paraphrase
1. In specific situations
   a. Before beginning important actions
   b. Before arguing or criticizing
   c. When partner has strong feelings or a problem
   d. When partner is speaking "in code" (technical jargon, abbreviations)
   e. When partner wants to understand your feelings and thoughts
   f. When talking to yourself
   g. When encountering new ideas
2. Using guidelines
   a. Use your own words
   b. Don't go beyond information communicated by speaker
   c. Be concise
   d. Be specific
   e. Be accurate

VII. Improving Your Responding Skills

A. Provide well-timed responses
1. Feedback is usually most effective offered at the earliest opportunity
2. If a person is sensitive or upset, delaying feedback can be wise
3. Use just-in-time (JIT) approach – provide feedback just before person might make another mistake

B. Provide useable information

1. What is useful and relevant
2. Selective feedback may be best

C. Be descriptive rather than evaluative

1. Focus on behaviour rather than personality

CHAPTER REVIEW: SECTION BY SECTION SUMMARY

I. Listening Defined

Hearing is the physiological process of decoding sounds. **Listening** is the process we use to make sense of what we hear. Listening involves four activities: (1) **selecting**, (2) **attending**, (3) **understanding,** (4) **remembering,** and (5) **responding**.

Selecting involves picking out sounds to focus on from the total volume of sound surrounding us. To select, we must "tune out" other sounds.

Attending involves bringing attention to bear on a selected sound or sounds. Information that is novel, humorous, intense, or personally relevant often commands our attention, making our task of maintaining focus easy and natural.

Understanding is the process of assigning meaning to the sounds you select. People understand best if they can relate what they hear to something they already know. For this reason, **analogy** and **comparison** are effective. Individuals with many similarities of cultural background, experience, and temperament have a greater likelihood of accurate mutual understanding.

Remembering. To remember is to recall information. Our memory consists of both **short-term** and **long-term** memory storage. Long-term memory storage includes significant, dramatic, and vital information and the details connection with such information.

Responding. Interpersonal communication is interactive. Responses can be either **verbal** or **nonverbal**.

II. Why You Listen

We listen for a variety of purposes. Some of these include (1) enjoyment, (2) learning, (3) evaluation, (4) empathy.

Listening to Enjoy -- television, music, movies, and the conversation of friends.

Listening to Learn --the more motivated you are to learn, the more likely you are to listen -- learning takes place both inside and outside the classroom -- one's daily life has educative value.

Listening to Evaluate -- we listen to make critical decisions -- to evaluate accurately we need to separate facts from inferences, identify fallacies in reasoning, and analyze evidence.

Listening to Empathize* -- supportive listening -- listening without judging or advising.

(***Empathy** means "to feel with" and is a more intense and engaged activity than sympathy.)

III. Six Barriers to Listening

Focussing on a Personal Agenda. We are focussing on personal agendas when we are waiting impatiently to take our turn in a conversation. Focussing on our internal messages can keep us from selecting and attending to the other's message.

Emotional Noise occurs when emotional arousal interferes with communication effectiveness. Sometimes it is our own emotional arousal that makes it difficult to attend to a message, especially messages that contain provocative, insulting, or obscene language (fighting words). Sometimes it is the emotional arousal of an angry or upset speaker that makes it difficult to attend to a message.

Criticizing the Speaker. Being critical of a speaker may distract us from focussing on the message. We are often critical of appearances: clothing, body size and shape, age, race, gender, ethnicity.

Speech Rate Versus Thought Rate. We all take in words faster than anyone can put them out. So, when someone is talking, our mind might wander away while waiting between words. The average speech rate is approximately 125 words a minute, our processing rate is up to 600 or 800 words a minute.

Information Overload. Multiple and simultaneous auditory stimuli can overload our capacity to receive, organize and remember information. Reading this workbook while listening to music, with the television going in the background and the neighbour's dog barking at the construction crew, might be too much to take in and keep separate and sensible.

External Noise. Some external noise is literal – e.g., all the ambient sounds of our household machines. Other external noise is figurative – all the distractions of conflicting desires and divided attention produced by environments with multiple stimuli.

Studies suggest men and women may communicate differently, and this may be a source of misunderstandings in relationships. Men seem to listen to solve a problem and give attention to identifying major ideas. Women listen to enhance understanding and give attention to details and nuance.

IV. Improving Your Listening Skills

Listening can be improved by the simple method of **STOP/LOOK/LISTEN**.

Stop – shut down the running interior commentary, the rude little voice inside our heads that's always talking while someone else is talking. Get off yourself long enough to really hear another. To acquire this skill takes time. Skills acquisition often proceeds in four stages: (1) **unconscious incompetence** [we're not good at something and don't even know we're not good at it], (2) **conscious incompetence** [we're not good at something but at least we know we're not], (3) **conscious competence** [we're good at something and we know we are], (4) **unconscious competence** [we're so good at something we don't even think about it].

Look – check the nonverbal messages coming in along with the verbal. Listen with your eyes. Notice facial expressions, vocal cues, eye contact, posture. Send nonverbal messages yourself that show your level of interest and attention to the speaker. Do it but don't overdo it. Avoid letting nonverbal cues distract you from the verbal ones.

Listen – mentally summarize the details of the message and weave these summaries into a focussed major point or series of major ideas. Use the time allowed you by the favourable speech/processing ratio to think about what's being said instead of what you're going to say.

V. Transform Listening Barriers into Listening Goals

Listening, although a natural capacity, requires conscious practice to improve. Seek out listening challenges such as documentaries and debates. Give an ear to something more than the ordinary conversation and entertainment.

In any listening situation, determine the appropriate goal. Listening to evaluate may not require the same skills and strategies as listening to support. Different situations call for different approaches.

VI. Responding with Empathy

Good listening is an other-oriented ability and is active not passive. The responses you offer in a listening situation can accomplish three things: (1) they measure how accurately you understand the message, (2) they indicate your agreement or disagreement with comments others make, (3) they tell speakers how they are affecting others. Just by being an active listener, you can help your partner clarify a problem.

Understand Your Partner's Feelings – imagine how you would feel in the same circumstances – put yourself in his or her place.

Ask Questions – ask to identify sequence of events – ask for definitions of unfamiliar words and terms – ask for examples – ask about feelings.

Reflect Content by Paraphrasing – check accuracy of understanding by using such phrases as "Are you saying . . . ?" and "You seem to be describing . . ." and "So the point you are making seems to be . . ." and "Here is what I understand you to mean . . ." and "So here is what seemed to happen. . . ."

Reflect Feeling by Paraphrasing – make certain you understand how others are feeling by using such phrases as "So, you are feeling. . ." and "You must feel. . ." and "So, now you feel . . ." and "Emotionally, you must be feeling. . . ."

VII. Improve Your Responding Skills

There are four ways to improve your responding skills.

Provide Well-Timed Responses. Feedback is usually most effective when offered at the earliest opportunity. Sometimes, however, if a person is already sensitive and upset about something, delaying feedback can be wise. Use the just-in-time (JIT) approach, which means providing corrective feedback before a mistake is made rather than afterwards when things cannot be changed.

Provide Useable Information. Feedback is useful if it is pertinent and productive. Sometimes less is more, and **selective feedback** can work where throwing in everything would topple the cart. Giving feedback should not be confused with blowing off steam. Steam is hot and usually leaves everyone burned.

Avoid Unnecessary Details. Cut to the chase. Again, less is more.

Be Descriptive Rather Than Evaluative. Describe behaviours that trouble you in others as objectively as possible. Avoid the language of condemnation and disapproval. For example: "When you read at the table, it is difficult for others not to feel excluded" instead of "Reading at the table is rude and insulting!"

TERMS TO LEARN

Listening
Hearing
Selecting
Attending
Understanding
Remembering
Short-Term Memory
Long-Term Memory
Responding
Sympathizing
Empathizing
Emotional Noise
Active Listening
Paraphrasing

Activity 4.1: Learning to Listen

Objectives:

1. To help you identify characteristics of your own and others' listening behaviours.
2. To explore the effect of different listening behaviours on others.

Instructions:

1. In the following activity, record examples of your listening behaviour over the next few days.
2. After you have finished, answer the questions at the end of the activity.

1. Situation:

Who is involved:

Subject:

My listening behaviours:

Others' listening behaviours:

Effect of these listening behaviours:

2. Situation:

Who is involved:

Subject:

My listening behaviours:

Others' listening behaviours:
Effect of these listening behaviours:
3. Situation:
Who is involved:
Subject:
My listening behaviours:
Others' listening behaviours:
Effect of these listening behaviours:
4. Situation:
Who is involved:
Subject:
My listening behaviours:
Others' listening behaviours:

Effect of these listening behaviours:
1. What effective and ineffective listening skills do you use most often?
2. What effect do these behaviours have on others?
3. What listening behaviours do you observe others using?
4. What effect do these behaviours have on you?

Activity 4.2 : Barriers to Listening

Objective:

1. To help you identify barriers to listening.

Part 1

Instructions:

1. Identify what the barriers to listening are in each of the following situations.

Example:

You have been struggling with your accounting course. You barely passed the last two tests. You are an excellent student and are very upset and embarrassed by this. A classmate approaches you in the cafeteria and begins complaining about how hard she is finding the course. You get defensive and say, "Why are you talking to me about this? Do you think I am having trouble with accounting? I am doing just fine."

Barrier: emotional noise

1. You and your husband would like to buy your first home. You want to begin your search by reading the real estate ads in the newspaper and going to a few open houses. Your husband wants to find a real estate agent to work with immediately. He says, "You are wrong. If we take your approach we will never find a house we like!"

   Barrier:____

2. Your brother has decided to accept a new job. He is eager to discuss this with you and begins by telling you about the increase in salary he will be receiving in this new position. You are reminded of the money you need to borrow from him so you can go to the movies tonight with friends. Your mind turns to this and you miss what he is saying to you.

   Barrier:____

3. You are beginning a new course. During the first session the instructor reviews the course outline with you. It is eight pages long. By the time you leave your mind is swimming with information. You turn to a friend and ask, "Can you remember what the assignment was for next week?"
   Barrier:____

4. You want to talk to your boss, Stephanie, about problems with a new computer program you are designing. As you meet in her office the phone begins to ring, her secretary interrupts with an important message and construction from the building next door begins. As you begin to describe the problem Stephanie says, "I'm sorry, I missed that. Could you repeat what you were saying?"

   Barrier:____

5. You are discussing buying a car with your friend. She is speaking about the advantages of buying a new car. You are listening to her but as she speaks you also find your mind wandering to your own reasons for wanting to buy a used car.

   Barrier:____

6. Your boyfriend tells you he wants to go to the hockey game Friday night with his friends because it is the final game of the series. You have been looking forward to going to a movie together as you had planned. Your boyfriend has been busy at work during the last month and you have not been spending as much time together. You are already feeling a little vulnerable in the relationship and wonder if this is just an excuse for him to distance himself from you. You say, "All you think about is hockey! What about me and my feelings?"

   Barrier:____

Part 2
Instructions:
Think of two situations in your own life where you encountered barriers to listening.

Situation:
Barrier:
Situation:
Barrier:

Activity 4.3: Improving Your Responding Skills

Objective:
1. To help you link your listening responses to your communication goals.

Part 1
Instructions:
1. In the following statements identify whether the listening response is consistent with the goal given. If it is not, suggest a more effective listening response.

Example:

You are in a group situation in a course. You and your group members are trying to brainstorm ideas for a class project. You want to generate some creative suggestions. When a quieter member voices her suggestion you say, "That is a stupid idea!"

Is this an effective response? *No*

If it is effective, why? If it is not effective, what response would be more appropriate and consistent with your goal? Why?

This is ineffective because it discourages the flow of ideas from this person and others in the group. Sometimes one idea that doesn't make much sense can lead to another, better idea. A better response would be "Good, let's keep going and see what other ideas we can generate."

1. Your son's grades at school are poor this term. You want him to be more motivated at school. You say, "You should stop skipping classes and get to work!"

Is this an effective response?____

If it is effective, discuss why. ____

____

____

____

If it is not effective, what response would be more appropriate and consistent with your goal?____

Why?____

2. A friend is telling you about her first date with a new admirer. You want to encourage her to talk about the relationship. You say, “Are you going to go out with him again?”

Is this an effective response?____________________________________

If it is effective, discuss why. ____________________________________

If it is not effective, what response would be more appropriate and consistent with your goal?____

Why?____

3. A friend of yours, Eric, tells you that a project they have been working on for their company for over two years has just been rejected, and on top of that the report evaluating the project was very cold and dismissive. Eric is very hurt and depressed. You want to empathize with him. You say, “Gee, that’s tough. Let’s take a careful look at the project and examine the areas where it might have been deficient. I had a successful project with these people a few years ago. Let me show you what I did that worked for them.”

Is this an effective response?____________________________________

If it is effective, discuss why. ____________________________________

If it is not effective, what response would be more appropriate and consistent with your goal?____________________________________

Why?____________________________________

4. Your colleague has just received a poor performance review. She is distraught and discouraged. You want to be supportive. You say, "Sounds like you are upset about your review."

Is this an effective response?____________________________

If it is effective, discuss why. ____________________________

If it is not effective, what response would be more appropriate and consistent with your goal?____________________________________

Why?____________________________________

5. A close friend is debating which university to attend in the fall. She has been accepted at both. One, a smaller university, offers a program which is more applied. The other is a more academically prestigious university. You have some experience with both. Your father teaches in the applied program. You want to give her the value of your knowledge and experience. You say, "Well, if what you are looking for is a job after you complete your B.A. you should go for the more applied focus. If you think you might want to do graduate work after the B.A., then the more prestigious university probably offers more opportunity for that."

Is this an effective response?____________________________

If it is effective, discuss why. ____

____

____

____

If it is not effective, what response would be more appropriate and consistent with your goal?____

____

____

____

Why?____

____

____

____

6. A friend that you have met through a writer's support group that you belong to is trying to get a manuscript for her first novel published. She has sent it to four publishers in the last six months. Today she received her fourth rejection notice. You want to empathize with her. You say to her, "Don't be too discouraged. I had fifteen rejections before my first manuscript was accepted. I believe in your book. Don't give up on it."

Is this an effective response?____

If it is effective, discuss why. ____

____

____

____

If it is not effective, what response would be more appropriate and consistent with your goal?____

____

____

____

Why?____

____

____

____

Part 2

Think of three real-life examples. Discuss what your goal is in the situation and identify an effective response. Discuss why this response is effective.

Example:

Effective Response:

Example:

Effective Response:

Example:

Effective Response:

Activity 4.4: Describing Behaviour

Objectives:

1. To help you recognize the difference between descriptive and evaluative responses.
2. To give you practice writing descriptive responses.

Part 1

Instructions:

1. In the following examples put a check mark beside those statements that contain a description of behaviour.

1. I noticed that you covered all the agenda items within the allotted time. ____
2. Bill feels insecure when he is not in charge of a project. ____
3. Jane's lack of motivation is causing difficulties for her staff. ____
4. You were rude with that customer right now. ____
5. You have been absent from work five days during the last month. ____
6. Sheila spends time with all new employees, introducing them to each department, during their first week of employment. ____
7. John's indifference is having an impact on company morale. ____
8. You finished that report two days before the deadline. ____
9. You can't be depended on at work. ____
10. You don't deliver. ____

Part 2

Instructions:

1. Record two real-life examples of specific behaviour you have observed.

One
Two

Activity 4.5: Listening Fishbowl

Objective:

1. To increase your awareness of effective and ineffective listening skills.

Instructions:

1. Choose a hot topic to discuss from the following list or select a topic of your own choosing.

Abortion

Capital Punishment

Legalization of Marijuana

Separation of Quebec from Canada

Lesbian and Gay Parenting

Euthanasia

Cloning and Reproduction Technologies

2. Have six students volunteer to debate this topic in a fishbowl setting (sitting in a circle in the middle of the room) for 10-15 minutes.
3. The rest of the class will act as observers attending to different effective and ineffective listening behaviours.
4. Observers should record their observations on the Observer's Guide (being as specific as possible in terms of who said what and how others responded) and be prepared to give verbal feedback at the end of the activity.
5. See Observer's Guide on next page.

Observer's Guide

Speaker:	ONE	TWO	THREE	FOUR	FIVE	SIX
Name:						
Effective Listening Behaviours						
Paraphrasing						
Empathizing						
Questioning						
Other Effective Behaviours						
Ineffective Listening Behaviours						
Interrupting						
Criticizing						
Excessive Information						
Reacting Emotionally						
Personal Agenda						
Inattention						
Other Ineffective Behaviours						

DIFFICULT POSITION 4

Your girlfriend has always wanted to be an actress and has just finished her first opening night performance in a local theatre. You were aware during the performance that she frequently mumbled her lines and that the audience was not impressed. Now she wants to tell you all about what she thinks made her performance outstanding, and she says she also wants your objective feedback. Her next and last performance is tomorrow night.

INSTRUCTIONS

1. What do you say? Do you offer feedback immediately or listen to her own self-analysis first? Do you use the JIT approach to feedback or delay feedback until after the play completes its run? When and if you offer feedback, if it causes pain, what communication skills can you use to help your girlfriend deal with her disappointment and hurt feelings? Would you consider not giving any feedback or the bare minimum? Would you be tempted to lie? If you were in the young actress' position, how do you think you would respond?

2. Discuss the issue in small groups and record your discussion.

Exercise 4.1: Learning Objective: General Review (**TRUE/FALSE**)

Instructions: Identify the following statements as either true or false.

1. The average individual spends almost 80 percent of communication time listening to others. ( )

2. One of the main obstacles to effective listening is interior commentary. ( )

3. A common cultural background guarantees mutual understanding. ( )

4. Empathy is the opposite of sympathy. ( )

5. Studies suggest we sometimes pay more attention to strangers than we do to our intimate life partners. ( )

6. The lowest level of skill acquisition is conscious incompetence. ( )

7. Paraphrasing involves the repetition of what other speakers say using as many of their exact words and phrases as possible. ( )

8. One of the possible dangers of paraphrasing is appearing unnatural. ( )

9. The information processing rate is almost infinitely faster than the rate of a speaker's verbal delivery. ( )

10. The JIT approach in feedback attempts to give careful empathetic analysis of what went wrong after a mistake has been made. ( )

11. "When you eat your food so quickly, you endanger your digestion." This remark is an instance of evaluative observation. ( )

12. "You eat like a pig!" This remark is an instance of descriptive observation. ( )

13. Nonverbal messages are often more persuasive than verbal ones. ( )

14. No matter what the situation, feedback offered at the earliest opportunity is most effective. ( )

15. Paraphrasing could be used as a way to hide one's thoughts and feelings from another. ( )

16. Asking questions directly of a speaker to clarify meaning is confrontational. ( )

Exercise 4.2: Learning Objective: General Review (**FILL-IN-THE-BLANKS**)

Instructions: Fill in the blanks using the appropriate term or terms from the following list.

listening	short-term memory	understanding	paraphrasing
hearing	long-term memory	remembering	JIT approach
selecting	sympathy	emotional noise	information overload
attending	empathy	active listening	

1. __________ is the basic physiological process of listening.

2. Everyone talked at once. I had to begin ___________ out sounds to understand.

3. When the student asked me questions, I knew he was involved in__________.

4. She tried to pay attention to what her mother was saying, but her mother's shaking voice and tear-stained eyes distracted her. The_____________ was too great for her to listen well.

5. Confronting multiple and simultaneous stimuli can cause __________________.

6. After the stroke, she lost much of her ____________ and had to look up my phone number every time she wanted to call, but her ______________ was still so strong that she knew every detail of my wedding even after 25 years.

7. Reflecting feeling and content in a discussion can be managed by__________.

8. Picking one instrument out of the orchestra is fairly easy, but ___________ to it throughout the concert is almost impossible.

9. Telling me what I did wrong after it was too late to change it was certainly not the ___________ to providing feedback!

10. ______________ requires an effort to assign meaning to the messages we hear.

11. No lecture will do us any good if we have no skill at _______________.

12. The ability to hear is not necessarily essential to all forms of __________.

13. ___________ is fine, but I need ___________ for you to really understand.

Exercise 4.3: Learning Objective: General Review (**MULTIPLE CHOICE**)

Instructions: Choose the best answer for each question below,

1. The process of reflecting feelings in communication is called

   a. empathy
   b. paraphrasing
   c. sympathy
   d. active listening

2. Recalling exactly what someone has said to you just moments earlier requires

   a. empathy
   b. the JIT approach to feedback
   c. short-term memory
   d. long-term memory

3. An upset or angry speaker is likely to convey his or her message mixed with

   a. information overload
   b. external noise
   c. distractors
   d. emotional noise

4. One of the most effective ways to achieve understanding of new material is to use

   a. selective feedback
   b. paraphrasing
   c. decentring
   d. analogy and comparison

5. One of the things to avoid when responding with empathy is

   a. nonverbal messages
   b. paraphrasing
   c. unsolicited advice
   d. descriptive observation

6. Listening effectively does *not* require

   a. selection
   b. attention
   c. understanding
   d. evaluation

7. All of the following are stages in skills acquisition except

   a. unconscious incompetence
   b. subconscious resistence
   c. conscious incompetence
   d. conscious competence

8. All of the following are possible phrases for reflecting feeling in paraphrasing except

   a. "You ought to feel. . ."
   b. "You must feel. . ."
   c. "So, now you feel. . ."
   d. "So, you are feeling. . ."

9. All of the following are aspects of effective response except

   a. feedback provided at earliest opportunity
   b. evaluative rather than descriptive observations
   c. selective feedback
   d. questions about sequence of events

10. All of the following are examples of listening barriers except

    a. emotional noise
    b. external noise
    c. information overload
    d. eye contact

11. All of the following statements about listening effectively are true except

    a. mentally summarizing message details aids understanding
    b. nonverbal cues may become distracting
    c. when nonverbal messages contradict verbal ones, the nonverbal are often believed
    d. empathy is always necessary to achieve understanding

Answers

CHAPTER 4

Exercise 4.1

1. (F)
2. (T)
3. (F)
4. (F)
5. (T)
6. (F)
7. (F)
8. (T)
9. (F)
10. (F)
11. (F)
12. (F)
13. (T)
14. (F)
15. (T)
16. (F)

Exercise 4.2

1. Hearing
2. Selecting
3. Active listening
4. Emotional noise
5. Information overload
6. Short-term memory/long-term memory
7. Paraphrasing
8. Attending
9. JIT approach
10. Understanding
11. Remembering
12. Listening
13. Sympathize/empathize

Exercise 4.3

1. b
2. c
3. d
4. d
5. c
6. d
7. b
8. a
9. b
10. d
11. d

Chapter 5

Communicating Verbally

CHAPTER OUTLINE

I. Words and Meaning

A. Words
1. Symbols -- words are symbols that represent something else
   a. Image, sound, concept, experience
2. Referents -- things symbols represent
3. Thoughts -- mental process of creating a category or idea for referent/symbol

B. Words are arbitrary
1. No logical connection now exists between word symbol and referent
2. English language evolved from Indo-European tongues

C. Words are context-bound
1. Symbols derive their meaning from the situation in which they are used

D. Words are culturally bound
1. Rules, norms, values, mores
2. Symbolic interaction
   a. We are bound together because of our common use of symbols
   b. We use our common understanding of symbols to form relationships
   c. The more similar the cultures of the communication partners, the greater the chance for a meeting of meanings

E. Words have denotative and connotative meaning
1. Denotative -- conveys content (literal)
2. Connotative -- conveys feeling (personal)

F. Words communicate concrete or abstract meaning
1. Concrete -- referent can be experienced with senses (bricks, wood)
2. Abstract -- referent cannot be experienced with senses (shelter)

G. Words have power
1. Power to create
   a. Symbolic vehicles to communicate creations and discoveries
   b. Self-worth with self-talk and self-labels
   c. Moods and emotional states with labels for feelings
   d. Health
2. Power to affect thoughts and actions
   a. The way a product is labelled affects our propensity to purchase it
   b. Can distort how we view and evaluate others
   c. Affect policies and procedures
3. Words have power to affect and reflect culture
   a. Linguistic determinism

(1) language shapes culture and culture shapes language

b. Word View

II. Word Barriers

A. Bypassing: One Word, Two Thoughts

1. Same words mean different things to different people

B. Bafflegab: High-Falutin' Use of Words

1. Highly abstract language
2. Overly formal language
3. Evasive phrases

C. Lack of Precision: Uncertain Meaning

1. Malapropism -- confusion of one word for another that sounds similar
2. Words out of context
3. Inappropriate grammar
4. Wrong word order
5. Restricted code
   a. Family's secret words
   b. Abbreviations
   c. Specialized terms
   d. Jargon

D. Allness: The Language of Generalization

1. Allness statements deny individual differences
2. Indexing acknowledges that each individual is unique

E. Static Evaluation: The Language of Rigidity

1. Statements that fail to recognize change
2. All-inclusive categories ("the map is not the territory")

F. Polarization: The Language of Extremes

1. Categorizing in bipolar extremes
   a. Good or bad
   b. Old or new
   c. Beautiful or ugly
   d. Brilliant or stupid
2. Leaving out the middle ground

G. Fact-inference confusions: jumping to conclusions

1. Determining the difference between a fact and inference
   a. Fact -- something observed
   b. Inference -- a conclusion based upon speculation

H. Biassed language: Insensitivity towards others

1. Stereotypical and discriminatory language
   a. Sexist
      (1) nonsexist language reflects nonsexist attitudes
      (2) nonsexist language will help you become more other-oriented
      (3) nonsexist language is more contemporary and unamibiguous

(4) nonsexist language will empower others

b. Racist

III. Using Words to Establish Supportive Relationships

A. Words contribute to feelings of supportiveness or defensiveness

1. Describe your own feelings rather than evaluating others
   a. Eliminate the accusatory "you" from your language
   b. Use "I" to describe your own feelings and thoughts about a situation/event
2. Solve problems rather than control others
   a. Ask open-ended questions ("What seems to be the problem?")
   b. Avoid critical comments ("Here's where you went wrong.")
3. Be genuine rather than manipulative
   a. Be yourself rather than someone you are not
   b. Take an honest interest in others
   c. Avoid generalizations
   d. Avoid hidden agendas
4. Empathize rather than remain detached from others
   a. Empathy a hallmark of supportive relationships
   b. Neutrality is indifference or apathy toward others
5. Be flexible rather than rigid toward others
   a. Avoid "you're wrong, I'm right" attitude
   b. Avoid making rigid statements
6. Present yourself as equal rather than superior
   a. Elaborated code -- explicit not condescending

IV. Using Words to Value Others

A. Demonstrating care to others a key skill in maintaining long-term relationships

1 . Confirming responses -- building self-esteem
   a. Direct acknowledgement -- mentioning the person by name in response
   b. Agreement about judgements -- confirming others' evaluations
   c. Supportive responses -- confirming others' feelings through reassurance
   d. Clarifying response -- seeking greater understanding of messages
   e. Expression of positive feeling -- participating in feelings of joy/excitement
   f. Compliment -- sincere appreciation/praise of another
2. Disconfirming responses -- (undermining self-esteem)
   a. Impervious response -- failing to acknowledge attempt to communicate
   b. Interrupting response -- interrupters imply their comments more important
   c. Irrelevant response -- nothing to do with statement made
   d. Tangential response -- minimally related response to statement
   e. Impersonal response, - - intellectualizes using third person (one)
   f. Incoherent response -- mumbling, rambling, unintelligible responses
   g. Incongruous response -- verbal message inconsistent with nonverbal

CHAPTER REVIEW: SECTION BY SECTION SUMMARY

I. Words and Meaning

Words may be considered to have three parts: (1) **symbol**, (2) **referent**, and (3) **thought**.

A symbol represents something other than itself, it "stands in" for something else. Each word is a symbol in this sense (word=symbol). The word "dog" is an abstract symbol for the concrete animal. The concrete animal is the referent, the thing to which the symbol refers. Thought is our process of bringing a picture or image of the referent into our head when a symbol (a word) has triggered it. If I say "dog" to you, the sound is a symbol of the animal, not the animal itself. The animal itself is the referent. When you form a mental image or picture in response to my saying "dog," you are creating a "thought" triggered by your idea of the referent.

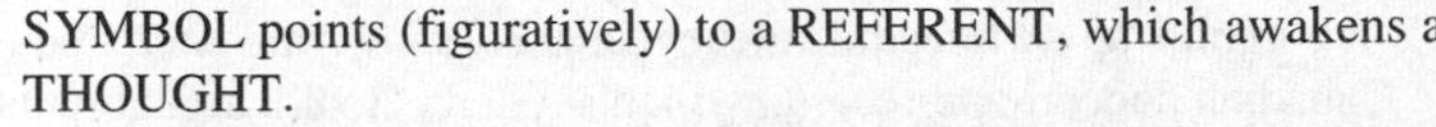

SYMBOL points (figuratively) to a REFERENT, which awakens a THOUGHT.

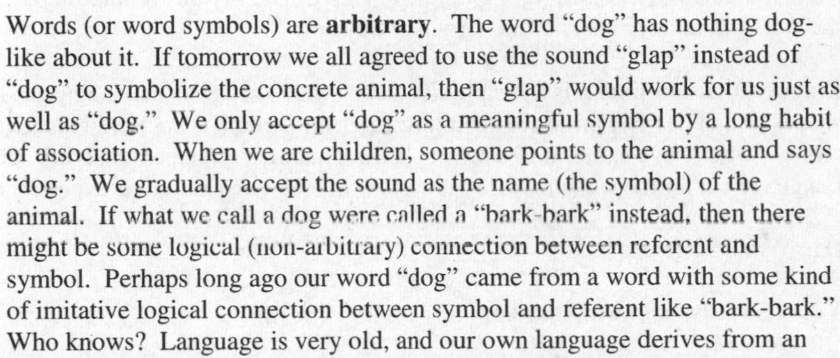

Words (or word symbols) are **arbitrary**. The word "dog" has nothing dog-like about it. If tomorrow we all agreed to use the sound "glap" instead of "dog" to symbolize the concrete animal, then "glap" would work for us just as well as "dog." We only accept "dog" as a meaningful symbol by a long habit of association. When we are children, someone points to the animal and says "dog." We gradually accept the sound as the name (the symbol) of the animal. If what we call a dog were called a "bark-bark" instead, then there might be some logical (non-arbitrary) connection between referent and symbol. Perhaps long ago our word "dog" came from a word with some kind of imitative logical connection between symbol and referent like "bark-bark." Who knows? Language is very old, and our own language derives from an ancient ancestral language linguists call Indo-European, because some scholars believe it originated in an area between India and Europe.

Words are **context-bound**. Symbols derive their meaning from the situation in which they are used. The word "great" has immediate positive connotations for most of us. It suggests something excellent or important or desirable – as in "He is just great!" However, there is nothing positive in the phrase "You are a great fool!" Words often mean what they mean in combination with other words around them. Sometimes words depend on nonverbal contexts or situations for their full meaning. If I say, "he is intelligent" with no particular gestures, that means one thing. If I say, "he is intelligent," and then roll my eyes, it may mean something else.

Words are **culture-bound**. A word which one cultural group uses to describe itself may become an insult if a member of another cultural group uses it. In the subculture of slang, words often mean something other than what they mean in standard usage. Words in one language may mean something quite different in another.

Words have **denotative** and **connotative** meanings. Denotative meanings are definition meanings, literal meanings. Connotative meanings are subjective and associational meanings. A prison is called a "house of correction" not "a home of correction." Why? "Home" has connotations of warmth and care that "house" does not. We speak of a police "squad" not a police "gang," although "gang" means essentially "group" as does "squad." The denotative meanings of gang and squad are similar, the connotative meanings are not. Words are **abstract** or **concrete**. If a word names a thing you can touch, taste, smell, hear or see, it is concrete: a tree. If a word names a thing you cannot access with any of your senses, it is abstract: beauty. Words can range on a continuum from very abstract to very concrete. Silk is very concrete, a dress is less so, fashion is rather abstract, beauty is very abstract.

Concrete > silk > dress > fashion > beauty > **Abstract**

II. Words Have Power

Words not only name things, they also create them. Until we have a name for something, it hardly exists for us. A word can create a new cognitive category. When Newton termed the attractant force of matter "gravity," he named something everyone had already experienced, but in isolating it with a name, he made us forever aware of it in a new way. What words we use to talk to ourselves (or describe ourselves to ourselves) can have profound effects on our health and happiness.

Words can influence our actions. Our decision to purchase a product is often influenced by the words associated with or identifying it. The Mustang automobile might not have sold so well if it had been named "mule." Words can distort how we view and evaluate others. When some Americans speak of Canadians as "Kanucks," it conjures up an image of hockey, canoes, snow, and beer, and tends to exclude the image of someone like Canadian concert and recording pianist Glenn Gould, arguably the greatest pianist of the twentieth century, or Northrop Frye, the famous University of Toronto literary critic and Biblical scholar, or the world-famous painters of the Group of Seven.

Linguistic determinism is a reciprocity theory which suggests that language shapes culture and culture shapes language. For instance, natural features throughout Canada and the United States – mountains and rivers -- often have names derived from several cultures reflecting differing cultural backgrounds. Language can influence our world view – our overall perspective on experience.

III. Word Barriers

Your text lists eight word barriers.

Bypassing occurs when the same words mean different things to different people.

Bafflegab is inflated and pretentious language, what the author Laurence Sterne called "tall, opaque words." For example, "the contractual labourers defenestrated the superannuated lumber of the chamber" for "workers threw the old wood out the window." Bafflegab often involves abstractions designed to hide unpleasant things. "Collateral damage" during the Gulf War referred to civilians killed in combat actions.

Lack of Precision: Uncertain Meaning sometimes involves **malapropism** – confusion of one word or phrase for another that sounds like it. People using bafflegab often fall into malapropism. Someone was once offered an award "in recognition of *meretricious* achievement." The word "meretricious" refers to prostitution. The word intended was "meritorious" – having merit. **Jargon** and **restricted codes** are private languages designed to exclude those not in the know. The language of law has some of these qualities. In a time of increasing specialization, private languages tend to increase. The word "bafflegab" is an example of communications jargon.

Allness statements are sweeping generalizations that overlook or deny individual differences or variations. Stereotypes are usually cast in the form of an allness statement. Example: All [ethnic group]s are[something unpleasant] or all [men/women] are [something unpleasant]. **Indexing** is the opposite of an allness statement and involves acknowledging that each individual is unique. Example: this particular police officer was intimidating, but it's the first time I've ever experienced that with a police officer.

Static evaluation is a judgement that fails to recognize change. Example: People sometimes carry nicknames with them from childhood that have long since ceased to be applicable. Example: We may be remembered by someone for our failure in some endeavour at which we have since come to excel. "The map isn't the territory." Our interpretations must change with the landscape, so to speak.

Polarization is the practice of casting things into extreme either/or formulas. Instead of recognizing various gradations in qualities, everything becomes black or white. The good is perfect, the imperfect is awful. Polarization is common in war when opponents become enemies who believe each other incapable of any good. This is why it has been said that the first casualty of a war is the truth.

Fact-inference confusion. A fact is something you can observe and have observed. An inference is a kind of guess based on speculation. If someone tells me it is a fact that water boils at 100 degrees Celsius, I can test this and find out. I can establish it as a fact. If someone tells me that it is a fact that women and men have different styles of communication, I can draw inferences based on my own experience of male and female communication, and I can also review the results of studies, but the scope of evidence required to establish this claim as a fact is so great that it must probably always remain a more-or-less reasonable inference. Inferences are often reasonable things to work with, but they are not facts.

Biased language. Sexists and racist language is biased. A bias is usually an unacknowledged prejudice. If I say "police*man*," I may not intend to exclude women from your mental image of a law enforcement officer, but I do. Many people will say "Eskimo" and mean no harm, but Inuit is the appropriate term. Biased language is not always easy to avoid. Sexist language affects both genders.

IV. Using Words to Establish Supportive Relationships

According to Jack Gibb words can be used to create communication environments characterized by **supportiveness** or **defensiveness.**

Supportive environments can be promoted in several ways.

Describe your own feelings rather than evaluating others. Avoid the verbal finger-pointing of saying "you." Example: "You always cut me off when I'm trying to speak." Try using "I-statements" instead. Example: "I feel I am often interrupted when I am talking to you."

Solve problems rather than control others. Adults aren't children and shouldn't be spoken to as if they were. Instead of giving commands, try asking open-ended questions. Example of command language: "You are going to have to stop being so trusting of people." Example of open-ended question: "Is there any way to help you avoid being taken advantage of by others?"

Be genuine rather than manipulative. Be yourself. Avoid generalizations and personal agendas. Treat people and their concerns as ends in themselves rather than as means to some end of your own.

Empathize rather than remain detached from others. Risk feeling with others. Indifference and apathy keep you at a distance, and it's hard to see things clearly from a distance.

Be flexible rather than rigid toward others. Avoid a "you're wrong, I'm right" attitude. The Greek philosopher Socrates was famous for often saying, "I don't know" in his conversations. Another philosopher, Friedrich Nietzsche, said that having the strength of your convictions is fine, but sometimes it is better still to have the strength for an attack on your convictions. Avoid rigid pronouncements.

IV. Using Words to Value Others

Words can demonstrate how we value others, which is an important skill for maintaining relationships. Our responses can either be **confirming** or **disconfirming** of others. Confirming responses build self-esteem, disconfirming responses break it down.

Your text lists six confirming responses:

1. **Direct Acknowledgement.** Use the person's name to whom you are speaking in your response to them. Example: "Certainly, Tom, I'd be pleased to help."

2. **Agreement about Judgements.** Confirm evaluations by agreement. Example: "Yes, that was the core of the whole film."

3. **Supportive Responses.** Confirm feelings by reassurance and understanding. Example: "I can imagine how hard it was to keep from feeling nervous out there on stage."

4. **Clarifying Response.** Seek greater understanding of another person's message. Example: "What was motivating you to take that action just then?"

5. **Expression of Positive Feeling.** Share feelings of joy and excitement. Example: "That was a great moment when you were named as one of the best auditors in the department."

6. **Compliment.** Sincere expression of appreciation and approval. Example: "You did a wonderful job developing the new computer system for us."

Your text lists seven disconfirming responses:

Impervious Response. Failing to acknowledge statements or attempt at communication. This is when someone acts as if you're not there or are beneath notice.

Interrupting Response. Not allowing people to finish phrases or have their say. Interrupters imply their message is too important to wait on yours.

Irrelevant Response. A response unrelated to a statement. This is when someone comes out of left field. You say, "I think we should eat at Joe's tonight," and he or she responds, "My wrist is hurting from playing tennis."

Tangential Response. Related to statement but barely. You say, "There was a fatal plane crash in Vancouver this morning," and he or she responds, "Vancouver has one of the largest bays on the west coast."

Impersonal Response. Intellectualizing and depersonalizing. You say, "I want to get some sun, " and he or she says, "Sunning is a practice peculiar to those who mistakenly think it indicative of health."

Incoherent Response. Mumbling, rambling, fumbling, whispering, unintelligibility. You say, "I like this new manager," and he or she responds, "Ah, yeah, uh, prabbleebesortalikelastguy, ya know, uh, bliflix."

Incongruous Response. Verbal message contradicted by nonverbal. Example: "Of course (ha ha ha), I'm taking you (snicker, snicker) very (ha ha) seriously."

TERMS TO LEARN

Symbol
Referent
Thought
High-Context Culture
Low-Context Culture
Denotative Meaning
Connotative Meaning
Symbolic Interaction
Linguistic Determinism
World View
Bypassing
Malapropism
Restricted Code
Jargon
Allness
Indexing
Static Evaluation
Polarization
Elaborated Code
Confirming Response
Disconfirming Response

Activity 5.1: Saying What You Mean

Objective:

1. To help you differentiate between abstract and concrete language.

Instructions:

1. In the following examples make each statement more concrete.

Example: *Ethan is lazy.*

Rewrite: *Ethan lies in bed until early afternoon every day. He hasn't completed any of his homework in three weeks and his dirty laundry just keeps piling up on his floor.*

1. You were very helpful.

2. Olivia likes to exercise.

3. Politicians cannot be trusted.

4. Dogs are loyal

5. Stephen is in good shape.

6. Big-city people are aggressive.

7. Camping is relaxing.

8. My mother is a good cook.

9. Knowledge is power.

10. Babies are cute.

Activity 5.2: Word Barriers

Objective:
1. To help you recognize word barriers.

Instructions:
1. In the following examples identify what the word barriers are.

Example: You are never there when I need you.

Word barrier: polarization

1. Headmistress Ms. Watkins tells Mrs. Smithers, "Here at the Clivemoor School for Girls we discourage social intercourse with boys." Mrs. Smithers replies, "I should think so! It's quite bad enough in private."

   Word barrier:____

2. Aqueous substances derived from common cyclic precipitation are the preferred means for the abatement of thirst among all living species including the hominid.

   Word barrier:____

3. A sign in a health club reads "This Way to Men's and Women's Change Room."

   Word barrier:____

4. "Sales people are so pushy."

   Word barrier:____

5. You husband is following a car on the freeway. The driver is a woman. She is speeding at about 120 km an hour; however, periodically, for no apparent reason, she will suddenly drop her speed to 100 km an hour. Your husband blurts out, " Women drivers are so erratic you can't count on them!"

   Word barrier:____

6. “Mary has always had Sunday dinner with her mom and dad ever since she was a child. I can’t believe she didn’t want to be here today.”

Word barrier:____

7. “You are either committed to this relationship or you are not.”

Word barrier:____

8. “It is a fact that you will not succeed at this job.”

Word barrier:____

9. “Let me introduce you to Mr. and Mrs. Sam Tillerman.”

Word barrier:____

Activity 5.3: Using "I" Instead of "You"

Objectives:

1. To give you practice using I-language.
2. To help you differentiate between evaluative and descriptive language.

Part 1

Instructions:

1. For each of the following evaluative "you" statements write an "I" statement. Include a description of the observed behaviour and a brief account of your reaction to it or feeling about it.

Example: *You are so lazy.*

I-statement: *I get frustrated when you don't do your share of the cleaning around the house.*

1. "You only want things your own way."
I-statement:
2. "You drink like a fish."
I-statement:
3. "You always hog the TV."
I-statement:
4. "You don't care about my needs."
I-statement:
5. "You are always late."
I-statement:

6. “You never pull your own weight.”
I-statement:
7. “You are always reading the newspaper when I want to talk.”
I-statement:
8. “You drive like a maniac.”
I-statement:
9. “Why can’t you listen to me?”
I-statement:

Part 2

Instructions:

Think of three real-life examples where you could use an I-statement. Record the I-statement below.

1.
2.
3.

Activity 5.4: Confirming and Disconfirming Responses

Objective:
1. To help you differentiate between confirming and disconfirming responses.

Part 1
Instructions:
1. For the following examples write a disconfirming response and a confirming one. Provide a rationale for why each statement is confirming or disconfirming.

Example: *"Did you see my article in the company newsletter?"*

Disconfirming response: *"I never read that rag."*

Rationale: impersonal

Confirming response: *"Yes, I was very impressed. I'd like to talk to you about it."*

Rationale: compliment

1. "There is nothing like hiking on the Bruce Trail on a spring day."

   Disconfirming response:____
   Rationale:____

   Confirming response:____
   Rationale:____

2. "I am so discouraged. My husband and I have been going to counselling for a year now and things are not getting any better."

   Disconfirming response:____
   Rationale:____

   Confirming response:____
   Rationale:____

3. "I am worried about my daughter. She has just started working the night shift."

   Disconfirming response:____

Rationale:____

Confirming response:____
Rationale:____

4. "I can't believe it. I got my first raise and I have only been working here three months."

   Disconfirming response:______________________________________
   Rationale:____

   Confirming response:____
   Rationale:____

5. "My cousin and I are going to Europe this summer. We are going to start in England and then work our way across the continent."

   Disconfirming response:______________________________________
   Rationale:____

   Confirming response:____
   Rationale:____

6. "I can't believe the mess that politicians are making of our economy."

   Disconfirming response:______________________________________
   Rationale:____

   Confirming response:____
   Rationale:____

7. "I saw *Tosca* last night. I was really disappointed in the lead female singer. She just couldn't project. Even though I was seated near the front it was hard to hear her."

   Disconfirming response:______________________________________
   Rationale:____

   Confirming response:____
   Rationale:____

8. "I just heard on the news that we are expecting a major snowstorm tonight and it is only the beginning of November!"

   Disconfirming response:______________________________________

Rationale:____

Confirming response:____________________________________
Rationale:____

9. "Would you like me to cook dinner tonight?"

   Disconfirming response:__________________________________
   Rationale:____

   Confirming response:____________________________________
   Rationale:____

Part 2

Instructions:

1. Give two examples of real-life situations where you received or gave a disconfirming response.
2. For each give an example of how you could change this to a confirming response.

Example:
Confirming response:
Example:
Confirming response:

DIFFICULT POSITION 5

A young woman, a junior partner in a new law firm, attends a conference of legal specialists in her field. The keynote speaker, a nationally prominent man in his middle sixties, presents a brilliant and impassioned summary of the current professional issues, but when referring to people in general he uses only the masculine pronoun "he" and speaks only of "man." The young woman is troubled by this. She knows that the influence of this speaker is broad and pervasive, and she feels his sexist language reinforces negative sexist attitudes in the profession. In the question-and-answer session which follows, she decides to bring this to the speaker's attention, since it is the only opportunity she will have to speak with him. She tells her colleague sitting next to her what she intends. This colleague, a young man and another junior partner of the firm, says, "You'll just look like an idiot; it's not important enough to bother him about it."

INSTRUCTIONS

1. What should the young woman do? Should she speak out? If so, what sort of things might she say to communicate her message effectively? What might be the consequences of speaking out? Is the goal important enough to justify the possible consequences? What are the consequences of not speaking out?

2. In an effort of both decentring and attribution, to what might you attribute the keynote speakers exclusive use of masculine nouns and pronouns? Would decentring help the young lawyer to make her message about sexist language more effective for the keynote speaker? If so, how so?

3. Consider these questions in small groups and write a brief summary of your discussion.

Exercise 5.1: Learning Objective: General Review (**TRUE/FALSE**)

Instructions: Identify the following statements as either true or false.

1. The relationship between a given word and its referent is intrinsic. ( )

2. The denotative meaning of a word corresponds with its various dictionary definitions. ( )

3. Abstraction in language is always a sign of deliberate obscurity. ( )

4. English is a member of the Indo-European family of languages. ( )

5. French is a member of the Indo-European family of languages. ( )

6. A malapropism involves the use of false generalization. ( )

7. No action or decision should ever be based on mere inference. ( )

8. Removing gender bias from our language will alone create gender equality. ( )

9. A fact is something susceptible and subject to direct observation. ( )

10. A tangential response to a statement is utterly unrelated to the statement. ( )

11. Declaring "All Canadians love hockey" is an instance of indexing. ( )

12. Polarization often excludes the middle ground from our consideration. ( )

13. Restricted codes are examples of biased language. ( )

14. Language forms culture, but culture also forms language. ( )

15. Communicating with someone who speaks only a little of your language may require you to use an elaborated code. ( )

16. All cultures rely equally on nonverbal cues to contextualize verbal meaning. ( )

17. Speaking a common language with others is a form of symbolic interaction. ( )

18. A confirming response to another could never be expressed in jargon. ( )

19. The word "home" has connotations of comfort that "house" does not. ( )

Exercise 5.2: Learning Objective: General Review (**FILL-IN-THE-BLANKS**)

Instructions: Fill in the blanks using the appropriate term or terms from the following list.

symbol	denotative meaning	malapropism	static evaluation
referent	connotative meaning	restricted code	polarization
thought	linguistic determinism	jargon	elaborated code
high-context culture	world view	allness	confirming response
low-context culture	bypassing	indexing	disconfirming response
			symbolic interaction

1. __________ refuses to take account of change in forming judgements.

2. When the student wrote that his grandfather suffered from "old-timer's disease" instead of "Alzheimer's Disease," he produced an example of __________.

3. The tendency to express things in either/or extremes is characteristic of __________.

4. When his father said, "get me a Phillips screwdriver," Tom ran next door to borrow a screwdriver from their neighbour, Mr. Phillips. Tom's father said, "I guess this is a case of __________."

5. "10/4 good buddy, watch out for smokies in the trees," is an example of truckers' __________.

6. When I was in Italy, my host at dinner used his hands so much in talking, he almost stabbed himself with his fork. I knew I was in a __________.

7. Whenever Mr. Smith made mistakes around the house, Ms. Smith would say to him, "I guess we need to train the dog." I never understood that as a kid, but now I know it was a part of their __________.

8. In the German language, there is no way to say that one is in the process of doing something. One can say "I ran" or "I run," but there is no way to say "I *am* running." I wonder if that's why many Germans seem so emphatic. Well, probably not, but if it were true, it would be a good example of __________.

9. Every word is an arbitrary __________ to represent a __________ which triggers a __________.

10. When I used diagrams drawn on a napkin with a crayon as part of my efforts to show Mr. Fukuyama the way to the CN Tower, I was using an __________________ to convey my meaning.

11. "Guard" had a better _______________ than "bouncer," so I insisted on being called a guard.

12. Professor Grimm read Schopenhauer and accepted the philosopher's claim that the universe was dominated by blind will as his own _______________.

13. Dr. Grand ignored my question entirely, which was a very ________________, but Dr. Deferent thanked me for my interest and agreed with me about the main issue, which was a very ________________.

14. Many doctors are like Dr. Grand, but many are also like Dr. Deferent. Remembering the difference between them helped me to avoid __________ statements about the coldness and remoteness of doctors. ___________ my evaluations to individuals allowed me to avoid stereotyping.

15. We went to the dictionary to find the exact _____________ of the word "bum."

16. Herr Schwartz from Berlin and Herr Klein from Dresden spoke for several hours without so much as moving a muscle. Although I could understand nothing of what they were saying, it was clear to me that their _________________ reflected a _______________.

Exercise 5.3: Learning Objective: General Review (**MULTIPLE CHOICE**)

Instructions: Choose the best answer for each question below.

1. The theory that language and culture are mutually influential is known as

   a. static evaluation
   b. symbolic interaction
   c. malapropism
   d. linguistic determinism

2. Restricting evaluations to particular instances and individuals is known as

   a. restricted code
   b. indexing
   c. polarization
   d. elaborated code

3. Denotation corresponds to

   a. biased language use
   b. the emotional associations of a word
   c. dictionary definitions
   d. categorizing by extremes

4. The tendency to categorize by extremes is characteristic of

   a. restricted codes
   b. denotation
   c. polarization
   d. connotation

5. Communication between speakers of different languages may involve use of

   a. elaborated code
   b. restricted code
   c. indexing
   d. linguistic determinism

6. Teenage slang most closely resembles

    a. malapropism
    b. polarization
    c. jargon
    d. bafflegab

7. All of the following can be barriers to good verbal communication except

    a. sweeping generalizations
    b. rigidity in evaluation
    c. deliberate abstractness
    d. symbolic interaction

8. All of the following can contribute to supportive communication except

    a. asking open-ended questions
    b. maintaining indifference
    c. avoiding generalizations
    d. practising empathy

9. All of the following are examples of confirming response except

    a. compliment response
    b. fulsome response
    c. supportive response
    d. clarifying response

10. All of the following are examples of disconfirming response except

    a. impervious response
    b. irrelevant response
    c. delayed response
    d. incoherent response

11. All of the following statements about words are true except

    a. as symbols, words arbitrarily represent something else
    b. the meaning of a word is often partially determined by context
    c. words can influence our sense of self-worth
    d. all words in all languages derive from a single parent language

Answers

CHAPTER 5

Exercise 5.1

1. (F)
2. (T)
3. (F)
4. (T)
5. (T)
6. (F)
7. (F)
8. (F)
9. (T)
10. (F)
11. (F)
12. (T)
13. (F)
14. (T)
15. (T)
16. (F)
17. (T)
18. (F)
19. (T)

Exercise 5.2

1. Static evaluation
2. Malapropism
3. Polarization
4. Bypassing
5. Jargon
6. High-context culture
7. Restricted code
8. Linguistic determination
9. Symbol/referent/thought
10. Elaborated code
11. Connotative meaning
12. World view
13. Disconfirming response/ confirming response
14. Allness/Indexing
15. Denotative meaning
16. Symbolic interaction/ low-context culture

Exercise 5.3

1. d
2. b
3. c
4. c
5. a
6. c
7. d
8. b
9. b
10. c
11. d

Chapter 6

Communicating Nonverbally

CHAPTER OUTLINE

I. Why Learn about Nonverbal Communication?

A. Nonverbal messages communicate our feelings and attitudes

1. As little as 7 percent of emotional meaning is communicated verbally
2. As much as 93 percent is communicated nonverbally
   a. As much as 55 percent is conveyed by facial expression
   b. As much as 38 percent is conveyed by vocal cues
      (1) voice volume
      (2) voice pitch
      (3) voice intensity
3. Our response to others is influenced more by their actions than their words
4. Nonverbal communication reflects our different relationships
   a. Informal with friends
   b. Formal in formal settings

B. Nonverbal messages are more believable

1. Actions speak louder than words
   a. It is difficult to manipulate and control nonverbal cues
   b. Nonverbal cues can "leak" meaning through key sources
      (1) face
      (2) hands
      (3) feet
   c. Nonverbal cues can suggest when someone is lying
      (1) greater lag time in response to a question
      (2) reduced eye contact
      (3) increased shifts in posture
      (4) unfilled pauses
      (5) less smiling
      (6) slower speech
      (7) higher pitch in voice
      (8) more deliberate pronunciation and articulation of words
   d. Nonverbal cues can indicate emotional arousal
      (1) dilating pupils
      (2) blushing
      (3) sweating
      (4) changes in breathing
   e. Nonverbal cues are used in polygraph (lie detector) tests
      (1) heart and breathing rates

(2) electrical resistance of skin (galvanic skin response)

f. Nonverbal cues may signal boredom or disinterest

(1) finger wiggling or toe wagging

(2) twiddling an object (pencil/pen)

C. Nonverbal communication plays a major role in interpersonal relationships

1. 65 percent of social meaning of messages based on nonverbal communication
2. Nonverbal cues form first impressions

   a. We begin making judgements about others immediately upon meeting them
3. Nonverbal cues develop and maintain mature relationships

   a. Use of nonverbal cues increases with increased intimacy of relationship
4. Nonverbal cues signal changes in level of satisfaction in relationships

   a. Desire to curtail or cool relationship may be indicated by nonverbal cues

   (1) less vibrant tone

   (2) reduced eye contact

   (3) reduced physical contact
5. Verbal and nonverbal cues work together in two primary ways

   a. Nonverbal cues *supplement* messages

   (1) substitute -- (gesture in place of word: hitchhiker's thumb)

   (2) repeat -- (gesture added to word: pointing while giving directions)

   (3) contradict -- (gesture contrary to word: frowning and saying, "I'm happy")

   (4) regulate -- (gesture signalling wish to participate or refrain from communication: raised finger to signal wish to speak: lowered head to signal wish not to)

   b. Nonverbal cues *complement* messages

   (1) accenting -- (gesture with word: pounding podium and saying, "This is important")

II. The Challenge of Studying Nonverbal Communication

A. Nonverbal messages are often ambiguous

1. Meaning of nonverbal messages may be known only to person displaying them
2. Nonverbal behaviours may have no meaning at all

B. Nonverbal messages are continuous

1. Words (verbal messages) are discrete entities with a clear beginning and end
2. Nonverbal messages flow seamlessly from one situation to another

C. Nonverbal messages are multichannelled

1. Nonverbal cues come simultaneously to our perception from various sources
2. We can only attend to one nonverbal cue at a time
3. Negative nonverbal messages command more attention than positive ones when the two compete
4. If nonverbal message contradicts verbal message, accurate interpretation of either message may be impossible

D. Nonverbal interpretation is culture-based

1. Humans from every culture share some nonverbal behaviours
   a. Smiling when happy
   b. Frowning when unhappy
   c. Raising eyebrows when meeting
   d. Children raising arms to be picked up
   e. Children sucking thumbs for comfort
2. Each culture may develop unique rules for nonverbal display and interpretation
   a. No common cross-cultural dictionary of nonverbal meaning
   b. Norms for nonverbal behaviour within each culture

III. Nonverbal Communication Codes

A. Body movement, posture, and gestures

1. Sign language used to communicate between speakers of different languages
   a. Captain Cook in the New Hebrides (1771 A.D.)
   b. Xenophon's Greeks in Asia Minor (400 B.C.)
2. Gestures help make points even among speakers of a common language
3. Kinesics – the study of human movement and gesture
   a. One kinesic paradigm identifies four stages of "quasi-courtship behaviour"
      (1) courtship readiness (tense muscles, erect posture)
      (2) preening behaviours (appearance checking and modification)
      (3) positional cues (posture, body orientation)
      (4) appeals to invitation (proximity, exposed skin, open body position, eye contact)
4. Kinesic behaviours influence our judgements about human warmth or coldness
   a. Warm people
      (1) face communication partner directly
      (2) smile often
      (3) make direct eye contact
      (4) do not fidget
      (5) do not make unnecessary hand movements
   b. Cold people
      (1) avoid eye contact
      (2) turn away from communication partner
      (3) smile infrequently
      (4) fidget
5. Posture and body orientation reveal important information
   a. Open body position communicates receptiveness and responsiveness
   b. Turning away communicates avoidance and rejection
6. Nonverbal cues contribute to perceptions of liking
   a. Open body and arm position
   b. Forward lean
   c. Relaxed posture
7. Movements and gestures can be classified according to five functions

a. Emblems – specific gestures with culturally understood meanings
  (1) raised and open palm = "do not interrupt"
  (2) applause = enthusiastic praise and appreciation
  (3) index finger to lips = "be silent"
b. Illustrators – contradict, accent, or complement messages
  (1) slamming a book shut and shouting, "I'm sick of reading!"
  (2) pounding a lectern and declaring, "This principle is absolutely vital!"
  (3) turning toward someone and saying, "Now it's your turn."
c. Affect displays – movements and gestures to communicate emotion
  (1) friendly – soft tone of voice, open smile, relaxed posture
  (2) neutral – minimal facial expression, monotone voice
  (3) hostile – harsh voice, frown with bared teeth, posture tense and rigid
d. Regulators – control flow of communication
  (1) desire to participate – eye contact, raised eyebrows, open mouth, raised index finger, forward lean
  (2) desire not to participate – averted eyes, closed mouth, crossed arms, backward lean
e. Adaptors – nonverbal behaviours to satisfy personal needs
  (1) adjusting glasses
  (2) combing hair
  (3) scratching mosquito bite

8. The five categories and interpersonal communication
  a. The five categories provide a precise way to think about your behaviour
    (1) note your use of emblems
    (2) note whether your use of nonverbal messages contradicts your verbal
    (3) be aware of how you display affect
    (4) notice how you use adaptors

B. Eye contact
1. Eye contact has four functions in interpersonal interactions
  a. cognitive – information about person's thought process
  b. monitoring – information about the reactions of others to us
  c. regulatory cues – eye signals of when we wish to talk or not talk
  d. expressive – information about emotions
    (1) crying
    (2) blinking
    (3) widening or narrowing eyes
2. Degree of eye contact is governed by various motives
  a. Reasons why one is likely to look at communication partner
    (1) physically distant from him or her
    (2) discussing easy, impersonal topics
    (3) nothing else to look at
    (4) interested in partner's reactions (interpersonally involved)
    (5) interested in partner (emotionally involved)

(6) trying to dominate or influence
(7) from a culture that emphasizes visual contact
(8) extroverted
(9) high affiliative or inclusion needs
(10) dependent on unresponsive partner
(11) listening rather than talking
(12) female

b. Reasons why one is not likely to look at communication partner
   (1) physically close
   (2) discussing difficult, intimate topics
   (3) other relevant objects, people, or backgrounds to look at
   (4) not interested in partner's reactions
   (5) talking rather than listening
   (6) not interested in partner because of dislike
   (7) from a culture that discourages visual contact in communication
   (8) introverted
   (9) low affiliative or inclusion needs
   (10) mental disorder like autism, schizophrenia, etc.
   (11) embarrassed, ashamed, sorrowful, sad, submissive, something to hide

C. Facial expressions

1. Face is the exhibit gallery for our emotional displays
   a. We may try to manipulate and control our facial cues
   b. Facial cues may betray real feelings despite efforts of control
   c. Face is versatile
      (1) capable of producing 250,000 expressions
   d. Facial expressions can be grouped under six emotional categories
      (1) surprise (wide-open eyes, raised and wrinkled brow, open mouth)
      (2) fear (open mouth, tense skin under eyes, wrinkled forehead)
      (3) disgust (raised or curled upper lip, wrinkled nose, raised cheeks, lowered brow, lowered upper eyelid)
      (4) anger (tensed lower eyelid, pursed lips or open mouth, lowered and wrinkled brow, staring eyes)
      (5) happiness (smiling, mouth open or closed, raised cheeks, wrinkles around lower eyelids)
      (6) sadness (trembling lip, corners of mouth turned downward, corners of upper eyelid raised)

D. Vocal cues

1. Voice is a major vehicle for communicating emotions
   a. Pitch
   b. Rate
   c. Volume
   d. Use of silence
2. Some vocal expressions of emotion are easier to identify than others

a. Joy and anger easy to identify
b. Fear often confused with nervousness
c. Love often confused with sadness
d. Pride often confused with satisfaction

3. Voice provides information about self-confidence and knowledge
   a. Mispronunciations and vocalized pauses negatively affect credibility
4. Voice has regulatory function in interpersonal situations
   a. Lowering pitch on final word often signals a speaker is finished
   b. Injected sounds ("ah ... ah ... ah ...") may signal wish to interrupt speaker
   c. Affirmative responses ("sure," "uh-huh") may signal impatience to assume a speaking role
5. Being silent may indicate many things
   a. Not knowing what to say
   b. Preparing a lie
   c. Seeking distance from others
   d. Opting out of conversation
   e. Taking time to think
   f. Showing respect
   g. Feeling words would diminish an experience
   h. Enjoying someone's company with no urgency to speak ("positive silence")

E. Personal space

1. How close we willingly to get to others relates to familiarity, power, and status
   a. Proxemics investigates four spatial zones in human relationships
      (1) intimate space – zero to one and one half feet – intimate communication
      (2) personal space – one and one-half feet to four feet – family and friends
      (3) social space – four to twelve feet – professional and group interaction
      (4) public space – from twelve feet – audience and classroom (impersonal)
2. Choosing or assigning specific space depends on variables
   a. We stand closer to those we like
   b. Persons of high status are assigned more space than those of lower status
   c. Large people are often accorded more space
   d. Women stand closer to others than men
   e. Everyone tends to stand closer together in a large room
   f. Dominant group members select seats at the head of a room or table

F. Territory

1. Territoriality concerns human and animal use of space to communicate ownership and boundaries
   a. Territorial markers – objects, signs, fences, locks, security systems

G. Touch

1. Normally, we use touch to express intimacy
2. If intimacy is not intended, we instinctively react to correct message
3. Touch is vital to well-being and development
   a. Breastfeeding

4. Amount of touch we need may be related to family background
5. We are more likely to touch others under specific circumstances
    a. When feeling happy or friendly
    b. When asking someone to do something for us
    c. When sharing rather than asking for information
    d. When trying to persuade someone to do something
    e. When talking about intimate topics
    f. When in voluntary social settings (party as opposed to business meeting)
    g. When sharing good news
    h. When listening to a troubled or worried friend

H. Appearance

1. In all our interactions with others, appearance counts
    a. We think attractive people more credible, happy, popular and prosperous
        (1) attractive females may persuade others more easily than less attractive
    b. Body shape and size affects how others perceive us
        (1) heavier people are perceived as older, talkative, conservative, jovial
        (2) thin people are perceived as suspicious, uptight, ambitious, negative
        (3) muscular people are perceived as adventurous, attractive
    c. Clothing affects how others perceive us
        (1) uniforms indicate rank and authority
        (2) fashionable or stylish clothing indicates social class and position

IV. Interpreting Nonverbal Communication

A. We synthesize and interpret nonverbal cues using three primary dimensions

1. Immediacy – behaviours communicating liking and engendering pleasure
    a. Proximity – close, forward lean
    b. Body orientation – direct, but could be side-by-side
    c. Eye contact – eye contact and mutual eye contact
    d. Facial expression – smiling
    e. Gestures – head nods, movement
    f. Posture – open, arms oriented towards others
    g. Touch – cultural- and context-appropriate touch
    h. Voice – higher pitch, upward pitch
2. Arousal – indications of responsiveness and interest
    a. Animation in face, voice, gestures
    b. Forward lean
    c. Flash of eyebrows
    d. Nod of head
3. Dominance – cues communicating status, position, and importance
    a. Use of space – height (platform or standing), facing a group, more space
    b. Eye contact – less with lower status, more when talking, more when initially establishing dominance, more when starting to establish power
    c. Face – no smile, frown, mature adult features

d. Touch – initiating touch
e. Voice – loud, low pitch, wide pitch range, slow, many interruptions, hesitation before speaking
f. Gesture – pointing at the other or at his or her property
g. Posture – standing, hands on hips, expanded chest, relaxed

V. Improving Your Ability to Interpret Nonverbal Messages

A. Consider nonverbal cues in context
1. Avoid drawing conclusions from isolated behaviours or a single cue

B. Look for clusters of nonverbal cues
1. Look for corroborating cues
2. Consider nonverbal behaviours in conjunction with other nonverbal cues
3. Consider the environment and the person's verbal message

C. Consider past experiences when interpreting nonverbal cues
1. Familiarity increases our sensitivity to nonverbal cues

D. Check your perceptions with others
1. Three stages of perception checking
   a. Observe nonverbal cues
   b. Attempt to interpret nonverbal cues
   c. If still uncertain, ask if your interpretation of nonverbal cues is accurate

CHAPTER REVIEW: SECTION BY SECTION SUMMARY

I. Why Learn about Nonverbal Communication?

Nonverbal messages do three things:

(1) communicate feelings and attitudes
(2) command more belief than verbal messages
(3) play a major role in our interpersonal relationships

Our face and voice are more important in communicating or revealing our feelings to others than our explicit verbal messages. Even when we are lying, the truth is often "written on our face." Sometimes we say that someone's voice or face "betrayed him." By this we mean a nonverbal message may contradict a verbal message and provide information contrary to the will of the speaker. Nonverbal gestures can be used to *supplement* words or *complement* words. If I point in response to a request for directions, I have used a gesture in place of a word (supplement). If I point at someone's chest while shouting, "You're responsible for this mess," I am using a gesture to accent my words (complement). Nonverbal cues form our first impressions and tend to be more persuasive than verbal messages.

II. The Challenge of Studying Nonverbal Communication

Nonverbal messages are often more powerful than verbal ones but are sometimes less easy to interpret. Four factors complicate the interpretation of nonverbal messages:

(1) Ambiguity
(2) Continuousness
(3) Multiplicity (multichannelled)
(4) Cultural context

Sometimes a nonverbal message may appear to mean something it does not. A man who frowns may be angry with us or only experiencing indigestion. A gesture we think meaningful may mean nothing at all. Remember the danger of **crediting irrelevant information** described in Chapter Three (91). A nonverbal message may mean a number of things or nothing. Be careful interpreting gestures. Nonverbal behaviours are continuous. Unlike words, which start and stop sharply in time, nonverbal behaviours flow along in a kind of stream – a smile becomes a frown, then a smile again, and again a frown. It is not always easy to follow this changing stream. Nonverbal messages also come thick and fast. We see facial expressions with our eyes, hear voice cues with our ears, and probably several at once. In the midst of multiple, simultaneous, and continuous messages, we are in danger of "information overload" and are forced by the natural limitation of our attention to make a selection. In selecting, we tend to give greater attention to negative messages if they are in competition with positive ones. Remember our disposition to **focus on the negative** described in Chapter Three (91). If these multichannel nonverbal messages are also accompanied by contradictory verbal ones (which can happen), our ability to interpret accurately may be overcome. Finally, a nonverbal message may have a particular cultural meaning unknown to us. In some cultures, a casual touch is courteous, in others, an insult. Smiling at a rebuke might seem impertinent in some cultures but would be understood as a sign of embarrassed shame in others. Nonverbal gestures and behaviours are often as context-bound as words in a sentence.

III. Nonverbal Communication Codes

Our bodies talk in various ways. The most literal use of body language is sign language. In the first contacts between European explorers and native peoples, sign language was often the only way to achieve understanding. Even today, a tourist visiting a foreign country where he or she does not speak the language may find sign language useful. In addition to intentional sign language, our bodies speak a less conscious and controlled language of gesture. The study of this language of gesture and movement is called **kinesics**.

Kinesic analysis has been applied to human courtship behaviours. Four distinct stages have been identified:

(1) courtship readiness (pull in that gut, stiffen that spine, tighten those muscles, look alive)
(2) preening behaviours (comb your hair, put on lipstick, adjust your clothes, check a mirror)
(3) positional cues (lean forward, get closer)
(4) appeals to invitation (get real close, look into the eyes, expose a little skin)

These behaviours can be more or less conscious depending on the individual and are used in any situation where we are trying to secure favourable attention from others. Kinesic analysis can also tell us about the gestures and behaviours that lead us to characterize others as either "warm" or "cold."

(1) Warm people: face communication partners, smile often, make direct eye contact, seldom fidget
(2) Cold people: face away from communication partner, seldom smile, avoid eye contact, often fidget

Posture and body orientation tells us about the responsiveness and receptiveness of others to our messages.
(1) Someone with his or her arms crossed, head down or turned away, probably doesn't want to hear us.
(2) Someone with arms uncrossed, head up and eyes on ours is probably ready to listen.

Nonverbal cues also contribute to perceptions of liking. If someone leans toward you with open body and arm position and has relaxed posture, it's easier to believe he or she likes you than if he or she stands stiffly with crossed arms and scowls.

Nonverbal cues can be categorized according to five functions:

(1) **Emblems** – generally understood nonverbal cues with fixed cultural meanings. A police officer directs traffic at an intersection with emblems. His raised hand, palm outward, means stop. His finger pointed right or left at arm's length means go in that direction. Every driver in North American (and probably elsewhere) knows this (or had better learn it!).

(2) **Illustrators** – gestures which accent, underscore, or complement a message. If a lawyer comes into her office, throws her arm in the air, and shouts, "We won the case," her raised arm illustrate the sense of triumph conveyed by her verbal message.

(3) **Affect displays** – nonverbal movements and gestures used to communicate emotion. Our facial expressions, vocal cues, posture, and gestures convey the intensity of our emotions and show if we are friendly, neutral, or hostile.

(4) **Regulators** – gestures controlling flow of communication. A raised index finger may indicate our desire to participate in a discussion or make an observation. Conversely, lowered eyes may indicate our desire not to participate.

(5) **Adaptors** – nonverbal behaviours that help us satisfy personal needs and adapt to an immediate situation. These nonverbal behaviours are not likely to be messages. If someone adjusts his glasses, it probably only means they were slipping on his nose. Of course, if it happens often and seems exaggerated, it may be a sign of impatience, disinterest, or boredom. Some adaptors, like using a toothpick to clean one's teeth, may be considered appropriate or inappropriate in different contexts and by different people.

Knowing these five categories can help us be more conscious of our own nonverbal behaviours. Ask yourself the following questions:

(1) Do I use emblems often? If I do, which ones?
(2) Does my nonverbal behaviour ever contradict my verbal messages? Is this intentional?
(3) How do I display affect? What do I look like when I'm feeling certain emotions?
(4) How do I use adaptors? What adaptors are habits with me? How do they appear to others?

One of the most powerful forms of nonverbal communication is eye contact. Eye contact serves four dominant functions:

(1) cognitive – we can sometimes guess what someone is thinking by watching his or her eyes
(2) monitoring – eye movement and expression will often tell us how others are responding to us
(3) regulatory – we use our eyes as signals to show when we want attention and when we don't
(4) expressive – emotion often shows most clearly in the eyes, from tears to glowing happiness

Another powerful form of nonverbal communication is the face itself. We may have as many as 250,000 distinguishable facial expressions, but all our expressions can be categorized under six primary emotional categories:

(1) surprise – wide-open eyes, raised and wrinkled brow, open mouth
(2) fear – open mouth, tense skin under eyes, wrinkles in centre of forehead
(3) disgust – raised or curled upper lip, wrinkled nose, raised cheeks, lowered brow and upper eyelid
(4) anger – tensed lower eyelid, pursed or open mouth, lowered and wrinkled brow, staring eyes
(5) happiness – smiling, mouth may be open or closed, raised cheeks, wrinkles around lower eyelids
(6) sadness – lip may tremble, corners of lips turn downward, corners of upper eyelid may be raised

Along with the eyes and face, the voice is another powerful nonverbal communicator. What we say is important. How we say it may be more so. Pitch, rate, and volume of voice communicate information along with the sound of words. Stopping and starting frequently when speaking, with many vocalized pauses ("ums" and "ahs"), may weaken one's credibility. Frequent mispronunciations may cause one's knowledge and competence to be questioned. Sounds and short responses may be used to indicate our impatience to assume a speaking role in a conversation ("uh-huh," "sure," "definitely, "I hear you"). Silence can mean many things, ranging from a pause to prepare a lie to sharing comfortable wordlessness with a friend or loved one. Comfortable silence is called "positive silence." Vocal cues, like all nonverbal cues, can be ambiguous. Shouts of anger and joy are hard to miss, but vocal expressions of fear, love and pride may be confused with nervousness, sadness, and satisfaction.

Another powerful nonverbal communicator is space. Where we place ourselves and where others place us is as important a message about who we are as our own physical posture and behaviour. Edward T. Hall in his study of human spatial dynamics called **proxemics** identifies four spatial zones:

(1) intimate space – zero to one and one-half feet – most intimate interpersonal communication
(2) personal space – one and one-half feet to four feet – friends and family interpersonal communication
(3) social space – from four to twelve feet – group and professional relationships
(4) public space – begins at twelve feet – audiences and classrooms, no interpersonal communication

Spatial relationships also reflect variables such as status. Individuals of higher status are accorded more space than those of lower status (for example, the large offices of senior members in law firms). Physically large people tend to be accorded more space. Women stand closer to others than men, and everyone tends to stand closer together in a large room. Dominant individuals seek out or are assigned seats at the head of a room or table.

Territoriality is another aspect of spatial relationships in both animal and human behaviour. We use territorial markers – objects, signs, fences, locks, security systems – to declare our ownership and boundaries. Our intimate and personal space is a territory we claim for ourselves and those we invite in. We speak of our personal space as being invaded when someone comes closer than we wish.

Touch is the most intimate form of nonverbal communication. When we touch a stranger accidentally we apologize for the unintentional "invasion" of their "space." Touching is necessary to our well-being and development. Breastfeeding strengthens the bond between mother and child. Different individuals have differing levels of need for touch, often depending on family background and training. We tend to touch others more often under specific circumstances:

(1) When feeling happy or friendly
(2) When asking someone to do something for us
(3) When sharing rather than asking for information
(4) When trying to persuade someone to do something
(5) When talking about intimate topics
(6) When in voluntary social settings (party as opposed to business meeting)
(7) When sharing good news
(8) When listening to a troubled or worried friend

Appearance is influential. We are biased in favour of people judged attractive. We think them more creditable, popular, happy, and prosperous. Attractive females may have an easier time persuading others than those perceived as less attractive. Our body size and shape affects how we are perceived by others. Heavier people are perceived as older, conservative, talkative, and good-natured. Thin people may be viewed as suspicious, ambitious, uptight, untalkative, and negative. Muscular types are seen as attractive and adventurous. You have probably heard the old saying, "Clothing makes the man (or woman)." Clothing does send nonverbal messages. Uniforms mean authority. Stylish and expensive clothing may send messages about social class and professional position. Even certain work clothes send status messages.

IV. Interpreting Nonverbal Messages

Nonverbal messages are interpreted along three primary dimensions:

(1) immediacy – cues communicating liking and engendering feelings of pleasure – eye contact, touch, forward lean, close distances
(2) arousal – cues expressing receptiveness and responsiveness – eye contact, varied vocal cues, animated facial expressions, forward lean, movement

(3) dominance – cues communicating status, position, and importance – protected and extended space, relaxed posture, status symbols (big chair, desk, corporate logo, secretarial support)

V. Improving Your Ability to Interpret Nonverbal Messages

There are four basic ways to improve your ability to interpret nonverbal messages:

(1) Consider nonverbal cues in context. Avoid drawing conclusions from isolated behaviours or a single cue. Look for clusters of nonverbal cues. Look for corroborating cues.
(2) Consider nonverbal behaviours in conjunction with other nonverbal cues. Consider the environment and the person's verbal message.
(3) Consider past experiences when interpreting nonverbal cues. Familiarity increases our sensitivity to nonverbal cues.
(4) Check your perceptions with others. Three stages of perception checking:
    1. Observe nonverbal cues
    2. Attempt to interpret nonverbal cues
    3. If still uncertain, ask if your interpretation of nonverbal cues is accurate

TERMS TO LEARN

Kinesics
Emblems
Illustrators
Affect Display
Regulators
Adaptors
Proxemics
Intimate Space
Personal Space
Social Space
Public Spaces
Territoriality
Immediacy
Arousal
Dominance
Perception Check

Activity 6.1: Effective Use of Nonverbal Behaviours

Objective:

1. To identify what you consider effective nonverbal behaviour in different contexts.

Part 1

Instructions:

1. In the following situations, what nonverbal messages could you use to communicate your message effectively?

Example: Being an attentive student

Non-verbal messages: *maintain eye contact with my professor, lean forward in my seat, nod my head, take notes as he lectures.*

1. Respect for a co-worker

Nonverbal messages:

2. A job interview with a panel of three interviewers

Nonverbal messages:

3. Teaching a science class

Nonverbal messages:

4. Encouraging a silent group member to participate in a small group discussion

Nonverbal messages:

5. Indicating your attraction to a person in whom you are romantically interested
Nonverbal messages:
6. Disapproval of someone's rude behaviour at the dinner table
Nonverbal messages:
7. Someone at work tries to engage you in a social conversation but you need to finish the report you are working on to meet a deadline.
Nonverbal messages:

Part 2

Instructions:

1. Describe three real-life situations you have experienced involving effective use of nonverbals and identify them here.

Example:
Nonverbal messages:
Example:
Nonverbal messages:
Example:
Nonverbal messages:

Activity 6.2: Nonverbal Diary

Objectives:

1. To help you become more aware of your own nonverbal messages.
2. To enable you to identify how your nonverbal messages help or hinder your communication.

Instructions:

1. Use the form below to keep a diary over the next few days. Record examples of your communication.
2. Identify what your nonverbal messages are.
3. Discuss whether these help or hinder the communication of your message.
4. Answer the questions following the exercise.

	Example	Nonverbals	Help or Hinder
Day One			
Day Two			
Day Three			
Day Four			
Day Five			

1. What impact did your nonverbals have on the communication of your messages?

2. If your nonverbals were ineffective, how could you have been more effective nonverbally?

Activity 6.3: Observing Nonverbals in Others

Objectives:
1. To help you increase your awareness of others' nonverbal communication.
2. To identify discrepancies between verbal messages and nonverbal messages.

Instructions:
1. Observe two people over the next several days. Record examples of their nonverbal behaviour in different situations. Note if there is any discrepancy between their verbal and nonverbal message.
2. Answer the questions at the end of the exercise.

Person A	***Observations Situations***	***Verbals***	***Nonverbals***	***Discrepancy***
1.				
2.				
3.				
4.				
5.				

Person B	***Observations Situations***	***Verbals***	***Nonverbals***	***Discrepancy***
1.				
2.				
3.				
4.				
5.				

1. Were there discrepancies between the verbals and nonverbals?

2. What were these discrepancies and to what do you attribute them?

3. What was the impact of this discrepancy?

Activity 6.4: Nonverbal Fishbowl

Objectives:
1. To increase your awareness of non-verbal behaviours in group meetings.

Instructions:

Part 1

1. Choose a hot topic from the list below or select a topic of your own choice.

Abortion

Capital Punishment

Legalization of Marijuana

Separation of Quebec from Canada

Euthanasia

Gay and Lesbian Parenting

Cloning and Reproductive Technologies

2. Have six volunteers debate this topic in a fishbowl setting (sitting in a circle in the middle of the room) for 10-15 minutes.
3. The rest of the class will act as observers attending to the nonverbal communication of the group members.
4. Observers should record their observations using the Observer's Chart (being as specific as possible in terms of what they observed) and be prepared to give verbal feedback at the end of the activity.

Part 2

1. Have the fishbowl group continue their discussion for 5 minutes; however, this time they may not use their hands. Have group members clasp their hands behind their chairs.

2. Observers should record their observations using the Observer's Chart (being as specific as possible in terms of what they observed) and be prepared to give verbal feedback at the end of the activity.

3. Answer the questions at the end of the exercise.

OBSERVER'S GUIDE

Person						
Body Movement						
Posture						
Gestures						
Eye Contact						
Facial Expression						
Vocal Cues						
Territory						
Touch						
Appearance						

1. What did you notice in Part 1 of the exercise?
2. What happened when participants were not allowed to use their hands?
3. What did you learn about nonverbal communication from this exercise?

DIFFICULT POSITION 6

You notice that whenever your new supervisor speaks to you she leans away from you and averts her glance. This makes you very uncomfortable. You feel you do not know her well enough to ask outright what these behaviours mean, but unless you can find out, you won't feel comfortable enough to concentrate on your assignments.

INSTRUCTIONS

1. In this situation, what kind of perception checking, short of direct questioning, might you do to gain an understanding of your supervisor's behaviour? What sorts of evidence derived from perception checking might make you less concerned about her nonverbal behaviour? What sorts of evidence might make you more concerned?

2. What sort of nonverbal behaviours within one's control might make an acquaintance or co-worker uncomfortable?

3. Consider these questions in small groups and write a brief summary of your discussion.

Exercise 6.1: Learning Objective: General Review (**TRUE/FALSE**)

Instructions: Identify the following statements as either true or false.

1. Unlike verbal messages, nonverbal messages are unambiguous. ( )

2. Nonverbal cues are impossible to manipulate or control. ( )

3. We make judgements about strangers within a second after meeting them. ( )

4. The frequency and understanding of nonverbal cues in a relationship is commonly relative to its degree of intimacy. ( )

5. An emblem in communication theory is a small picture of an action or gesture. ( )

6. Mispronunciations and vocalized pauses make effective communication impossible. ( )

7. Our judgements based on appearance are always accurate. ( )

8. The face is capable of an infinite range of expression. ( )

9. Polygraphs (lie detectors) rely primarily on measures of eye motion. ( )

10. Leaning toward another while speaking is always a sign of dominance. ( )

11. The kinesic behaviours of courtship are always unconscious. ( )

12. The rules governing interpretation of nonverbal messages are universal. ( )

13. Pounding a lectern to emphasize a point is an instance of adaptor function. ( )

14. A chief symptom of mental illnesses like autism and schizophrenia is staring. ( )

15. Immediacy cues are behaviours related primarily to establishing dominance. ( )

16. Nonverbal cues tend to be multiple, simultaneous, and continuous. ( )

17. The amount of touch a person requires varies from individual to individual. ( )

18. Our body size and shape often influences how others see us. ( )

19. Territorial markers are boundary indicators used during courtship rituals. ( )

Exercise 6.2: Learning Objective: General Review (**FILL-IN-THE-BLANKS**)

Instructions: Fill in the blanks using the appropriate term or terms from the following list.

nonverbal communication	affect display	intimate space	territoriality
	regulators	personal space	immediacy
kinesics	adaptors	social space	arousal
emblems	proxemics	public space	dominance
illustrators			perception check

1. _____________ is the area between zero and one and one-half feet from our person.

2. Leaning forward, making eye contact, touching, and standing close to another in an effort to elicit and engender liking are elements of _____________.

3. Subtle gestures in a conversation, like raising a finger slightly to indicate a desire to speak, are instances of nonverbal_____________.

4. When Jack started picking his teeth in the boardroom, it was certainly an example of an_____________that was out of place.

5. When he left briefly to get a drink of water, he left a towel draped over the barbell he was still using to indicate_________________.

6. Understanding the spatial dynamics of human behaviour is the study of___________.

7. When the professor answered us in a monotone without even looking at us, we knew that these were not signs of ___________.

8. Charles Darwin was one of the first to study animal and human expressions of emotion which we now classify as ______________.

9. When I told them the story of my first solo flight, I bent my knees and moved my hand through the air to show how I glided over the water. I used these two gestures as _____________ to give accent to my words.

10. I am happy to have my friends in my ________________, but I prefer that most of my coworkers remain in_________________ at meetings.

11. I walked in the enormous museum and looked at the pictures behind ropes and glass. The few tourists there besides myself kept their distance as did I. We behaved as we knew we should in that vast _____________.

12. The arrangement of the rooms with their huge oak desks and bookcases were intended to demonstrate the _____________ of senior partners in the firm of Lordly and Grand.

13. Because __________________ is often ambiguous, I always resort without hesitation to a careful_______________________ when using it to make important decisions.

Exercise 6.3: Learning Objective: General Review (**MULTIPLE CHOICE**)

Instructions: Choose the best answer for each question below.

1. A generally understood nonverbal gesture used in place of a word is called an

    a. illustrator
    b. emblem
    c. expressive
    d. adaptor

2. Nonverbal movements used to communicate emotion are called

    a. proxemics
    b. kinesics
    c. affect displays
    d. perception checks

3. A relationship between employees and their supervisor is likely to take place in

    a. social space
    b. intimate space
    c. public space
    d. personal space

4. One of the chief obstacles to interpreting nonverbal messages is

    a. irrelevance
    b. positional cues
    c. immediacy
    d. ambiguity

5. Of the following, a polygraph (lie detector test) chiefly measures

    a. eye movement
    b. facial expressions
    c. heart rate
    d. vocal cues

6. Which of following is the best example of an illustrator?

    a. a man shrugs his shoulders in response to a question about what he wants to eat
    b. a woman's face turns bright red when she realizes her dress is split along the seam
    c. a police officer riding a motorcycle points for a motorist to pull over
    d. a man rubs his stomach and says, "let's eat."

7. All of the following are complicating factors in interpreting nonverbal cues except

    a. continuousness
    b. ambiguity
    c. arousal
    d. multiplicity

8. All of the following are spatial zones identified in proxemics except

    a. interior space
    b. social space
    c. personal space
    d. intimate space

9. All of the following are examples of immediacy behaviours except

    a. forward lean
    b. fidgeting
    c. touching
    d. eye contact

10. All of the following are examples of adaptors except

    a. adjusting glasses
    b. loosening a tie
    c. removing a shoe and rubbing one's foot
    d. holding your hand palm outward to communicate a wish not to be disturbed

11. All of the following statements about touch are true except

    a. the amount of touch an individual needs or desires varies
    b. touching can contribute to our sense of well-being
    c. initiating touch can be a sign of dominance
    d. touch can only occur in intimate space

Answers

CHAPTER 6

Exercise 6.1

1. (F)
2. (F)
3. (T)
4. (T)
5. (F)
6. (F)
7. (F)
8. (F)
9. (F)
10. (F)
11. (F)
12. (F)
13. (F)
14. (F)
15. (F)
16. (T)
17. (T)
18. (T)
19. (F)

Exercise 6.2

1. Intimate space
2. Immediacy
3. Regulators
4. Adaptor
5. Territoriality
6. Proxemics
7. Arousal
8. Affect display
9. Illustrators
10. Personal space/social space
11. Public space
12. Dominance
13. Nonverbal communication/ Perception check

Exercise 6.3

1. b
2. c
3. a
4. d
5. c
6. d
7. c
8. a
9. b
10. d
11. d

Chapter 7

Conflict Management Skills

CHAPTER OUTLINE

I. What Is Conflict?

A. Interpersonal conflict occurs when people disagree on how to meet their needs

1. Needs may be incompatible
2. Too few resources may be available to satisfy needs
3. Individuals in conflict may opt to compete instead of cooperate
4. Intensity of conflict relates to intensity of unmet need
5. Bedrock of all conflicts is difference

B. Goals and conflict

1. Psychologists agree we are need-driven and goal-oriented
2. Most of what we do is based upon achieving a desirable goal
3. Most conflict is goal-driven
4. Colliding goals cause conflict

C. Experiences and conflict

1. Inherited differences, coupled with our experiences, cause conflict
   a. Different inherited religious practices
   b. Different inherited cultural and family traditions

II. Types of Conflict

A. Most conflicts fit into three categories

1. **Pseudo Conflict** – triggered by lack of understanding
   a. Unless we clear up misunderstandings, a real conflict might ensue
   b. Listening and asking questions to test understanding can contain conflicts
2. **Simple Conflict** – stems from different ideas, definitions, perceptions, goals
   a. Simple conflicts can be unravelled by keeping focus on issues at hand
3. **Ego Conflict** – based upon personal differences
   a. Pseudo and simple conflicts can become ego conflicts unless contained
      (1) refrain from hurling personal attacks and emotional epithets
      (2) take turns expressing feelings without interrupting
      (3) take time to cool off

B. Gender differences influence responses to conflict

1. Partnership perspective emphasizes keeping communication channels open between men and women

C. Different cultures have different approaches to conflict

1. Expressive conflict focusses on relationship issues
2. Instrumental conflict focussing on achieving goals and objectives

III. Myths About Conflict

A. Conflict myths contribute to our negative feelings about conflict

1. Myth 1: Conflicts should always be avoided
   a. Evidence suggests conflict arises in virtually every relationship
   b. Contentment in marriage relates to how conflict is managed not the amount
   c. Conflict is normal and productive in group interactions and deliberations
2. Myth 2: Conflict always occurs because of misunderstanding
   a. Sometimes real differences not merely misunderstandings cause conflicts
3. Myth 3: Conflict is always a sign of a poor interpersonal relationship
   a. Disagreements do not necessarily signal a relationship is on the rocks
   b. Overly polite, stilted conversation more likely signals a poor relationship
   c. Free expression of honest disagreement is a mark of a healthy relationship
4. Myth 4: Conflict can always be resolved
   a. Not all differences can be resolved by listening or paraphrasing
5. Myth 5: Conflict is always bad
   a. Conflict is a healthy component of our relationships
   b. If a relationship is conflict-free, it may indicate dishonesty between partners
   c. Conflict can lead to negotiation and fresh insights into a relationship

IV. Constructive and Destructive Conflict

A. Constructive conflict helps build new insights and new patterns in a relationship

1. Well-managed disagreements can benefit a relationship
   a. Disagreement may lead a couple to examine and repledge commitment
   b. Disagreement may revitalize a relationship
   c. Disagreement may enable people to see conflict from various perspectives

B. Destructive conflict dismantles relationships without restoring them

1. A hallmark of destructive conflict is lack of flexibility in responding to others
   a. In destructive conflict, people see their conflict from a win-lose perspective
   b. In destructive conflict, competition precludes cooperation
2. Escalation in destructive conflicts reduces flexibility
   a. Blocks off options for managing differences
   b. Makes a win-win solution more elusive

V. Understanding Conflict as a Process

A. Source: Prior Conditions

1. First phase is a dawning awareness of differences between you and another
   a. Different role expectations
   b. Different perceptions
   c. Different goals
   d. Different demands on limited resources
2. Many potential sources of conflict may be smouldering below the surface
3. These potential sources may be compounded with other concerns

B. Beginning: Frustration Awareness

1. Self-talk noting and concerning a problem engenders frustration

2. Realizing you may not achieve important goal engenders frustration
3. Someone else has resources you need engenders frustration
4. Recognizing differences in perception engenders frustration
5. Differences interfering with accomplishing goals heighten frustration

C. Middle: Active Conflict
1. Conflict brought to awareness of others is active, expressed struggle
   a. Active conflict does not necessarily involve shouting and intense emotion
   b. Expression of disagreement may be verbal or nonverbal
   c. Timely, active conflict may keep frustration levels from peak intensity
   d. Intense emotions and frustration add to difficulty of managing conflict
2. If frustrations remain only as thoughts, the conflict is passive or repressed

D. End: Resolution
1. Attempting to manage conflict is the resolution stage
2. Not all conflicts can be neatly resolved
   a. Divorce
   b. Dissolution of business corporation
   c. Separation of friends and roommates

E. Aftermath: Follow-up
1. Follow-up involves dealing with hurt feelings or managing simmering grudges
   a. Check with other person to confirm frustration is not reactivated
   b. Resolutions can backslide unless you confirm understandings

VI. Conflict Management Styles

A. Conflict styles can be organized into three dominant types
1. **Nonconfrontational Style** (avoiding, withdrawing, being indirect)
   a. Placating – attempting to please
      (1) placaters uncomfortable with negative emotions
      (2) placaters fear rejection if they rock the boat
      (3) placaters seek approval and avoid threats to their self-worth
      (4) placaters are so controlled they seem unresponsive to situations
      (5) placaters agree with others quickly to avoid conflict
      (6) placaters appear other-oriented but seek self-protection
   b. Distracting – looking away
      (1) distracters attempt to change the subject rather than face stressful issue
      (2) distracters hope problem will just go away
   c. Computing – remaining aloof and cool
      (1) computers refuse to be provoked or ruffled even under intense pressure
      (2) computers avoid expressing genuine feelings
      (3) computers respond to emotional issues with impersonal language
      (4) computers demonstrate low empathy and minimal involvement
2. **Confrontational**(controlling, manipulating, intimidating)
   a. Confrontational people always want to dominate and triumph
      (1) confrontational people have a win-lose philosophy

(2) confrontational people want to win even at the expense of others
(3) confrontational people claim victory over their opponents
(4) confrontational people are focussed on themselves
(5) confrontational people ignore the needs of others
(6) confrontational people resort to blaming and seek scapegoats
(7) confrontational people resort to intimidation
(a) name-calling
(b) personal attacks
(c) threats
(d) warnings

3. **Cooperative** (seeking mutually acceptable solutions)
a. Cooperative people view conflicts as problems to be solved not contests
b. A cooperative approach to conflict resolution involves four strategies
(1) separate the people from the problem – leave personal grievances out
(2) focus on shared interests – emphasize common interests, values, goals
(3) generate many options to solve problems – brainstorm alternatives
(4) base decisions on objective criteria – establish standards of measure

VII. Conflict Management Skills

A. Manage Your Emotions

1. Avoid taking action in emotionally charged states
a. Actions taken when emotionally upset are often cause for regret
b. Actions taken when emotionally upset may escalate conflict
c. Emotional outbursts may feel good but can foreclose rational negotiation
d. Five specific strategies can help minimize damaging effects of emotion
(1) Select a mutually acceptable time and place to discuss conflict
(a) avoiding ambushing someone with an angry attack
(b) give yourself time to cool off before trying to resolve a conflict
(c) whenever possible, make sure person is ready to receive message
(2) Plan your message
(a) take care to organize your message
(b) identify your goal and determine desired outcome
(c) talk with trusted friend or colleague first
(d) consider writing down key ideas
(3) Monitor nonverbal messages
(a) monitoring can help de-escalate an emotion-charged situation
(b) speak calmly and use direct eye contact
(c) maintain a natural facial expression
(d) be sure nonverbal message supports verbal message
(4) Avoid personal attacks, name-calling, and emotional overstatement
(a) threats and name-calling can turn a simple conflict into ego conflict
(b) avoid exaggerating emotions

(5) Use self-talk

(a) talk yourself down, ask if emotional tirade will achieve your goal

B. Manage Information

1. Clearly describe the conflict-producing events
    a. Think of delivering a brief, well-organized minispeech
    b. Describe events in chronological order
    c. Think of yourself as a journalist
    d. Describe events dispassionately
2. "Own" your statements by using descriptive "I" language
    a. Beginning a statement with "you" sets a listener up for a defensive response
    b. Not using "I" is a way of not taking responsibility for anger
3. Use effective listening skills
    a. Give your full attention to the speaker
    b. Tune out your internal messages
    c. Wait for a response
    d. Understand the major point the speaker is making (not just details)
    e. Stay other-oriented
4. Use effective response skills
    a. Ask questions
    b. Summarize your understanding
    c. Check key points to ensure that you have understood

C. Manage Goals

1. Identify your goal and your partner's goal
    a. Phrase goal statements in terms of wants and desires
    b. Balance value of achieving goal with value of maintaining good relationship
2. Identify where your goal and your partner's goal overlap
    a. Focus on shared interests (common goals)
    b. Develop objective rather than subjective criteria

D. Manage the Problem

1. Define the problem
    a. Think of problem as a "deviation" from your desired situation or condition
    b. Define the "real" problem and not just symptoms
2. Analyze the problem
    a. Break problem down into smaller components
    b. Decide what type of conflict it is (pseudo, simple, or ego)
    c. Ferret out all symptoms, effects, and obstacles
    d. Determine if problem stems from subproblems or one major problem
3. Determine the goals
    a. Generate objective criteria

        (1) measurable

(2) verifiable

4. Generate multiple solutions
   a. Brainstorming
      (1) make sure the problem and the goals are clear to both of you
      (2) suspend judgement and evaluation temporarily; do not censor thoughts
      (3) specify a certain time for brainstorming
      (4) have each partner brainstorm and write ideas down prior to meeting
      (5) develop at least one unique or far-out idea – you can tame them later
      (6) piggyback off your partner's ideas – encourage partner to do the same
      (7) write down all ideas suggested
      (8) review ideas, note ways to combine, eliminate, or extend them
5. Select the best solution and try it
   a. Make repeated efforts to generate a mutually agreeable solution
   b. Consider taking the issue to an impartial person
   c. Agree to disagree if necessary, drop it, and move on

VIII. When Others Aren't Other-Oriented: How to Be Assertive

A. Assertion informs a communication partner when he or she is violating rights
1. We each have rights in interpersonal communication
   a. Right to refuse a request someone makes of us
   b. Right to express feelings which do not trample on the feelings of others
   c. Right to have personal needs met if they do not infringe on other's rights

B. Aggressiveness pursues self-interest at the expense of others' rights
1. Aggressive people use coercive verbal means to get what they want
   a. Blaming
   b. Judging
   c. Evaluating
   d. Accusatory "you-statements"
2. Aggressive people use intimidating nonverbal cues to get what they want
   a. Steely stares
   b. Bombastic voice
   c. Flailing gestures

C. Five steps in assertive behaviour
1. Describe how you view the situation
   a. Monitor nonverbal messages, especially voice
   b. Avoid sarcasm or excessive vocal intensity
   c. Calmly, yet confidently, describe the problem
2. Disclose your feelings
   a. Disclosing feelings builds empathy
   b. Disclosing feelings helps avoid harangues about unjust treatment
3. Identify effects

4. Wait
    a. Monitor nonverbal cues expressive of impatience
    b. Make sure facial expression does not contradict your verbal message
5. Reflect content and feelings
    a. Reflect your understanding using paraphrase
    b. If person is evasive, unresponsive, or aggressive, go through steps again
    (1) describe what other person is doing that is not acceptable
    (2) disclose how you feel
    (3) identify the effects
    (4) wait
    (5) reflect and clarify as needed

CHAPTER REVIEW: SECTION BY SECTION SUMMARY

I. What Is Conflict?

Interpersonal conflict occurs when two people cannot agree upon a way to met their needs. The intensity of conflicts is related to the intensity of the unmet needs involved. Conflicts can range in intensity from mild differences to litigation and even armed struggle. Conflicts are commonly generated by a collision of goals. Our conflicts are often influenced by our inherited differences, preferences, and experiences. Culture, religion, gender, ethnicity, family background, and economic class are aspects of our inherited differences.

II. Types of Conflict

There are three basic types of conflict: (1) pseudo, (2) simple, and (3) ego. These three varieties represent an ascending series of conflict intensity.

Pseudo conflict is a matter of misunderstanding. If the misunderstanding is resolved, the conflict vanishes. If the misunderstanding is not resolved, a pseudo conflict may escalate into simple or ego conflict.

Simple conflict is conflict about different ideas, definitions, perceptions, and goals. Simple conflict is conflict in its pure state: the collision of difference. A simple conflict is best managed by focussing closely on the specific issues involved and seeking mutually acceptable resolution.

Ego conflict is personal. It involves antagonism. An ego conflict may arise from a simple conflict, but it tends to become all-embracing. To avoid these vicious and unproductive conflicts refrain from hurling personal attacks or trading emotional epithets; take turns expressing feelings without interrupting; and take time to cool down.

III. Myths About Conflict

There are five dominant myths about conflict:

Myth 1: Conflict should always be avoided. This is both unwise and probably impossible. Virtually every relationship involves conflict. It is largely unavoidable. One study suggests that contentment in marriage relates not to the amount of conflict, but to the ways in which partners manage it. Conflict can be a normal and productive part of interaction in group deliberations.

Myth 2: Conflict always occurs because of misunderstanding. Unfortunately, this is not true. Sometimes conflicts involve real differences that cannot be cleared away by understanding.

Myth 3: Conflict is always a sign of a poor interpersonal relationship. Again, not true. Fear of conflict and anxious efforts to avoid it at all costs is more likely to destabilize a relationship. Free expression of honest disagreement is an indication of a healthy relationship.

Myth 4: Conflict can always be resolved. Sadly, no. Some disagreements are so intense and perceptions so fixed that individuals may have to agree to disagree and live with it. Sometimes even that is impossible. Marriage partners and even nations sometimes have irreconcilable differences that can lead to intense and destructive conflict.

Myth 5: Conflict is always bad. A broken bone sometimes heals and is stronger than it was before the break. This can be true of relationships as well. Conflict can help us identify issues that need further discussion and can lead to negotiations that provide fresh insights.

IV. Constructive and Destructive Criticism

Constructive criticism may sometimes be painful or challenging, but it builds and strengthens relationships. Destructive criticism only hurts and leaves nothing behind but ruins.

A well-managed disagreement can lead couples and friends to first examine and then repledge their commitment to one another; revitalize a relationship; and provide different perspectives. Constructive criticism in relationships is like growing pains in childhood, a necessary part of healthy development.

Destructive criticism occurs in an atmosphere of competition, in which those involved want to win and fear to lose. In such circumstances, cooperation becomes impossible. Without a willingness to cooperate, the disputants become rigid and inflexible in their views and attitudes. In this tug-of-war, conflicts tend to escalate into ego battles.

V. Understanding Conflict as a Process

Conflicts, like stories, have a beginning, a middle, and an end. Unlike most stories, they also have a beginning before the beginning (source) and an end after the end (aftermath).

Source (beginning of the beginning). Before a conflict can exist between people, someone has to recognize it. This may take time. Differences between people are always a potential source of conflict. Differences tend to produce conflict only when they involve a collision of goals. If someone listens to music I dislike, it means nothing to me unless I hear it. When differences involve people's differing goals, they become sources of conflict. Sometimes we may not even be fully aware that a conflict exists; we merely feel some unidentified dissatisfaction or irritation. In this state, we may not be sure exactly what's troubling us and may think it quite a number of things all mixed together.

Frustration awareness (beginning). In our uncomfortable irritation, we may start a process of self-talk trying to identify and define what's amiss. We may realize that some goal of ours is not being achieved because someone else has the resources we need to achieve it or is behaving in ways that prevent its achievement. If the thwarted goal is part of our system of needs, and the need is intense, then frustration builds. Frustration is conflict becoming conscious.

Active conflict (middle). If you are aware of a conflict but say nothing about it, it might go away, but probably not. In this condition, your conflict is passive and is more likely to intensify. Expressing your frustration openly to another makes the conflict active. Active conflict need not be expressed with shouting and emotional intensity. In fact, it is probably best, all things being equal, to acknowledge and express a conflict before frustration levels escalate to peak intensity.

Resolution (end). If you and the person with whom you have a conflict agree to discuss possible solutions, you move into the resolution stage. If all goes well, the conflict will end. Sometimes a conflict ends only when those in conflict disengage entirely (divorce, dissolution of a business corporation, etc.) In this case, the conflict is not *re*solved but *dis*solved.

Aftermath (the end of the end). Like shoelaces on running shoes, conflict resolutions can unravel unless they are periodically tightened. Conflicts can hurt feelings, and hurt feelings are like smouldering coals – they can start a fire up again. Check with the other person now and then to ensure that frustrations are not reviving , clarify your understandings, offer a peace gesture.

VI. Conflict Management Styles

Your text identifies three conflict management styles: (1) nonconfrontational, (2) confrontational, and (3) cooperative. Although your text is not explicit about its evaluations, it is clear from context that only the cooperative style is considered "good."

Nonconfrontational style. This really isn't a management style at all. Conflict here isn't managed, it's avoided. There are three types of nonconfrontationals: (1) placaters, (2) distractors, and (3) computers. All three types seek to avoid conflict.

1. Placaters attempt to please because they are uncomfortable with negative emotions. They fear rejection, seek approval, and try to avoid threats to their self worth. They give in easily. They may appear other-oriented, but they seek self-protection above all.

2. Distractors try to look the other way in a conflict. They change the subject. They believe, if they can keep focus away from the conflict long enough, it may just disappear.

3. Computers keep cool and impersonal. They refuse to be provoked, avoid genuine emotional expression, and respond to the emotion of others with impersonal words and phrases. Of the three nonconfrontational types, computers are the most extreme. Placaters recognize conflict and seek to end it by easy compliance; distractors know a conflict is there but don't want to look at it; computers simply refuse to acknowledge that a conflict exists.

Confrontational style. The confrontational type wants to dominate and make sure his or her objectives are achieved come what may. Conflict for confrontationals is a contest, a test of wills, a battle. They think in win-lose terms. They are willing to win at the expense of others, think only of themselves, and ignore or deny the needs of others. They freely use coercive methods, including blame-casting, scapegoating, name-calling, threats and warnings. Their threats concern possible actions they can actually carry out: "I am going to leave you." Their warnings are dire predictions of doom about things in general: "you better do this my way or the boss will murder you."

Cooperative style. After your text's description of nonconfrontationals and confrontationals, it's a pleasure to turn to the cooperative. Conflict for cooperatives is about solving problems not avoiding uncomfortable feelings or triumphing over others. There are four techniques which characterize cooperative management of conflict.

1. Separate the people from the problem. Leave out personal grievances and emphasize description over evaluation.

2. Focus on shared interests. Emphasize common ground where it exists.

3. Generate many options to solve problems. Come up with alternatives, be creative.

4. Base decisions on objective criteria. Establish standards for an acceptable solution to a problem – these may involve cost, timing, and other factors.

VII. Conflict Management Skills

Good conflict management involves management of four things: (1) emotion, (2) information, (3) goals, and (4) problems.

Manage Emotion. The toughest challenge in conflict management is emotion. Avoid taking action when emotionally distraught. It usually leads immediately to conflict escalation and later to regret. Thomas Jefferson used to repeat the alphabet twice before speaking when his temper was up, but here are five other strategies.

1. Select a mutually acceptable time and place to discuss a conflict. Try not to ambush someone with an angry attack. Whenever possible, make sure your audience is ready to hear your message. Let yourself cool off before trying to address a serious conflict.

2. Plan your message. Identify your goal and determine what outcome you would like. Talk with a trusted friend. Write out your thoughts. Thinking about what you want to say has two benefits: (1) it will force you to calm down enough to think and (2) it might help to keep you from getting flustered when you finally have your say.

3. Monitor nonverbal messages. Remember your face and body talk even when your mouth is shut. Be aware of what your posture and expression might be saying to others. When you do speak, keep your voice calm and moderate. Maintain reasonable eye contact. Controlling affect display can help de-escalate an emotion-charged situation. Be sure verbal and nonverbal messages agree. Saying you accept a decision while scowling ferociously probably won't inspire trust.

4. Avoid personal attacks, name-calling, and emotional overstatement. Threats and insults turn simple conflicts into ego wars. If you attack, expect a counterattack. Stay away from inflationary language about your outrage, shock, disgust and dismay. Use moderate words to moderate emotion.

5. Use self-talk. Ask yourself whether an emotional tirade and escalating conflict will produce the results you want. Talk yourself down like an air traffic controller to a pilot in trouble or a police negotiator to a hostage taker. Remember our self is a composite of different components. Even in the most extreme emotional situations, most of us have access to a more sensible self.

Manage Information. There are four basic ways to manage information.

1. Clearly describe the conflict-producing events. Instead of blurting out your complaints at random, think of delivering a brief, well-organized speech. Describe events dispassionately in clear chronological order, like a journalist writing a news story.

2. "Own" your statements by using descriptive "I" language. Do you know the United States Army recruiting poster with the words "I want you!" printed under a picture of Uncle Sam pointing his finger? Actually, this poster was first used during World War One in England and its dominions (including Canada) and had a picture of Lord Kitchener over the same slogan. Well, the point is that's just what saying "you" in a conflict is like; it's like pointing your finger at someone's chest and shouting. Instead of telling your partner what he or she did, say how you think and feel using "I." That way you take responsibility for your thoughts and feelings while making your partner less defensive.

3. Use effective listening skills. Give full attention to the speaker and tune out your own internal messages. Attend to the major point of the speaker's message, don't get stuck on details. If you've said something, give your partner a chance to respond. Stay other-oriented.

4. Use effective response skills. Ask questions, summarize understanding, check key points.

Manage Goals. There are two main components to goal management: (1) identify goals and (2) identify where goals overlap.

1. Identify and clarify your own goal. What is it you want? Get down to something specific and concrete. Ask yourself whether achieving this goal is worth the possible damage it may cause to the relationship.

2. Identify your partner's goal. What is it he or she wants?

3. Once goals are identified, look for common ground to start from.

Manage the Problem. There are six components of problem management: (1) definition, (2) analysis, (3) goal determination, (4) generating multiple solutions, (5) selecting, and (6) setting time to evaluate solution.

1. Define the problem. Look at a problem as a deviation from some desired condition, as something more or less than you want. Be sure to define the "real" problem and not just symptoms.

2. Analyze the problem. Break the problem down into its components. Decide what kind of conflict you're dealing with (pseudo, simple, or ego). Decide if the conflict stems from several subproblems or from one major issue.

3. Determine the goals. Generate objective criteria for a solution. Criteria should be measurable, verifiable, and objective.

4. Generate multiple solutions. Brainstorm alternatives. The old saying is right, there's more than one way to skin a cat. (See outline for brainstorming suggestions.)

5. Select the best solution and try it. If at first you don't succeed, try again. If one solution doesn't work, try another. If no solution works, take the problem to an impartial person who might help solve the problem. When labour and management cannot agree, they go into arbitration and submit their case to others. If nothing works, admit it and give up gracefully (if possible) and drop it.

6 Set a time to evaluate the chosen solution. Periodic checks are useful in keeping a long-term solution on course. Set reasonable time frames for measuring achievement of resolutions.

VIII. When Others Aren't Other-Oriented: How to Be Assertive

Assertion is sometimes necessary to safeguard our rights in interpersonal communication. We have the right to refuse a request made of us, the right to express feelings as long as they do not trample on the feelings of others, and the right to have personal needs met if they don't infringe upon the rights of others.

We usually have to be assertive when someone else is being aggressive. Aggressiveness means pursuing self- interests by denying the rights of others. Aggressive people use both verbal coercion and nonverbal intimidation, including blame-casting, judgemental evaluation, steely stares, a bombastic voice, and flailing gestures. Aggressive people prefer accusatory "you-statements" to less confrontational "I-statements."

There are five basic steps to assertive behaviour.

1. Describe how you view the situation. Monitor nonverbal messages, especially those of the voice. Avoid sarcasm and excessive vocal intensity. Calmly, yet confidently, describe the problem.

2. Disclose your feelings. Disclosing feelings can help to build empathy by shifting emphasis away from the failings of your partner to your own responses.

3. Identify effects. Establish the effect of behaviours.

4. Wait. Allow your partner an opportunity to respond while monitoring nonverbal cues that may be suggestive of anger, boredom, or impatience.

5. Reflect content and feeling. Use paraphrasing to express understanding of your partner's messages in terms of both meaning and feeling.

TERMS TO LEARN

Interpersonal Conflict
Pseudo Conflict
Simple Conflict
Ego Conflict
Expressive Conflict
Instrumental Conflict
Conflict Myths
Constructive Conflict
Destructive Conflict
Nonconfrontational Style
Confrontational Style
Cooperative Style
Assertiveness
Aggressiveness
Placating
Distracting
Computing

Activity 7.1: Conflict Management Styles

Objectives:
1. To help you identify conflict styles.
2. To help you identify the effect of different conflict styles.
3. To help you be aware of your own style of dealing with conflict.

Part 1

Instructions:
1. In the following examples identify the style being used.
2. Discuss the possible consequences of this style, whether it is effective or ineffective in this situation. If it is ineffective discuss what style would be more effective.

Example: *You and your new roommate agree to share garbage duty. She promises to put out the garbage every second week. You take the garbage out the first week. However, you notice that the next week she doesn't deal with the garbage. You wait. The following week the garbage is still there. By this time you are annoyed. You aren't going to put out the garbage – it is her turn. Three weeks go by and the garbage continues to pile up.*

Style: *non-confrontational*

Possible consequences: *neighbours may complain and we might get evicted*

Effective or ineffective: *ineffective*

More effective style: *cooperative. I should address the issue with her before it gets out of hand*

1. Your boss has just called to say you will have to work this weekend because Javed is sick and cannot take his shift. You respond angrily into the phone: "I always work for Javed. He never works for me. Find someone else!" and then slam down the receiver.

Style:

Possible consequences:
Effective or ineffective:
More effective style:
2. Your neighbour's leaves keep blowing into your yard which has been meticulously raked. Last weekend at your request he promised to rake and dispose of his leaves. Nothing has been done. Today you raked up a huge pile of leaves and deposited them all on his front doorstep.
Style:
Possible consequences:
Effective or ineffective:
More effective style:
3. Gerta who heads up the advertising department and Amir who heads up sales are always at each other's throats. Amir accuses Gerta of not meeting deadlines. Gerta says Amir does not give her enough lead time. Stephanie, a senior manager in the firm, takes them out for lunch to help mediate their differences. For the first time they take an opportunity to listen to each other's needs.
Style:
Possible consequences:

Effective or ineffective:
More effective style:

4. You want your eighteen year old daughter to go to university right after highschool. She wants to take a year off to work and travel. You are worried if she does this she won't get back to school. She feels that having more life experience will increase her motivation at school. You have argued about this until you are both blue in the face.
Style:
Possible consequences:
Effective or ineffective:
More effective style:

Part 2

1. Think of a situation in your own life where you have experienced conflict.
2. Describe the situation and answer the following questions.

Situation:
What are your behaviours?

What are others' behaviours?

What conflict style are you using?

What are the consequences of this style?

How is this style effective or ineffective in this situation?

If your style is ineffective what style would be more effective?

Activity 7.2: The Shape of Conflict

Objectives:
1. Identify types, processes, and management approaches to conflict.

Instructions:
1. Analyze a real life conflict that you have experienced recently with one other person.
2. Answer the following questions in the space provided on the next page.

Option: Roleplay this situation with a partner.

Part 1

Describing the Conflict

Describe the situation and how the conflict developed:

Who is involved?

What are the issues?

Is it pseudo, simple, or ego conflict?

What are the behaviours you are observing?

What are the consequences of these behaviours?

Part 2

Managing the Conflict

Instructions:
Use the following guidelines to help you manage your conflict.

1. Define the problem.
2. Analyze the problem.
3. Determine goals: Identify your goal and your partner's goal; identify where your goal and your partner's overlap.
4. Generate multiple solutions.
5. Select the best solution and try it.
6. Evaluate the solution.

Description of Conflict:

Management of Conflict:

Activity 7.3: Being Assertive

Objective:
1. To help you see the kinds of interactions created by aggressive, assertive and non-assertive behaviour.

Part 1
Instructions:
1. For the following situation write out three interactions as outlined below.

2. Roleplay each of these three interactions with a partner.

Situation:
A report that was due next week is now due today at 5:00 p.m. because your boss is going of town tomorrow morning. The boss is telling you about the new report deadline.

Assertive Boss to Aggressive Subordinate:
Aggressive Boss to Non-assertive Subordinate:
Assertive Boss to Assertive Subordinate:

Part 2
Instructions:

1. Imagine a situation in which you could assertively express your wants.

2. Describe this situation below.

3. Roleplay this with a partner.

Situation:

Activity 7.4: Learning Assertion

Objective:
1. To practise assertive behaviour.

Part 1

Instructions:
Analyze a real life situation that you have experienced using the five steps of assertive behaviour.

1. Describe how you view the situation.

2. Disclose your feelings.

3. Identify effects.

4. Wait.

5. Reflect content and feeling.

Part 2

1. Roleplay this with a partner.
2. Have an observer give you feedback using the list in the communication experience box on p. 248 of your textbook.

Activity 7.5: Fighting Fair

Objective:
1. To help identify and apply rules for fighting fairly.

Instructions:
1. In the following examples identify what barriers to "fighting fairly" are apparent.
2. Restate each example using the rules for fighting fairly as outlined on p. 247 of your textbook.

Example: *"You never do your share of the work around here."*

Rule broken: *Be specific*

Restatement: *"You promised to vacuum the living room today and there are still crumbs all over the rug."*

Rule broken:

Restatement:

1. There is absolutely no way we are going to do it your way. I am going to take the car to work. If you need it too, well, that is your problem. Take the subway.

Rule broken:

Restatement:

2. I don't care about what you think or feel in this situation. We have got to complete this report on schedule.

Rule broken:

Restatement:

3. You don't care about me. You don't help out around the house. We haven't been out together in months. You never ask me how I feel. And now you want to go out with your friends tonight.

Rule broken:

Restatement:

4. We have been through this before. You are angry because I am not home enough. You think I work too much. You feel neglected.

Rule broken:

Restatement:

5. You are an idiot to think that I'm going to give up my yoga class so I can watch the kids while you go golfing. You just want to control me.

Rule broken:

Restatement:

6. You still didn't get this done on time. It is just like last month and the month before. I can't trust you.

Rule broken:

Restatement:

7. I feel like I could explode. You are such a brute!"

Rule broken:

Restatement:

Activity 7.6: Constructive and Destructive Conflict

Objective:
1. To help you identify constructive and destructive elements of conflict.

Instructions:
1. Identify constructive and destructive elements of conflict in the following examples.

1. Liban and Wendy have been married for two years. Wendy likes to go to the cottage on weekends. Liban likes to stay home and watch T.V.. They used to get into fights until one or the other gave in and then they would be angry all day. Finally they decided to sit down at the dinner table one afternoon and talk it out. They agreed that they would go to the cottage alternate weekends. Liban found that he enjoyed going to the cottage and Wendy learned to like watching television Saturday afternoons.

Constructive conflict:
Destructive conflict:

2. Pauleen and Andrew have been married for two years. Pauleen enjoys the ballet. Andrew is a hockey fan. Pauleen used to talk Andrew into going to the ballet. Andrew sometimes talked Pauleen into going to hockey games. Afterwards they always fought because neither could stand what the other liked. Eventually when it came time to go to a hockey game or the ballet neither would go with the other nor go alone so they would spend the evening fighting. They were sick of each other and spent less and less time together.

Constructive conflict:
Destructive conflict:

DIFFICULT POSITION 7

You and your husband can only afford one home computer, but you both need to use it frequently. Sometimes you both need it at the same time. Whenever this happens an argument usually ensues about who is working harder or who is more selfish than the other. That can go on for hours and then neither one gets much work done.

INSTRUCTIONS

1. What steps might you use in this situation to resolve your conflict using your knowledge about conflict types, conflict process, and brainstorming?

Exercise 7.1: Learning Objective: General Review (**TRUE/FALSE**)

Instructions: Identify the following statements as either true or false.

1. The root cause of all conflicts is misunderstanding. ( )
2. Unresolved pseudo conflicts can escalate into ego conflicts. ( )
3. Unlike destructive criticism, constructive criticism is always painless. ( )
4. It is always best to avoid confrontation in conflict situations. ( )
5. One way to manage an intense emotion is to self-talk your way through it. ( )
6. The absence of conflict in a marriage is an indicator of marital contentment. ( )
7. Competition for limited resources is a common cause of conflict. ( )
8. Keeping a conflict passive helps to keep frustration from reaching peak levels. ( )
9. Someone who responds to emotion with impersonal language is relying on distraction to avoid possible conflict. ( )
10. Assertion sometimes requires the use of coercion and intimidation . ( )
11. Appearing other-oriented may be a mask to hide fear of rejection. ( )
12. One of the best ways to keep conflicts simple is to trade insults openly. ( )
13. There is always only one mutually agreeable solution to a conflict. ( )
14. Using the strongest language possible to express your emotions is a good way to keep a conflict from escalating. ( )
15. In seeking a resolution in a conflict, it is important to keep your focus on the differences instead of what little you may have in common with others. ( )
16. In brainstorming even seemingly ridiculous ideas should be admitted. ( )
17. Sometimes the best solution possible for a conflict is to just drop it. ( )
18. Giving in immediately in a conflict is a strategy of distraction. ( )

Exercise 7.2: Learning Objective: General Review **(FILL-IN-THE-BLANKS)**

Instructions: Fill in the blanks using the appropriate term or terms from the following list.

interpersonal conflict	conflict myths	confrontational style	placating
pseudo conflict	constructive conflict	cooperative style	distracting
simple conflict	destructive conflict	assertiveness	computing
ego conflict	nonconfrontational style	aggressiveness	

1. When he said "noses," I thought he said "roses," so I said, "Your girlfriend has a big red one." After a brief shouting match, we both realized it was a pseudo conflict. ____________.

2. We talked for hours about how we felt. We both raised our voices a few times, but in the end, because of this____________________, we understood each other better and are more committed now than ever.

3. When Howard looked at me from behind his glasses and said, "Well I imagine the prospect of being fired could distress one a bit," I knew he was ___________ to avoid dealing with the coming conflict with our boss.

4. Mary decided it was time for some ______________, so she turned to her manager and said, "I understand your frustration, but it is not fair for you to demand that I work overtime. I have a right to refuse."

5. In a fine instance of __________________ in conflict management, the committee members put aside their individual differences and personal grudges in an effort to discover a solution for the company's personnel problems.

6. In 1938, when Britian's prime minister Neville Chamberlain gave in to Adolf Hitler's demand that Czechoslovakia be divided, it was denounced by some as appeasement. Perhaps it is the most famous example of ___________ to avoid a conflict.

7. We cornered Pierre and asked him what he thought about the last referendum vote on Quebec sovereignty. "Ah," he said, "I'm glad to see you both. I often think about our canoe trip last summer. Let's plan another soon." Later, we agreed that Pierre is a master at ___________ to avoid conflict.

8. I tried to work with Milton, but if I disagreed with him, he inflated his chest, called me an idiot, and said I'd be responsible if the project failed. He even went so far as to predict I'd be fired and threatened to write a negative report on my performance. Finally, after one meeting, he pointed his finger at me and screamed, "You are the cause of every problem in this firm!" Well, this was ________________ beyond anything I'd ever seen. When it came to conflict management, Milton definitely had a______________________.

9. My mother always said a happy household is a peaceful one. Well, our house was quiet, but it wasn't peaceful. There was lots of anger and resentment simmering under the surface. I often thought that if we just once fought things out in the open, things might have been better. I guess _______________ like my mother's about fighting always being negative kept us from constructive conflict.

10. No matter what, Brad never says anything at our meetings. At most, he nods and smiles at everyone. His ___________________ in conflict situations is no help at all.

11. At the weekly meeting, Juan shouted, "Becky, you're a disgrace to this department, all you do is gossip and whine about your students!" Becky shot back, "You loudmouth phoney, you're just a bootlicking little chameleon!" These two always managed to turn a simple conflict about departmental policy into _________. Of course, what they said to each other in these battles was often true, but it was only _______________ because they never resolved their issues.

12. ______________________ is unavoidable in human relationships. We must learn to manage it. Attempting to escape or eliminate it only makes it worse.

Exercise 7.3: Learning Objective: General Review (**MULTIPLE CHOICE**)

Instructions: Choose the best answer for each question below.

1. The final stage in the process of conflict is

   a. source
   b. resolution
   c. aftermath
   d. agreement

2. The six levels of the struggle spectrum are

   a. mild differences, disagreement, dispute, campaign, assaults, annihilation
   b. frustration, disagreement, passive conflict, active conflict, resolution
   c. mild differences, disagreement, dispute, threat, litigation, fight
   d. mild differences, disagreement, dispute, campaign, litigation, fight

3. The dominant cause of interpersonal conflict is

   a. conflicting opinions about sports
   b. conflicting preferences in clothing
   c. conflicting religious training
   d. conflicting goals

4. Conflicts centring on the quality of relationships and interpersonal tensions are

   a. instrumental
   b. expressive
   c. controlling
   d. assertive

5. Conflicts which involve real, often objective, differences are

   a. pseudo conflicts
   b. simple conflicts
   c. ego conflicts
   d. expressive conflicts

6. Responding evasively and shifting focus from the issue is characteristic of

   a. placating
   b. computing
   c. controlling
   d. distracting

7. All of the following are techniques of cooperative conflict management except

   a. separate the people from the problem
   b. focus on shared interests
   c. generate many options to solve a problem
   d. anticipate objections and avoid all confrontation

8. All of the following are myths about conflict except

   a. conflict is essentially unavoidable
   b. conflict is always a sign of a poor interpersonal relationship
   c. conflict can always be resolved
   d. conflict is always bad

9. All of the following are examples of rights in interpersonal communication except

   a. right to refuse a request someone makes of you
   b. right to express feelings as long as they do not trample on the feelings of others
   c. right to have personal needs met if they don't infringe on the rights of others
   d. right to empathy as long as you are willing to offer empathy to others

10. All of the following are steps in assertive communication except

    a. describe how you view a situation
    b. be ready to placate
    c. disclose your feelings
    d. wait

11. All of the following statements about aggression in conflict are true except

    a. aggressive individuals blame, judge and evaluate to get what they want
    b. aggression often involves a violation of the communication rights of others
    c. aggressive people tend to use accusatory "you-statements" when communicating
    d. aggressive people almost never get what they want by using aggressive means

Answers

CHAPTER 7

Exercise 7.1

1. (F)
2. (T)
3. (F)
4. (F)
5. (T)
6. (F)
7. (T)
8. (F)
9. (F)
10. (F)
11. (T)
12. (F)
13. (F)
14. (F)
15. (F)
16. (T)
17. (T)
18. (F)

Exercise 7.2

1. Pseudo conflict
2. Constructive conflict
3. Computing
4. Assertiveness
5. Cooperative style
6. Placating
7. Distraction
8. Aggressiveness/ Confrontational style
9. Conflict myths
10. Nonconfrontational style
11. Ego conflict/ Destructive conflict
12. Interpersonal conflict

Exercise 7.3

1. c
2. d
3. d
4. b
5. b
6. d
7. d
8. a
9. d
10. b
11. d

Chapter 8

Interpersonal Communication and Cultural Diversity: Adapting to Others

CHAPTER OUTLINE

I. The Nature of Culture

A. Culture: a learned system of knowledge, behaviour, attitudes, beliefs, values, and norms shared by a group of people

B. Anthropologist Edward T. Hall suggests communication and culture inseparable

C. We derive our cultural identity from three factors

1. **Cultural Elements**: things and ideas of most profound cultural influence
   a. Five basic categories of cultural elements
      (1) material culture: things and ideas
      (2) social institutions: schools, governments, religious organizations
      (3) individuals and the universe: system of beliefs
      (4) aesthetics: music, theatre, art, dance
      (5) language: verbal and nonverbal communication systems
   b. Enculturation: process of communicating culture across generations
      (1) family, friends, colleagues, and media
      (2) Enculturation process conveys information and advocates choices
   c. Cultures are not static
      (1) changes result from scientific discoveries
      (2) changes take place through acculturation
      (3) changes result from contact with other cultures
2. **Cultural Values**: the things and ideas valued and appreciated by a culture
   a. Researcher Geert Hofstede identifies four variables for measuring cultural values in almost all cultures
      (1) value assigned to masculine and feminine perspectives
         (a) some cultures emphasize traditional male values, some female values
         (b) these values not about biological sex differences but overarching approaches to dealing with others
         (c) masculine cultures value achievement, assertiveness, heroism, and material wealth
         (d) feminine cultures value relationships, caring for less fortunate, and overall quality of life
         (e) rarely is a culture on the extreme end of male/female continuum
         (f) for centuries most countries in Europe, Asia, and the Americas have had masculine cultures
         (g) these cultures now moving toward the middle

(h) legal and social rules now encourage greater gender balance/equality

(2) value assigned to avoidance of uncertainty

(a) some cultures tolerate more ambiguity and uncertainty than others

(b) some cultures enforce rigid behaviour rules to minimize uncertainty

(c) cultures tolerating uncertainty are more relaxed and informal

(d) Portugal, Germany, Peru, Belgium, and Japan need high certainty

(e) Scandinavian countries tend to tolerate uncertainty

(3) value assigned to distribution of power

(a) some cultures value equal or decentralized power distribution

(b) some cultures accept concentrated and hierarchical power

(c) Russia, France, and China are high on concentrated power scale

(d) Australia, Denmark, New Zealand, and Israel minimize power differences

(4) value assigned to individualism

(a) traditionally, North Americans champion individual accomplishment

(b) Asian cultures often value collective or group achievement

(c) individualistic cultures are more loosely knit socially

(d) collectivist cultures expect support and loyalty from others

(e) teamwork approaches work especially well in collectivist cultures

3. **Cultural Contexts**

a. Different cultures use cultural contextual cues in varying degrees to enhance messages and meaning

b. Edward T. Hall categorizes cultures as either high- or low-context

(1) high-context cultures place a high value on nonverbal cues

(2) low-context cultures rely heavily on language

(3) individuals of high-context culture may regard low-context individuals as less attractive, knowledgeable, and trustworthy because they violate unspoken rules of dress, conduct, and communication

(4) individuals from low-context cultures often unskilled in interpreting unspoken, contextual messages

II. Barriers to Effective Intercultural Communication

A. Ethnocentrism: a conviction that one's own culture is superior to others

1. The opposite of other-orientation
2. Inhibits communication

B. Different Communication Codes

1. Language
2. Gesture

C. Stereotyping and Prejudice: inflexible, all-encompassing categories

1. Stereotyping "prints" the same judgement over and over again

a. Fails to consider the uniqueness of individuals, groups, or events

b. Is a barrier to effective intercultural communication

2. Anthropologists suggest every person is in some respects:

a. Like all other people
b. Like some other people
c. Like no other people
(1) our challenge is to discover how others are alike but also unique

3. Prejudice: inhibits effective communication in most situations
a. Certain prejudices are almost universal
(1) females are prejudged to be less valuable than males
b. Gender and racial discrimination in hiring and promotion now illegal in Canada
c. Social attitudes have not kept pace with the law
d. Stereotyping and prejudice still barriers to effective communication

D. Assuming Similarity: assumption that others think and act as you do
1. Focussing on superficial factors
a. Appearance
b. Clothing
c. Occupation
2. We must explore a person's background and cultural values before we can determine what we really have in common

III. Improving Intercultural Competence

A. Intercultural communication is the transactional process of listening and responding to people with different cultural backgrounds
1. The greater the cultural difference between two people, the greater the potential for misunderstanding and mistrust

B. There are three sets of strategies to help bridge cultural differences
1. **Developing Knowledge**: strategies to understand others different from us
a. Seek information about culture
(1) every person has a world view based on cultural beliefs about universe
(a) death
(b) God
(c) meaning of life
(2) Carley Dodd claims, "A culture's world view involves finding out how the culture perceives the role of various forces in explaining why events occur as they do in a social setting."
(3) world view beliefs shape thoughts, language, and behaviour
(4) only intercultural communication allows us to understand world views
(5) when speaking to a person from another culture, think of yourself as a detective watching for implied, unspoken messages
(a) values, norms, roles, rules
(6) if you are going to another country, study the culture
(a) history, anthropology, art, geography
(7) if communicating with someone closer to home from different culture
(a) study magazines, music, and food

(b) exchange visits

(8) learn about another language

b. Seek information about co-culture

(1) a co-culture is a group within larger culture

(2) men and women are each a separate co-culture

(a) men more likely to develop friendships through participation in common activities

(b) women more likely to develop friendships through talking

(3) read books about differences between male/female communication

(a) Deborah Tannen, *You Just Don't Understand*

(b) John Gary, *Men Are from Mars, Women Are from Venus*

(4) it is important not to develop rigid gender stereotypes and categories

c. Ask questions and listen effectively

(1) asking then pausing is simple technique for gathering information

(2) better to ask about expectations than assume to know

(3) when asking for information, share information about yourself

(4) communication helps reduce uncertainty in relationships

(5) uncertainty in cross-cultural communication is particularly high

(6) continuing to ask questions will reduce this uncertainty

(7) asking for and sharing information is not sufficient, listening needed

d. Develop a "third culture"

(1) third culture is created when communication partners join aspects of separate cultures to create a new culture that is more comprehensive and inclusive than the other two alone

(2) third culture reduces "us" versus "them" mentality about culture

(3) third culture seeks to create a new understanding for both participants

(4) Benjamin Broome describes third culture "as . . . unique values and norms that may not have existed prior to dyadic relationship."

(a) Broome labels essence of new relationship rational empathy

(b) Rational empathy permits varying degrees of understanding rather than requiring complete comprehension of another's culture

(5) third culture seeks to develop a common code

(a) learning something of communication partner's language

(b) discussing meanings of nonverbal communication

(c) perception checking (Chapter 3)

(6) third culture acknowledges different cultural contexts and interactions

2. **Developing Motivation**: strategies to accept others who are different from us

a. Tolerate Ambiguity

(1) communication with others from another culture produces uncertainty

(2) it may take several exchanges to clarify a message

(3) be patient and expand your capacity to tolerate ambiguity

b. Develop Mindfulness

(1) to be mindful is to be aware of cultural differences

(2) William Gudykunst suggests being mindful is among the best ways to approach any new cultural encounter
(a) remember that there will be cultural differences
(b) try to keep them in your consciousness
(c) consider the other individual's frame of reference
(d) use the other's cultural priorities and assumptions in communication
(e) adapt behaviour to minimize cultural noise and distortion
(f) mindfulness can be promoted by self-talk

3. **Developing Skill**: strategies to adapt to others who are different from us
   a. Develop flexibility
      (1) you must be willing to learn as you communicate
      (2) cultural generalizations learned from research may not always apply
      (3) pay close attention to the other's nonverbal cues
      (4) adjust communication style and language as needed
   b. Become other-oriented
      (1) social decentring: a cognitive process which takes into account the other's thoughts, feelings, values, backgrounds, and perspectives
      (2) there are three ways to socially decentre
         (a) develop an understanding of others, based on how you have responded in similar situations
            (i) to the degree the other person is similar to you, your reactions will match
            (ii) understanding your own reactions must be tempered by awareness of how similar or dissimilar other person is to you
         (b) base your understanding of others upon knowledge you have about a specific person
            (i) draw on memory of other's previous behaviour in similar situation
            (ii) increased intimacy of relation increases accuracy of predictions
            (iii) the more intercultural interaction you have with another, and the more you learn about his or her culture, the more your ability to socially decentre will increase
         (c) make generalizations about others based upon your understanding of how most people would feel and behave
            (i) each of us develops implicit personality theories, constructs, and attributions of how people act (Chapter 3)
            (ii) draw upon these conceptualizations to decentre
            (iii) avoid developing inaccurate, inflexible stereotypes
      (3) Empathy: an *emotional* reaction as contrasted with the *cognitive* reaction of social decentring
         (a) some emotional reactions are almost universal and cross-cultural
         (b) empathy can enhance interpersonal interactions in several ways
            (i) it provides a bond between you and the other person
            (ii) it is confirming

(iii) it is comforting and supportive
(iv) it can increase your understanding of others
(v) it can strengthen a relationship
(c) we empathize most easily with those who are similar to us, and in situations in which we have had similar experiences
(d) developing empathy is different from sympathizing with others
(i) sympathy acknowledges others' feelings
(ii) empathy is an emotional reaction similar to others' feelings
(4) Adaptation: adjusting behaviours to accord with individuals, situations, and relationships
(a) adapt predictively: modification of behaviour in anticipation of event
(b) adapt reactively: modification of behaviour after event
(c) there are several reasons we adapt our communication to others
(i) to make our messages understandable
(ii) to accomplish our message goals effectively
(iii) to conform message to feedback in intercultural communication
(d) we adapt nonverbal as well as verbal cues
(e) adaptation across intercultural contexts is usually more difficult than within one's own culture

CHAPTER REVIEW: SECTION BY SECTION SUMMARY

I. The Nature of Culture

Culture is a learned system of knowledge, behaviour, attitudes, beliefs, values, and norms shared by a group of people. Anthropologist Edward T. Hall suggests that communication and culture are inseparable. We derive our cultural identity from three factors: (1) elements, (2) values, and (3) contexts.

Cultural Elements are the things and ideas of greatest cultural influence. There are five basic categories of cultural elements: (1) material culture, (2) social institutions, (3) individuals and the universe, (4) aesthetics, (5) language.

These five categories are the *avenues* of **enculturation**, which is the process of communicating a group's culture from generation to generation. *Agents* of enculturation include family, friends, colleagues, and the media. A child born into a particular culture goes through a process of enculturation in which parents, friends, and others begin to expose him or her to the range of cultural elements. The child is given information and influenced by his or her cultural agents. When a child grows into full possession of his or her culture elements, he or she is **acculturated**.

Cultures, like people, are subject to change. Scientific discoveries can cause cultural change. For instance, many students of culture feel the invention of the birth control pill profoundly altered cultural rules about reproduction in technically developed nations. Inter-cultural contact and exchange also causes change. The introduction of the horse into North America by Spanish explorers profoundly altered the cultures of native peoples.

According to Geert Hofstede, there are four variables for measuring cultural values in almost every culture: (1) masculine and feminine perspectives, (2) avoidance of uncertainty, (3) distribution of power, and (4) individualism.

Some cultures (**masculine cultures**) emphasize traditional male values, which include achievement, assertiveness, heroism, and material wealth. Other cultures (**feminine cultures**) emphasize traditional female values, which include relationships, caring for the less fortunate, and overall quality of life. These masculine and feminine cultural values are not really about biological sex differences but overarching approaches to interacting with others. Rarely is a given culture either exclusively masculine or feminine. For centuries, most Western and Asian cultures have been masculine in orientation, but these cultures are now moving slowly toward greater balance, which is reflected in new legal and social rules encouraging gender equality.

Some cultures have very low tolerance for uncertainty and require rigid rules of behaviour and elaborate codes of conduct to bolster and enhance security. Other cultures are more tolerant of uncertainty and tend to be more relaxed. Portugal, Germany, Peru, Belgium, and Japan have high certainty needs. In contrast, Scandinavian countries tend to tolerate uncertainty.

Some cultures emphasize individual achievement. Other cultures favour group achievement. North Americans traditionally champion individual achievement. Asian cultures traditionally value collective or group achievement. In individualistic cultures, kinship and other social ties are loose; immediate family and oneself are the limit of social responsibility. In collectivist cultures, community-wide loyalty and support are expected and required. Teamwork approaches to business often succeed better in collectivist cultures.

All cultures use cultural contextual cues in varying degrees to enhance messages and their meaning. Edward T. Hall has categorized cultures as either high- or low-context.

High-context cultures consider nonverbal cues extremely important.
Low-context cultures rely more explicitly on language.
Individuals from high-context cultures may perceive persons from low-context cultures as less attractive, knowledgeable, and trustworthy, because they violate unspoken rules of dress, conduct, and communication.

Individuals from low-context cultures often are not skilled in interpreting unspoken and contextual messages.

Cultural diversity has many facets, including (1) age, (2) language, (3) religion, (4) disability, (5) social class, (6) gender, (7) sexual preference, (8) race, and (9) ethnicity.

Cultural diversity is reflected in differing marriage structures. Some cultures allow and encourage *polygamy*, the marriage of more than one spouse, either (1) *polygyny* -- more than one wife or (2) *polyandry* -- more than one husband. The concept of "marriage" seems universal, but its forms have varied widely over time and still do today in different regions.

II. Barriers to Effective Communication

Your text lists four main barriers to communication: (1) ethnocentrism, (2) different communication codes, (3) stereotype and prejudice, and (4) assuming similarity.

Ethnocentrism is the unshakeable conviction that your way is the best way. An extreme ethnocentrist believes his or her own culture is superior to all others in all ways. Ethnocentrism is the opposite of other-orientation and makes meaningful communication impossible.

Different Communication Codes. Language and gestures vary widely in this world. The more you know of other languages and cultures, the more communication-literate you will be.

Stereotyping and Prejudice. Rigid, inflexible categories are stereotypes. We sometimes use these to categorize individuals from other cultures, failing to recognize the uniqueness of individuals. We should remember that every person is, in some respects (1) like all other people, (2) like some other people, (3) like no other people. Our challenge when meeting others is to discover how they are alike and how they are unique. Some prejudices seem almost universal, such as the prejudgement of females as inferior to males.

Assuming Similarity. In a sense, assuming similarity is the most extreme form of ethnocentrism, for assuming similarity suggests not merely that your culture is superior but that it is the only one. People and cultures are different, but assuming similarity does not recognize this. Superficial factors may suggest cultural similarity and lead to false assumptions.

III. Improving Intercultural Competence

Your text recommends three strategies to improve intercultural competence.

ONE: Developing Knowledge: Strategies to Understand Others Who Are Different from Us

Seek knowledge about culture
Learn about differing world views: cultural beliefs about the universe and key issues such as death, God, and the meaning of life. Become a "culture detective" examining implied and unspoken messages that provide information about cultural values, norms, roles, and rules.

Study the culture of a foreign country through courses in history, anthropology, art, or geography. When communicating with an immigrant from another country, consider exchanging visits to one another's homes, learning something of each other's language, and sharing cultural products such as music, magazines, and food.

Seek knowledge about co-cultures. A co-culture is a cultural group within a larger culture. Men and women are each a co-culture. Read books about the differences between men and women. Recognize co-cultural differences but do not construct rigid categories or stereotypes.

Ask questions and listen effectively

Asking questions and then pausing to listen is a simple and effective technique for gathering information. It is better to ask what cultural expectations are than assume your own good manners will see you through. When you ask for information, be prepared to share information about yourself. When you communicate with someone from another culture, uncertainty levels are high. Communication helps reduce this uncertainty.

Develop a "third culture"

A third culture is created when the communication partners join aspects of separate cultures to create a "new" culture that is more comprehensive and inclusive than either of the two separate cultures. The goal of developing a third culture is to reduce the "us" versus "them" mentality. Benjamin Broome describes the third culture as "characterized by unique values and norms that may not have existed prior to the dyadic relationship." Broome labels the essence of this new relationship **relational empathy**.

A third culture seeks to develop a common code. Participants in developing a third culture learn about each other's language and nonverbal meanings. A third culture involves recognition that there are different cultural contexts and interactions.

TWO: Developing Motivation: Strategies to Accept Others Who Are Different from Us

Tolerate ambiguity

Communicating with someone from another culture produces uncertainty. It may take time and several exchanges to clarify a message. Be patient and try to expand your capacity to tolerate ambiguity.

Develop mindfulness

To be mindful is to be aware of cultural differences. William Gudykunst suggests that being mindful is among the best ways to approach a new cultural encounter. There are five key elements of mindfulness: (1) remember and be actively conscious of cultural differences, (2) consider the other person's frame of reference or world view, (3) use his or her cultural assumptions and priorities when communicating, (4) adapt your behaviour to minimize cultural noise and distortion, and (5) use self-talk to promote mindfulness.

THREE: Developing Skills: Strategies to Adapt to Others Who Are Different from Us

Develop flexibility

To develop flexibility, you must be willing to learn while you communicate. Cultural generalizations you have learned from reading and research may not always apply to particular individuals. Pay close attention to the nonverbal cues of others and adjust your communication style and language if necessary and appropriate.

Become other-oriented

Remember the discussion of decentring in Chapter 1? Well, there is a form of **social decentring** which makes cultural communication more effective. Social decentring is a cognitive process in which we take account of the other person's thoughts, feelings, values, background, and perspectives. There are three ways to socially decentre: (1) develop an understanding of others based upon how you have responded under similar circumstances, (2) base your understanding of others upon the knowledge you have a specific person, and (3) make generalizations about someone based upon your understanding of how you think most people would feel or behave. Approach (1) is effective to the extent that the person is similar to you. Approach (2) is effective in more intimate relationships in which we have experience of the person's prior behaviour in similar circumstances. Approach (3) draws on our implicit personality theories, which are effective provided they are not inflexible stereotypes incapable of correction.

Practice empathy
Empathy is an *emotional* reaction similar to what another is experiencing, in contrast to social decentring, which is *cognitive*. One could say that empathy involves the heart and social decentring involves the head. Empathy is facilitated by the fact that some emotional reactions are almost universal and cut across cultural boundaries. Empathy enhances interpersonal relationships in a number of ways: it provides a bond between you and your communication partner; it comforts and supports; it increases understanding of others; and strengthens relationships. Of course we empathize most easily with those who are similar to us and in situations where we have had similar experiences. Empathy is a more engaged activity than sympathy. Sympathy *acknowledges* feelings, but empathy *shares* them.

Practice adaptation
Adaptation involves adjusting our behaviour to accord with the individual, the relationship, and the situation. When you modify your behaviour in anticipation of an event, you **adapt predictively**. When you modify your behaviour after an event, you **adapt reactively**. We adapt for several reasons: to make our messages easier to understand; to accomplish our communication goals effectively; and to accord with information derived from feedback or reactions we receive. Adaptation also extends to our nonverbal communication. Cross-cultural adaptation is usually more difficult than intracultural adaptation.

TERMS TO LEARN

Culture
Co-culture
Cultural Elements
Enculturation
Acculturation
Cultural Values
Masculine Cultural Values
Feminine Cultural Values
Cultural Context
High-Context Culture
Low-Context Culture
Ethnocentrism
Stereotype
Prejudice
Intercultural Communication
World View
Third Culture
Relational Empathy
Empathy
Sympathy
Adaptation
Adapt Predictively
Adapt Reactively

Activity 8.1: Barriers to Intercultural Communication

Objective:
1. To help you identify barriers to effective intercultural communication.

Instructions:
1. Identify barriers to effective intercultural communication in the following examples.

1. You live in Montreal and as far as you are concerned Canadians are more polite, considerate and civilized than Americans. On business trips to New York you are always appalled by the noise, rudeness, and aggression. In the many years you have been going there you have not gotten to know a single American well.

Barrier:____

2. My friend from Minnesota stood outside the cathedral in Morelia, Mexico, built in 1744, one of the most outstanding examples of Spanish Reniassance architecture and said, "Don't they ever pick up the garbage around here?" That is all he had to say.

Barrier:____

3. Mary was always in the habit of tousling the hair of her three young sons. When she tried doing this as a gesture of friendliness to a stranger's child in Thailand, she was surprised when the parents started yelling at her and made threatening gestures.

Barrier:____

4. When I went to Michoacan, Mexico my friend's father Emilio Flores prepared fish for supper. The fish still had the head on it. Emilio suggested I eat the eyes first. He wanted me to have the best part. I was horrified.

Barrier:____

5. The word "barbarian" derives from the ancient Greek language. The ancient Greeks thought that the languages of all other peoples sounded like nothing but "bar-bar-bar." So anyone who did not speak Greek they called a "barbarian."

Barrier:____

6. Timothy O'Rourke was late for the meeting. His supervisor said, "You know the Irish.

O'Rourke probably just had one too many down at the pub."

Barrier:____

7. When Pierre hugged and kissed my friend Jake from Texas, Jake looked a little green.

Barrier:____

8. You are attending a conference in Prague. You go out to lunch with a group of conference participants. The menu is in both Czech and English. You ask the waiter how to pronounce the Czech names of the various dishes. After the waiter leaves one of the conference participants says to you, "That language sounds like nothing but gobbledygook to me. I wouldn't waste any time on it even for fun."

Barrier:____

Activity 8.2: Intercultural Diary

Objective:

1. To heighten your awareness of intercultural communication.

Instructions:

1. For the next several days record your observations about any intercultural encounters that you may have.

2. After you complete your observations interview one person whom you have observed. Check your interpretations of his or her behaviour. Discuss what you have learned from this.

Encounter	Observations

Activity 8.3: Learning About Cultural Perspective

Objective:
1. To help you understand differences in cultural perspective and values.

Part 1

Instructions:
1. Interview one person from a culture different from your own.
2. In your interview consider the following issues:

a. masculine vs. feminine perspective
b. tolerance of uncertainty vs. avoidance of uncertainty
c. concentrated vs. decentralized power
d. individual vs. group achievement

Part 2

Instructions:
1. Consider how you could communicate more effectively with this person using the following guidelines.
2. Develop Knowledge -- ask questions and listen effectively -- develop a third culture
3. Develop Motivation -- tolerate ambiguity -- develop mindfulness
4. Develop Skills -- develop flexibility -- become other-oriented
5. Summarize the circumstances of your interview and its results.

Activity 8.4: Dealing with Diversity

Objective:
1. To give you practice in dealing with intercultural situations effectively.

Part 1

Instructions:
1. Describe how you would handle the following intercultural situations.
2. Give two examples of intercultural communication from your own life. How did you handle these situations? Were you effective?

Example:

You are a professor. A student approaches you at the beginning of class and informs you that she will need to leave during the middle of your lecture to pray.

How would you handle this situation?

I would accede to her request this first time without question, but I would ask that she would see me after the class so we could discuss ways to accommodate her needs without disrupting the class.

1. A new staff member has just joined your department. You are working in a fast-paced environment where deadlines need to be met yesterday. Your co-worker is from a slower-paced culture and does not understand the demands of your department. You have to work closely together on projects and are concerned about meeting deadlines.

How would you handle this situation?

2. An older Middle Eastern man enters a bank and approaches the teller who is a young woman. He tells her he wants to speak to a man. She tells him he has to speak with her. "No," he responds, "Get me the manager." When the manager arrives she too is a woman. Imagine you are this manager.

How would you handle this situation?

3. A British and a U.S. company have merged. The British company's way of doing business is steady but slower-paced. The U.S. company is always on the go, even frantic. The combined companies are experiencing personnel difficulties. Your job is to help make this merger work.

How would you handle this situation?

4. You are a female engineer in Canada and your company has offered you a lucrative position in the Middle East. You are informed that it is a condition of your employment that in certain situations you will have to wear a veil in public. You believe in and have fought for gender equality in your own country. This request makes you uncomfortable.

How would you handle this situation?

5. Your company in Vancouver has just been purchased by a multinational corporation with its headquarters in Japan. The new owners introduce a cooperative team-based approach to production. Managers from Japan are sent over to implement and facilitate this process. They bring a strong collectivist perspective to business operations. While you consider yourself a team player, you are used to and welcome a higher degree of open competition than is now favoured or allowed.

How would you handle this situation?

Part 2

Personal example:

How did you handle this situation?

Was this effective?

Personal example:

How did you handle this situation?

Was this effective?

DIFFICULT POSITION 8

In a history course about nineteenth-century colonialism, a professor is lecturing about the old East Indian practice of *suttee*, in which a window was burned alive on the funeral pyre of her deceased husband, sometimes against her will. The professor informs his students that this custom was forcibly abolished by the British in 1829 when India was still a colony of the British Empire. At this, a student in the back of the class snaps out, "That shows that Western culture is superior because it respects human rights!" A visiting Indian student in the class responds, "If the West respects human rights so much why did the British murder defenceless women and children at Amritsar and make it so hard for Gandhi to nonviolently end colonial domination?"

INSTRUCTIONS

1. Imagine you are the professor in this course. Drawing on what you have learned about ethnocentrism, social decentring, and third culture, how might you assist these two students to understand each other better?

2. In small groups, cooperatively develop a mini-lecture for the professor using the techniques of intercultural communication.

Exercise 8.1: Learning Objective: General Review **(TRUE/FALSE)**

Instructions: Identify the following statements as either true or false.

1. The idea of romantic love as a motive for marriage is a cultural universal. ( )

2. Developing a "third culture" requires substituting reason for emotion. ( )

3. Western and Asian cultures are becoming less exclusively masculine in values. ( )

4. Enculturation only occurs in formal educational environments. ( )

5. North Americans are incapable of teamwork approaches to problem solving. ( )

6. Latin America and China are co-cultures. ( )

7. A large multinational corporation might have characteristics of a co-culture. ( )

8. Minimizing ambiguity is perhaps Denmark's highest cultural value. ( )

9. Social attitudes about gender in Canada have not kept pace with new laws. ( )

10. Only Americans, Canadians, and Europeans are guilty of ethnocentrism. ( )

11. People from low context-cultures need many nonverbal cues to communicate. ( )

12. Only highly developed cultures have world views. ( )

13. Assuming similarity is a form of adaptation to cultural difference. ( )

14. Ambiguity is likely to be highest in cross-cultural communication. ( )

15. Implicit personality theories are a chief obstacle to social decentring. ( )

16. Someone from Japan is likely to tolerate uncertainty better than a Dane. ( )

17. Australians require highly articulated hierarchies in government. ( )

18. Collectivist values are superior to individualistic values. ( )

19. Families tend to be larger and more stable in collectivist cultures. ( )

20. Punctuality is a high value in most uncertainty-tolerating cultures. ( )

Exercise 8.2: Learning Objective: General Review (**FILL-IN-THE-BLANKS**)

Instructions: Fill in the blanks using the appropriate term or terms from the following list.

culture	cultural values	ethnocentrism	empathy
co-culture	masculine cultural values	stereotype	sympathy
cultural elements	feminine cultural values	prejudice	adaptation
enculturation	cultural context	world view	adapt predictively
acculturation	high-context culture	third culture	adapt reactively
intercultural communication	low-context culture	relational empathy	

1. __________ is a learned system of knowledge, behaviour, attitudes, beliefs, values, and norms that is shared by a group of people.

2. The creation of a new culture combining aspects of two separate cultures creates a more comprehensive ____________ which allows __________ .

3. The recognition of Quebec as a "distinct society" acknowledges the existence of a clearly defined ______________ within the Canadian federation.

4. It would probably be fair to describe the culture of Montreal as a ________________ relative to the________________ of Toronto.

5. The warlord culture of the Muromachi period in Japanese history, domination by the heroic military ethos of the samurai class, represented _________________________.

6. I was aware that showing up on time was actually considered rude, so I slowed my pace and deliberately came a little late. You can ________________ and avoid giving offense by appearing too concerned about punctuality.

7. I insisted on going to bed after my long drive and refused my host's invitation to see the city. I had no idea they would be offended. Once I understood the cultural importance of such an invitation, I managed to ______________ and forced myself to stay awake.

8. Attending one of the famous English public schools was a part of________________ for young aristocrats like Lord Byron, whose arrogance and sense of absolute superiority showed that he had undergone thorough __________.

9. The concern for social justice and the rights of the oppressed which were prominent in North American reform movements of the nineteenth century showed a cultural shifting the direction of_______________________.

10. Advocacy of capitalism as the only possible economic system may be an indication of____________________ that prevents some economists from understanding how a different ___________ may make capitalism impractical for some cultures.

11. The basic __________________ were easy to recognize, but it took a real effort of sustained_______________ to understand the ______________ they expressed.

12. __________________ is especially difficult between uncertainty-tolerant and uncertainty-intolerant cultures.

13. My father's ______________ about Catholics was the cause of a ____________ he had about priests being friends of reactionary government.

14. The only productive course was ________________ if I wanted our message to be understood and appreciated by the islanders, so I dropped those aspects I knew would offend them.

15. Everything I had been taught told me this practice was wrong, but by an heroic effort of _______________ I could muster some _____________ for why it seemed necessary and important in this environment.

16. Staying ___________ is the best way to recognize the _______________ that can contribute so much to explicit verbal messages.

Exercise 8.3: Learning Objective: General Review (**MULTIPLE CHOICE**)

Instructions: Choose the best answer for each question below.

1. The practice of a man's having multiple wives is called

   a. polygonal
   b. polygamy
   c. polyandry
   d. polyphemos

2. Refusing or being unable to recognize significant cultural differences characterizes

   a. ethnocentrism
   b. relational sympathy
   c. assuming similarity
   d. prejudice

3. The process of communicating a group's culture from generation to generation is

   a. intercultural communication
   b. acculturation
   c. adaptation
   d. enculturation

4. Strong reliance on nonverbal cues is characteristic of

   a. high-context cultures
   b. low-context cultures
   c. social decentring
   d. intercultural communication

5. Social decentring involves a

   a. cognitive process
   b. emotional reaction
   c. spiritual renewal
   d. expressive disorientation

6. Which of the following countries is generally the least tolerant of uncertainty?

   a. Iceland
   b. Norway
   c. Sweden
   d. Germany

7. All of the following are values associated with masculine cultures except

   a. heroism
   b. material wealth
   c. assertiveness
   d. ethnocentrism

8. All of the following are aspects of mindfulness in interpersonal communication except

   a. being actively conscious of cultural differences
   b. being open to cultural assumptions and priorities other than your own
   c. being considerate of someone else's world view and frame of reference
   d. being careful not to express your own ideas and assumptions

9. All of the following are recognized forms of cultural diversity except

   a. age
   b. language
   c. education
   d. sexual preference

10. All of the following are true statements except

    a. every person is like all other people in some respect
    b. every person is like some other people in some respects
    c. every person is like one other person in all respects
    d. every person is like no other people in some respects

11. All of the following statements about culture are true except

    a. men and women each represent a separate co-culture
    b. collectivist cultures expect and require a high degree of group loyalty
    c. the highest value of all cultures is empathy
    d. cultures can be categorized as favouring masculine or feminine values

Answers

CHAPTER 8

Exercise 8.1

1. (F)
2. (F)
3. (T)
4. (F)
5. (F)
6. (F)
7. (T)
8. (F)
9. (T)
10. (F)
11. (F)
12. (F)
13. (F)
14. (T)
15. (F)
16. (F)
17. (F)
18. (F)
19. (T)
20. (F)

Exercise 8.2

1. Culture
2. Third culture/Relational empathy
3. Co-culture
4. High-context/low-context
5. Masculine cultural values
6. Adapt predictively
7. Adapt reactively
8. Acculturation/Enculturation
9. Feminine cultural values
10. Ethnocentrism/world view/
11. Cultural elements/empathy/ cultural values
12. Intercultural communication
13. Prejudice/stereotype
14. Adaptation
15. Social decentering/sympathy
16. Mindful/cultural context

Exercise 8.3

1. b
2. c
3. d
4. a
5. a
6. d
7. d
8. d
9. c
10. c
11. c

Chapter 9

Understanding Interpersonal Relationships

CHAPTER OUTLINE

I. Relationships of Circumstance and Relationships of Choice

- **A.** Relationships of circumstance are formed not from choice but because our lives overlap with others
  1. Family members, teachers, classmates, and co-workers
- **B.** Relationships of choice are intentionally developed
- **C.** We act and communicate differently in these two types of relationship
- **D.** Relationships of circumstance can also be relationships of choice
  1. Your brother or sister can also be your friend
  2. You can break off interacting with family members or co-workers
  3. Someone might redefine or terminate a relationship with you
     - a. Your boss might fire you
     - b. A relative might cut you off
     - c. A lover might desert you

II. Trust, Intimacy, and Power in Relationships

- **A.** Trust
  1. Interpersonal trust is the degree to which we feel safe in disclosing personal information
  2. We exhibit a variety of trusting behaviours
     - a. Revealing intimate information about ourselves
     - b. Displaying our vulnerability to another
     - c. Displaying confidence in another
  3. As a relationship develops, we look for proof that our partner is trustworthy
     - a. He or she accepts our feelings without exploiting them
     - b. He or she protects our vulnerability
     - c. He or she does not cheat
     - d. He or she protects information we have disclosed
     - e. He or she maintains affection even when we reveal negative information about ourselves
  4. To sustain a close relationship both partners must exhibit mutual trust
  5. The more we trust, the more intimate information we are willing to share
     - a. Sometimes this sharing is selective
- **B.** Intimacy
  1. Intimacy means the degree to which we can be ourselves in front of another
  2. We depend upon intimate relationships to bolster our self-confidence
  3. We communicate intimacy directly and indirectly, verbally and nonverbally

a. We might tell someone how we feel
b. We might use nonverbal cues (proximity, eye contact, tone of voice, etc.)

4. Mutual trust is relative to intimacy and strength of emotional bond
5. Emotions sometimes fly in the face of reason

C. Power

1. Interpersonal power means the ability to influence another to obtain your ends
2. All interactions involve power
3. Every relationship falls somewhere on a power continuum
   a. At one extreme you have more power than your partner
   b. At the other extreme your partner has more power than you
4. In some relationships there is a predefined power imbalance
   a. Teacher and student
   b. Doctor and patient
5. There are three distinct relationship categories (Chapter 1)
   a. Complementary – one partner willingly hands power over to the other
   b. Parallel – power continually shifts between partners
   c. Symmetrical – power is equalized
      (1) this attempt often backfires
      (2) partners feel they have equal power over every decision
      (3) the negotiation process can become time-consuming and ineffective
6. In all relationships the balance of power affects how and what we talk about
7. Information is a source of power
8. Nonverbal behaviours and speech patterns reflect an individual's perception of his or her power
   (1) Our culture judges men's speech patterns as more powerful than women's
      (a) masculine speech is loud, forceful, deep, authoritarian, blunt
      (b) feminine speech is gentle, smooth, friendly, warm, gossipy, high-pitched
      (c) individuals of both sexes are liable to adopt either style

D. Researchers have identified five distinct power sources

1. Legitimate Power: based upon an appointed, elected, or designated position
   a. Prime ministers, senators, mayors, deans, principals, CEOs, etc.
   b. Parent-child and other dependent relationships
2. Referent Power: based on the liking others have for us
   a. If others like us we have power over them in managing conflicts
   b. People rarely acknowledge the role of interpersonal attraction
3. Expert Power: based upon specialized knowledge and competence
   a. Experts have great influence over decisions in matters related to their field
4. Reward Power: based on resources to manage conflicts
   a. Gifts, money, status, power
   b. Bosses, parents, teachers
5. Coercive Power: based on sanctions and punishments
   a. Often the same individuals who can reward you can also punish you
   b. Some people use coercive power in interpersonal relationships

(1) not returning phone calls
(2) giving the silent treatment
(3) verbal assaults

III. Interpersonal Attraction: The Spark of a Relationship

A. Interpersonal attraction is the degree to which you desire to form or maintain an interpersonal relationship

B. There is a strong correlation between level of intimacy and level of attraction

C. Feelings of attraction change as relationship changes

1. Short-term initial attraction is degree to which we sense a potential for developing an interpersonal relationship
2. Long-term maintenance attraction is the level of liking or positive feeling that motivates us to maintain or escalate a relationship

D. Seven elements of interpersonal attraction

1. Physical attraction
   a. Body size, height, clothing, hairstyle, makeup, jewellery, vocal qualities
   b. Each culture has its own definition of the physical ideal
      (1) North America promotes a slender ideal for both males and females
      (2) in some cultures and times attractiveness is synonymous with bulk
   c. Physical attractiveness acts as a filter reducing relationship possibilities
      (1) we tend to seek out those who represent our own attractiveness level
   d. Physical image of a person can reflect substantive qualities
      (1) body type and condition bespeaks other values about diet, etc.
2. Credibility, competence, and charisma
   a. Competence, credibility, and often, physical attractiveness = charisma
   b. Political and other leaders often depend on charisma to attract support
3. Proximity
   a. Any circumstance increasing interaction possibilities increases attraction
      (1) good chance two people will become friends if they share a room
      (2) information exchange increases ability to assess relationship value
4. Similarity
   a. We are attracted to people whose personalities, values, upbringing, experiences, attitudes, and interests are similar to our own
      (1) we assess relative similarities and dissimilarities and arrive at level of attraction which may change over time
      (2) in initial stage of relationship, we emphasize positive information about ourselves to create a positive and attracting image
      (3) we save revelations about important aspects of ourselves for later
      (4) attitude similarity is a stronger source of long-term maintenance attraction than short-term initial attraction
5. Complementary needs ("opposites attract")
   a. Three interpersonal needs motivate us to form and keep relationships
      (1) inclusion -- the need to include others in our activities, or us in theirs

(2) control -- need to make decisions or accept decisions of others
(3) affection -- need to love or to be loved

b. No perfect match, only degrees of compatibility relative to needs

6. Relationship potential
   a. **Outcome Value Theory** claims we assess the potential of any relationship to meet relational needs and weigh that assessment against potential costs
   b. We pursue attractions beyond interaction stage if we think they can yield positive outcomes, and we avoid or terminate relationships for which we predict negative outcomes
7. Reciprocation of liking
   a. One way to get people to reciprocate liking is to show we like them
   b. In initial interactions, we may hold back from fear of rejection or of giving the other person power over us
   c. We may underestimate how much a new acquaintance is attracted to us

E. Communication of Attraction

1. Strategies for communicating attraction
   a. We use several direct and indirect strategies to communicate liking
      (1) reduce physical distance between ourselves and another
      (2) increase eye contact and touch
      (3) lean forward and keep an open body orientation
      (4) smile
   b. We also use the various quasi-courtship behaviours (Chapter 6)
      (1) readiness, preening, positional cues, and appeals to invitation
   c. We communicate our attraction through language
      (1) we use informal and personal language
      (2) we address individuals by name and use "you and I" and "we"
      (3) we ask questions to show interest and probe for details
      (4) we listen responsively
      (5) we refer to information shared in past interactions
   d. Sometimes we simply tell people we like them
2. Affinity seeking
   a. Methods of communicating attraction may double for affinity-seeking
      (1) Control – present yourself as in control, with ability to reward
      (2) Visibility – look and dress attractively, increase visibility
      (3) Mutual trust – present yourself as honest, self-disclose
      (4) Politeness – follow conversational rules, let other person speak
      (5) Concern and caring – show interest, help the other person
      (6) Other-involvement – put positive spin on shared activities
      (7) self-involvement – arrange encounters and interactions
      (8) commonalities – point out similarities, establish equality
3. Uncertainty reduction
   a. Research team theory of Berger, Calabrese, and Bradac explains

relational development

(1) theory based on cause-effect assumption that we like to have control and predictability in our lives; when face with uncertainty we seek information to reduce uncertainty

b. In initial reactions we follow predictable scripts to reduce uncertainty

c. Gathering cognitive and emotional information reduces uncertainty

(1) cognitive information relates to thoughts, attitudes, and opinions

(2) behavioural information relates to situational reactions and remarks

(3) we gather information in pre-interaction stage of relationship through observations and conversations with others who know the person

(4) Later, we observe behaviours in direct interaction

(5) We also ask direct questions

d. We gather behavioural information through observation and cognitive information through interactions

IV. Self-Disclosure: A Foundation for Relational Escalation

A. Principles of self-disclosure

1. Self-disclosure is a building block of intimacy

a. There is more self-disclosure activity in early relationship stages

b. We proceed from low-risk to high-risk, then to intimate information

c. The more intimate the relationship the greater the intimate disclosure

d. Not all relationships progress uniformly

e. Dramatic increase or decrease in self-disclosure reflects relationship change

f. Even long-term relationships have significant increases and decreases in self-disclosure

g. Interpersonal relationships cannot achieve intimacy without self-disclosure

(1) Without self-disclosure, we form only superficial relationships

(2) Self-concepts in relationships can be mutually confirmed only with mutual self-disclosure

2. We expect self-disclosure to be reciprocal and appropriate

a. When we share information, we expect others to share

b. If other person does reciprocate, both people may feel resentful

c. Mutual self-disclosure maintains equal balance of power

d. If self-disclosure is not mutual, power imbalance may cause discomfort

e. We must assess relationship and situation to determine appropriateness of any disclosure

3. We assess self-disclosure risks differently

a. Judging what and when to disclose means realizing different people have different standards about what is appropriate and inappropriate

b. Be sensitive to others when you choose what and when to disclose

(1) consider how the other person may react to information

(2) when partner reveals information, determine if it is highly personal

(3) personal information shared openly may cause partner to feel betrayed

c. Degree of self-disclosure is not dependent on gender

(1) some men are highly self-disclosing

(2) some women are quite closed

(3) treating people as individuals increases communication effectiveness

4. We base self-disclosure on an analysis of costs and rewards

a. There is an optimal level of self-disclosure in each relationship stage

b. If optimal level is exceeded one or both partners may be dissatisfied

c. We disclose because we believe benefits of disclosure greater than costs

(1) we might disclose negative information about ourselves because we believe in the long run it may be better for the relationship

(2) you are likely to share information about yourself with another if you have found it rewarding to do so in the past

(3) you will be reluctant to self-disclose to someone if you have been harmed in the relationship with him or her, or in other relationships

V. Two Models for Self-Disclosure

A. Social Penetration Model

1. Irwin Altman and Dalmas Taylor developed a model of social penetration to illustrate how much and what kind of information we reveal in various stages of a relationship

a. Model starts with a circle representing totality of information about you

b. The circle is subdivided like a pie into pieces

(1) pieces represent particular aspects of self (family, religion, school, etc.)

(2) these pieces represent the breadth of information available about you

c. Concentric circles within circle represent depth of information

d. Each of your relationships represents a degree of social penetration

(1) number of concentric circles = depth

(2) number of pie pieces = breadth

B. Johari Window: named for model developers Joe and Harry

a. The four panes of the model window represent the totality of self (known and unknown)

b. One axis divides what you know about yourself from what you do not yet know about yourself

c. The other axis divides what some other knows and does not know about you

d. The intersection of categories creates the four panes of model window

(1) open quadrant represents known part of self revealed to others

(a) open quadrant grows larger as relationship intimacy increases

(2) hidden quadrant represents known part of self not revealed to others

(b) hidden quadrant shrinks as relationship intimacy increases

(3) unknown quadrant represents as yet undiscovered part of self
    (a) individuals who are not introspective will have large unknown quadrant
    (b) unknown quadrant will always exist because we can never know ourselves completely
(4) blind quadrant represents unintentional self-disclosure
    (a) this quadrant does not include misperceptions about us, but real aspects of ourselves we fail to recognize

C. Both the social penetration model and the Johari Window represent relationships

CHAPTER REVIEW: SECTION BY SECTION SUMMARY

I. Relationships of Circumstances and Relationships of Choice

There are two dominant types of relationships: (1) those determined by circumstances and (2) those created by choice. No one can choose his or her parents. Family membership is a relationship of circumstance. If you joined the armed forces, the men and women you served with would be relationships of circumstance. In contrast, husbands, wives, best friends, and lovers are -- in most cultures now -- relationships created by choice. Circumstantial relationships can become relationships of choice. If you become friends with a co-worker, you transform circumstance into choice. We behave differently in these different relationships. Bad behaviour can end a friendship, but even the worst behaviour cannot end your membership in a family.

II. Trust, Intimacy, and Power Relationships

Trust

Interpersonal trust is the degree to which we feel safe in disclosing personal information to another person. We exhibit trust in another when we reveal intimate information about ourselves and display our vulnerabilities. We look for signs that our partner is trustworthy, that he or she accepts our feelings without exploiting them, keeps personal information confidential, and continues to show us affection even when we reveal negative information about ourselves. An intimate relationship requires that both partners exhibit trust by sharing information openly, although this sharing might reasonably be selective.

Intimacy

Intimacy means the degree to which we can be ourselves in front of another person. We depend on intimate relationships to bolster our self-confidence and strengthen our self-image. We communicate intimacy directly and indirectly, verbally and nonverbally. We may tell a person outright that we like him or her, but we may also use less direct means such as eye contact, physical proximity, word selection, and tone of voice. The more intimate a relationship, the stronger the emotional bond and mutual trust. Emotions may not always be rational, but they are certainly real.

Power

Interpersonal power means the ability to influence another in the direction you desire – to get another person to do what you want. All relationships involve power and range somewhere between (1) an extreme where you have power over your partner to (2) the opposite extreme where your partner has power over you. Some relationships have a built-in power imbalance: teacher and student, doctor and patient, enlisted soldier and officer. Power in interpersonal relationships is distributed in three distinct relational forms: (1) complementary, (2) parallel, and (3) symmetrical (Chapter 1).

Complementary relationships, as the name implies, involve the idea of "completion." In a complementary relationship, partners' lifestyles fit together in a compatible way because one partner predominantly does what the other does not and vice versa. Power is willingly surrendered. In symmetrical relationships, partners do not behave in complementary ways but in the *same* way, whether that way is competitive or submissive. Power is balanced but conflicting. Parallel relationships involve reciprocal sharing and alteration of functions, responsibilities, and privileges between partners. Power shifts and alternates. Symmetrical relationships may involve high levels of conflict requiring time-consuming and inefficient negotiation.

In all relationships, the balance of power affects how we talk and what we talk about. Who possesses what information is also a source of power. Nonverbal behaviours and speech patterns also reflect a person's perception of his or her power relative to the person with whom he or she acts. Traditionally, our cultural norms classify men's speech patterns a more powerful than women's. To be masculine is to be loud and forceful; to speak in deeper tones, and to be authoritarian and blunt. Feminine speech is gentle, smooth, friendly, warm, quick, gossipy, high-pitched, nonverbally expressive, and frequent. Individuals of both sexes are apt to adopt either style.

Your text identifies five principal power sources: (1) legitimate, (2) referent, (3) expert, (4) reward, and (5) coercive.

Legitimate Power is power based on an appointed, elected, or designated position. Ministers, senators, mayors, deans and principals. Also dependent relationships such as parent and child.

Referent Power is based on interpersonal attraction. If people like us, we may have influence over them.

Expert Power is based on expertise, on special knowledge within a given field. Experts are also authorities within their special area.

Reward Power is based on the power to reward. Whoever has something to give that others want has power. Money, status, power, and those who command them, have influence.

Coercive Power is based on the power to punish. Those who can reward can also punish.

III. Interpersonal Attraction: The Spark of a Relationship

Your text lists seven elements of interpersonal attraction: (1) physical attraction, (2) charisma, (3) proximity, (4) similarity, (5) complementary needs, (6) relationship potential, and (7) reciprocation of liking.

1. **Physical Attraction.** The degree to which we find another person's physical self appealing represents our physical attraction to him or her. Appeal might be based on size, height, clothing, hairstyle, makeup, jewellery, vocal qualities, gestures, and so on. Different cultures have different ideals of physical attractiveness. We tend to seek out others who represent the same level of physical attractiveness as ourselves.

2. **Charisma.** Competence, credibility, and, sometimes, physical attractiveness are all important elements in the composite quality we call charisma. Political and other types of leaders depend upon charisma to gain support.

3. **Proximity.** Any circumstance that increases the possibilities for interacting is also likely to increase attraction. There is a good chance that two individuals will become good friends simply because they share living accommodations.

4. **Similarity.** We are often attracted to people whose personalities, values, upbringing, personal experiences, attitudes, and interests are similar to our own. We assess the relative weight of similarities and differences and arrive at a level of attraction that may change over time as we continue to discover more information. In the initial stages of a relationship, we try to emphasize positive information about ourselves to create a positive and attractive image. We save our revelations about important attitudes and issues for later relationship stages. Attitude similarity is a more likely source of long-term maintenance attraction than short-term initial attraction.

5. **Complementary Needs.** "Opposites attract." There are three interpersonal needs which motivate us to form and maintain relationships: (1) inclusion, (2) control, and (3) affection. Inclusion refers to our need to include others in our activities, or to be included in theirs. Control refers to our need to make decisions and take responsibility, or our willingness to accept others' decision making. Affection refers to our need to be loved and accepted by others, or our need to give love and acceptance to others. There are no perfect

matches in relationships, only degrees of compatibility relative to type and degree of needs.

6. **Relationship Potential.** We use Predicted Outcome Value theory to assess the potential for any given relationship to meet relational needs against potential costs. We use a cost/benefits analysis in assessing which relationship we pursue and which we terminate.

7. **Reciprocation of Liking.** We like people who like us. One way to get other people to reciprocate is to show we like them. In initial interactions, we tend to hold back from showing interest because we fear rejection or are afraid of giving someone power over us.

Communication of Attraction. Feeling attraction is one thing, showing it is another. Your text lists three dominant strategies for communicating attraction:

1. **Strategies for communicating attraction.** We use direct and indirect means to communicate liking. We use immediacy cues (Chapter 6) and quasi-courtship behaviours (Chapter 6). We use personal and informal language making heavy use of "you and I" and "we." We listen responsively and ask questions, referring to information shared in past interactions. Sometimes we simply tell people we like them.

2. **Affinity seeking includes eight categories.** (1) Control – presenting ourselves as in control, with the ability to reward, (2) Visibility – looking and dressing attractively and increasing our visibility, (3) Mutual trust – presenting ourselves as honest, sharing self-disclosure, (4) Politeness – following conversational rules, letting others speak, (5) Concern and caring – showing interest and helping the other person, (6) Other-involvement – putting a positive spin on shared activities, (7) Self-involvement – arranging encounters and interactions, and (8) Commonalities – pointing out similarities and establishing equality.

3. **Uncertainty reduction.** We all seem to share a fear of the unknown. The research team of Berger, Calabrese, and Bradac developed a theory based upon one basic cause-effect assumption: we like to have control and predictability in our lives; therefore, when face with uncertainty, we are driven to gain information to reduce uncertainty. In initial interactions we often follow scripts (Chapter 3) to reduce uncertainty. We further reduce uncertainty by gathering information both directly and indirectly about others, by asking about them and by observing them.

IV. Self-disclosure: A Foundation for Relational Escalation

Self-disclosure is an indispensable element of relationships. Your text identifies four distinct aspects of self-disclosure:

1. **Self-disclosure is a building block for intimacy.** Self-disclosure increases with the increase in relational intimacy. In a sense, self-disclosure is intimacy. Increases and decreases in self-disclosure reflect changes in a relationship. Even long-term relationships have increases and decreases. You can confirm another person's self-concept, and have your own confirmed, only if both you and your partner have revealed your selves to each other.

2. **We expect self-disclosure to be reciprocal and appropriate.** When we share information about ourselves, we expect the other person to share similar information. If one person in a relationship does not reciprocate, both people might feel resentful and uncomfortable with the resulting power imbalance. We must disclose only what seems appropriate in the context of a specific relationship.

3. **We assess self-disclosure risks differently.** In judging what and when to disclose, you need to realize that different people have different standards. Be sensitive to the other person when you choose what and when to disclose. Consider how the other person might react to the information. When your partner reveals information try to determine whether it is highly personal to them; if it is, keep it confidential. There is

nothing inherent in men or women that leads them to self-disclose more or less. Some men are highly self-disclosing; some women are quite closed.

4. **We base self-disclosure on an analysis of costs and rewards.** In each stage of a relationship, there is an optimal level of self-disclosure. If we exceed this level, discomfort and dissatisfaction may result for both partners. We make disclosures (even of unpleasant information) if we judge it will be good for the relationship in the long run. We are likely to share information with someone who has proved themselves receptive and supportive. We are unlikely to share information with others if someone has harmed us, either in the present relationship or in the past.

V. Two Models of Self-Disclosure

There are two models for visualizing self-disclosure: (1) the **social penetration** model of Irwin Altman and Dalmas Taylor and (2) the **Johari Window** developed by Joe and Harry.

1. The social penetration model is a series of bisected concentric circles. The concentric circles represent depth of information about the self; the pie-shaped wedges created by bisection represent diversity and breadth of information about the self.

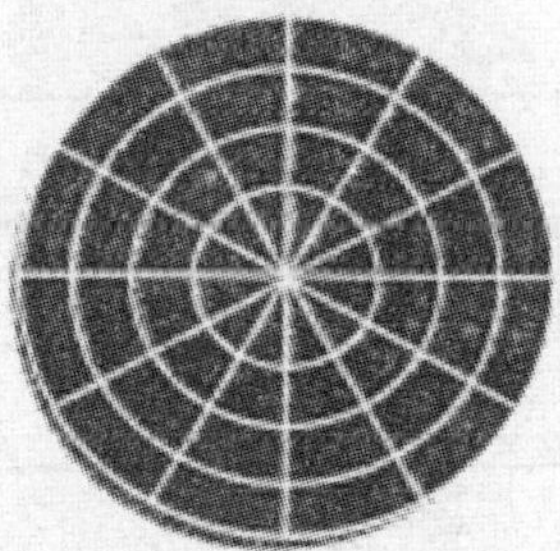

2. The Johari Window is a square divided into four quadrants by the intersection of a vertical and horizontal axis. Each of the quadrants represents a different dimension of the self in relation to others.

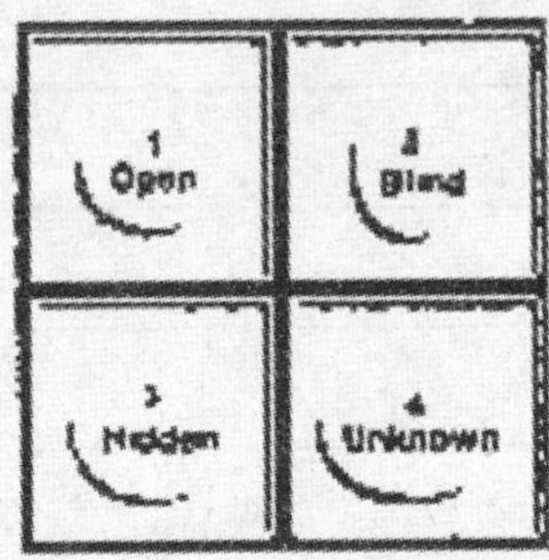

1. Quadrant One = Open Quadrant: known to self and revealed to others
2. Quadrant Two = Hidden Quadrant: known to self but not revealed to others
3. Quadrant Three = Blind Quadrant: unknown to self but evident to others
4. Quadrant Four = Unknown Quadrant: unknown to self and others

The dimensions of the various quadrants vary in different relationships and between different individuals.

TERMS TO LEARN

Relationships of Choice
Relationships of Circumstance
Interpersonal Trust
Trustworthy
Intimacy
Interpersonal Power
Legitimate Power
Referent Power
Expert Power
Reward Power
Coercive Power
Interpersonal Attraction
Short-Term Initial Attraction
Long-Term Maintenance Attraction
Physical Attraction
Proximity
Similarity
Complementary Needs
Relationship Potential (Predicted Outcome Theory)
Reciprocation of Liking
Communicating Attraction
Affinity Seeking
Uncertainty Reduction
Self-Disclosure
Social Penetration
Johari Window

Activity 9.1: Powerful and Powerless Speech

Objective:

1. To help you explore the difference between powerful and powerless speech.

Instructions

1. In the following situations identify elements of the "powerful" and "powerless" speaker.

Example	Powerful	Powerless
You are in a meeting of the marketing department of your company. Jim is suggesting a new marketing strategy. Eileen interrupts him to promote her own idea. She spends the rest of the meeting discussing her suggestion.	*Eileen interrupting; dominating speaking time*	*Jim doesn't talk much*

Situation	Powerful	Powerless
1. Stephan is asking Sylvia out for a date for the first time. He says, "I wondered if you might like to go to the movies if you've got the time? Maybe?"		

Situation	Powerful	Powerless
2. Laura is in a job interview. She responds well to the interviewer's questions and is well prepared. At one point she asks, "Could you give me more insight into what you are looking for?"		

Situation	Powerful	Powerless
3. There have been problems handling customer complaints lately. There are a lot of them and staff just does not have the time and resources to manage them. Ian, the general manager, has invited Inez and Francois, two managers, to help problem-solve in this situation. He opens the discussion by saying to them, "So what are your thoughts on this?" Francois jumps in with his ideas. Throughout the meeting Inez says barely a word.		

Situation	Powerful	Powerless
4. Brian has been bothered nightly by his neighbour Alan's barking dog. He approaches Alan to discuss the issue. He begins by asking Alan if he is aware of the problem. Alan responds with, "Well, um, perhaps she's been a bit noisier than usual but no one else has complained."		

Situation	Powerful	Powerless
5. Louise is part of an Employee Satisfaction Committee at work delegated to deal with employee concerns. At the first meeting Jason and Ivan nominate her to chair their monthly meetings. She responds with, "I am not very good at leading groups. I don't think I can do it."		

Situation	Powerful	Powerless
6. Indira is asked to make recommendations on company policy as a member of the Policy Review Committee. During her presentation she picks up and drops a pencil, shifts her papers on the lectern, and frequently adjusts her glasses.		

Situation	Powerful	Powerless
7. Daphne says, "I rather suspect that there may be no great readiness to hear proposals which do not correspond to those of management."		

Situation	Powerful	Powerless
8. "You will bloody well do it my way or I will see you rot in hell!"		

Activity 9.2: Analyzing Interpersonal Attraction

Objective:
1. To help you analyze the different elements of interpersonal attraction.

Instructions:
1. Reflect on a significant interpersonal relationship in your life.
2. Analyze the elements of interpersonal attraction in this relationship.

Example:

Relationship:
My friend Ming: We met at the beginning of the school year. She came to Canada a year ago from Hong Kong to study. I am also from Hong Kong and have been here two years.

Physical attraction:
We are both in good shape and enjoy swimming and biking.

Credibility, competence, and charisma:
We are both quiet but very diligent students to whom others seem attracted.

Proximity:
We share two classes this term and live in the same residence.

Similarity:
We are both women. We are similar in terms of our nationality and background and in our quiet temperaments, although Ming can be more persuasive than I am when she wants something. We both appreciate art and often like to visit the local art gallery. We both hate accounting.

Complementary needs:
Ming is patient and tolerant, works well with others, whereas I am more independent and a self-starter.

Relationship potential:
Strong. We will know each other for the next three years in school and if we return to our families in Hong Kong as we plan we will continue the friendship there.

Reciprocation of liking:
We have both acknowledged that we enjoy each other's company and are both relieved to have found a compatible friend in a new country.

Communication of attraction:
We caught each other's eye the first day of class, and when the instructor asked us to find a partner for an introductory exercise, we naturally gravitated toward each other.

Relationship:
Physical attraction:
Credibility, competence, and charisma:
Proximity:
Similarity:
Complementary needs:
Relationship potential:

Reciprocation of liking:
Communication of attraction:

Activity 9.3: Applying the Social Penetration Model

Objective:
1. To apply the social penetration model to different relationships.

Instructions:
1. Choose two relationships in your life from different contexts.
2. Analyze each relationship using the social penetration model.
3. Draw concentric circles to indicate relationship depth and section lines for breadth.

1. Describe the depth and breadth of this relationship.
2. How comfortable are you with the depth and breadth of this relationships?
3. What would you like to change about this relationships?
4. If you would like to change something, how could you do this?

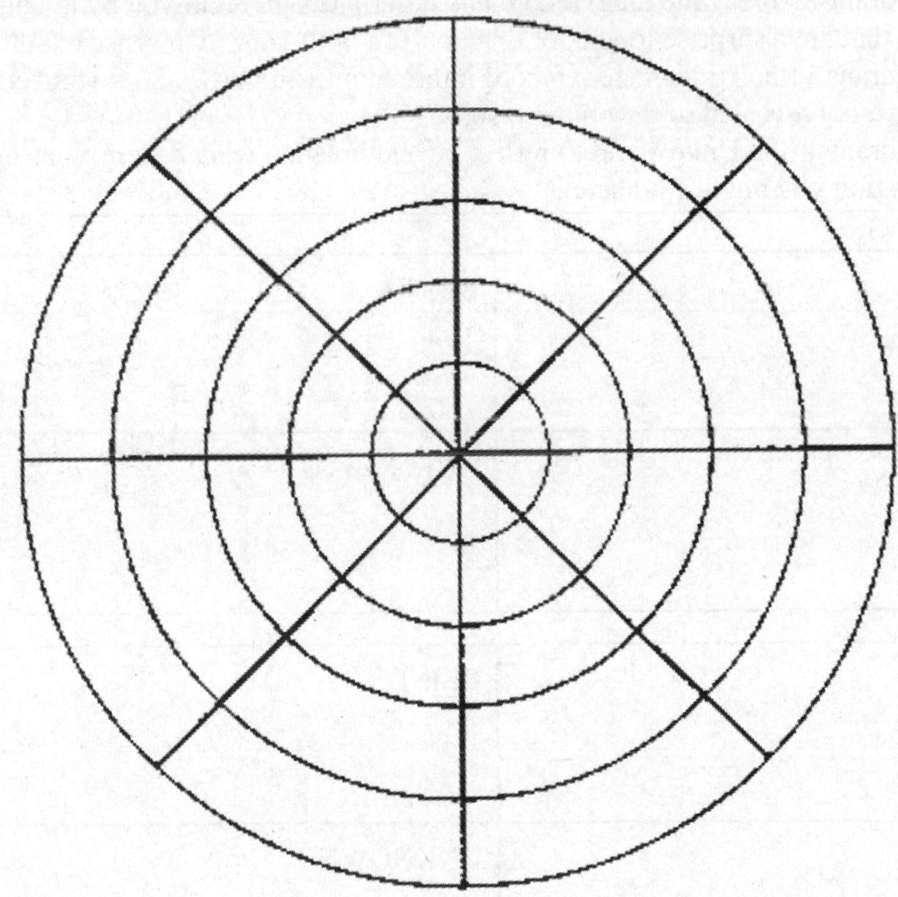

Activity 9.4: Building a Johari Window

Objectives:
1. To help you analyze relationships using the Johari Window Model.

Part 1

Instructions:
1. Interview two people who know you in different contexts of your life (e.g. family, friends, co-workers, etc.)
2. Ask each person to provide you with a list of descriptors that they would use to describe you.
3. Ask each person you interview how open or closed they perceive you to be in your relationship.
4. Complete a Johari Window for each relationship.
5. In Quadrant 1 (the Open area) of your Johari Window record adjectives and phrases that represent the part of self that you know and have revealed to the other person.
6. In Quadrant 2 (the Blind area) record any descriptors given to you by the other person that are a surprise to you, or that don't fit with your own sense of self.
7. In Quadrant 3 (the Hidden area) record information you know about yourself that you have not revealed to the other person.
8. In Quadrant 4 (the Unkown area) reflect on and imagine what descriptions or information you might find here.

OPEN	BLIND
HIDDEN	UNKNOWN

OPEN	BLIND
HIDDEN	UNKNOWN

Part 2

Instructions:

1. Using information gathered in Part 1, draw a Johari Window for each relationship in the space provided on the next page. Remember that in relationships where there is greater disclosure and feedback, the Open area will be much larger than in relationships where there is less. For example, your Open area might be smaller than with a manager at work than with your best friend.

2. When you have completed your Johari Windows, return to this page and answer the following questions.

1. How do these Johari Windows differ?
2. To what do you attribute these differences?
3. What have you learned about yourself here?

Johari One

Johari Two

Activity 9.5: Giving and Receiving Feedback

Objective:
1. To give you practice in giving and receiving feedback.

Instructions:

1. Form a small group (5-6 people) in your class with people you have worked with over the term.
2. Have one person (Person A) begin the exercise by asking for feedback. Person B will give feedback to Person A. Then Person B will ask Person C for feedback and so on until everyone in the group has given one item of feedback and received one.
3. Feedback messages should contain a description of observed behaviour, your reaction to or feeling about that behaviour, and your wants, (what you would like the person to change or continue).
4. Record feedback you receive below.

Example:

Denvan, when you encouraged me to present in front of the class I felt encouraged. Please continue to support me.

Indira, when you interrupt me when I am giving my ideas in a meeting I feel annoyed. Please wait until I finish speaking before you make your point.

Feedback Received:

DIFFICULT POSITION 9

Andre and Leo have been good friends for almost ten years. In that time, they have worked together on many common projects and even vacationed together with each other's families. Quite suddenly, Leo announced to Andre that he was leaving his wife, Marilyn, for a younger woman he had met at a conference in Vienna several years before and with whom he had kept up a daily e-mail correspondence ever since. This was the first Andre had ever heard of this mysterious woman, and the whole thing came as a shock to everyone. Andre's wife, Clare, said that Leo why behaving shamefully and she never wanted him in her home again. Andre asked Leo why he never told him about his plans to divorce, and Leo said, "I just felt I couldn't trust anyone, not even you." Andre was hurt by this, and he also felt sorry for Leo's wife. What with Clare telling him Leo was someone she could never respect again, and with his own pride hurt because Leo had not trusted him enough to confide in him, Andre felt bitter and confused.

A few months later, after Leo's divorce (and almost immediate remarriage), Andre got a call from Leo saying he was sorry about how things had worked out, but he really needed a friend now more than ever, especially since his new relationship seemed to be off to a rocky start. Andre knew Clare would be upset if he went to see Leo and his new wife, so he said he would try to come by but that he might not be able to make it. Andre felt torn.

INSTRUCTIONS

1. Identify, analyze, and discuss the dynamics of this relationship in terms of trust, intimacy, and power. Based on what you know about Leo's and Andre's relationship, what would you think appropriate and reasonable at this stage? How would you feel yourself under such circumstances? What would you do?

2. Discuss these questions in small groups and record your discussion points.

Option:

1. Have two students roleplay Andre and Leo. Centre the roleplaying around a discussion between Andre and Leo in which they try to repair the relationship.

Exercise 9.1: Learning Objective: General Review (**TRUE/FALSE**)

Instructions: Identify the following statements as either true or false.

1. In all our lives, relationships of circumstance precede those of choice. ( )
2. All human relationships involve power issues. ( )
3. Symmetrical relationships with power sharing are usually the most efficient. ( )
4. Legitimate power may be reinforced by referent and charismatic power. ( )
5. Tyrants and dictators can sometimes command charismatic power. ( )
6. Reward power is often another face of coercive power. ( )
7. Similarity is the only reliable basis for a long-term maintenance relationship. ( )
8. All relationships progress uniformly through stages of increasing intimacy. ( )
9. Self-disclosure is always necessary if relationships are to become intimate. ( )
10. Self-disclosure or the lack of it can be an instrument of control. ( )
11. Introspection would most affect the hidden quadrant of a Johari window. ( )
12. In the social penetration model, concentric circles represent relationship breadth. ( )
13. Dissimilarity can be a factor in attraction. ( )
14. Complete self-disclosure should always be achieved as quickly as possible. ( )
15. Men are inherently less likely to self-disclose than women. ( )
16. Judgements based on physical attractiveness are invariably unreliable. ( )
17. Nonverbal behaviours convey an individual's sense of power. ( )
18. Initial apparent similarities may mask significant differences. ( )
19. We apply cost/benefit measures to determine the value of our relationships. ( )

Exercise 9.2: Learning Objective: General Review (**FILL-IN-THE-BLANKS**)

Instructions: Fill in the blanks using the appropriate term or terms from the following list.

relationships of choice	expert power	physical attraction	uncertainty reduction
relationships of circumstance	reward power	proximity	self-disclosure
	coercive power	similarity	social penetration
trustworthy	interpersonal attraction	complementary needs	Johari Window
intimacy	short-term initial attraction	relationship potential	interpersonal trust
interpersonal power		reciprocation of liking	
legitimate power	long-term maintenance attraction	communicating attraction	
referent power		affinity seeking	

1. "Jack Sprat could eat no fat, his wife could eat no lean, and so between the two of them, they licked the platter clean" could be seen as a nursery rhyme version of a relationship based on ______________________.

2. In aristocratic societies, birth confers authority and is regarded as a source of ______________________regardless of any special gifts or competence.

3. ______________ involves at least eight distinct strategies ranging from manifestations of control to a search for commonalities.

4. When the boy-next-door marries the girl-next-door (and he often does), it is a demonstration of the importance of ______________ in fostering relationships.

5. The teacher had grades which she could use as either ______________ to promote certain behaviours or as ______________ to discourage others.

6. Kafka always kept confidences, and over the years he proved himself to be supportive and ______________.

7. Jane was raised in Alberta and has a love for breeding and racing horses, just like I do. Our relationship is based on this strong ______________.

8. The famous Victorian writer John Ruskin once said that good books are like companions. Relationships with authors we like to read are__________________ unlike the__________________ that we have with most people in our daily lives.

9. I felt I could tell her the truth about myself, and she felt the same way about me. We had arrived at a high level of __________________.

10. I know that I am understood and appreciated for who I am by at least one man in this world, and I understand and appreciate him. Our marriage is the outward and visible sign of our_________________.

11. It is sad to realize that evil men sometimes command considerable _______________ based on the _______________ they have over those who admire and willingly follow them.

12. Lawyers know that the_____________ commanded by scientists in assessing material evidence in criminal trails is seldom appropriately respected by juries.

13. Some organizations require a formal act of _______________ before one can become a member. One must show a willingness to share information about oneself openly with others in the organization.

14. I had met William at the party and liked him, but I knew almost nothing about his background, so I asked around. I wanted to gather information so I could achieve some degree of __________________________.

15. The boss thinks I'm about the best thing going, and I admit I think he's the best guy alive. I guess there's no disputing our ________________________.

16. I like going out with her, but she has a temper. I enjoy spending time with her, but she doesn't leave me time to myself. I weigh the pros and cons of this new relationship back and forth trying to assess the ______________________.

17. The moment we saw each other, we recognized a high degree of ________________ but it turned out to be _______________________ that lasted only a month. It had a lot to do, I'm afraid, with how we were dressed. It was based mostly on _____________ and we found that there were not enough fundamental similarities to sustain ____________________.

18. If you stand close to someone, use his or her name frequently, speak in a quiet and personal tone, and say openly how much you admire him or her, you are almost certainly involved in _________________________.

19. Thinking of my relationships in visual terms helps clarify their dynamics. The ________________ model helps me think about depth and breadth of my relationships with others, and _________________ helps me think of the various dimensions of my self in my relationship with others.

Exercise 9.3: Learning Objective: General Review (**MULTIPLE CHOICE**)

Instructions: Choose the best answer for each question below.

1. The form of interpersonal power used to compel others by use of sanctions is

    a. referent power
    b. coercive power
    c. reward power
    d. legitimate power

2. In the Johari Window model of relationships, the blind quadrant represents

    a. things unknown to the self but evident to others
    b. things unknown to the self and to others
    c. things known to the self but hidden from others
    d. things known to the self but misrepresented to others

3. If two people are close friends and one is forceful and the other passive, their relationship probably best exemplifies

    a. affinity seeking
    b. reciprocation of liking
    c. complementary needs
    d. charisma

4. In the social penetration model of relationships, concentric circles represent

    a. the various aspects of the self
    b. the unconscious areas of our behaviour
    c. the breadth of our relationship
    d. the possible depth of a given relationship

5. Physical attraction is often the basis of

    a. self-disclosure
    b. short-term initial attraction
    c. long-term maintenance attraction
    d. coercive power

6. Shifts in the level of self-disclosure

   a. follow a uniform pattern in all relationships
   b. vary depending upon gender
   c. disappear in long-term maintenance relationships
   d. indicate significant changes in a relationship

7. All of the following statements are true except

   a. self-disclosure is a building block of intimacy
   b. we expect self-disclosure to be reciprocal
   c. we assess self-disclosure risks differently
   d. self-disclosure is easier in relationships of circumstance

8. All of the following statements are true except

   a. reward power and coercive power are often commanded by a single individual
   b. different cultures may have different standards for assessing physical attractiveness
   c. physical attractiveness is an essential aspect of charisma
   d. interpersonal relationships cannot achieve intimacy without self-disclosure

9. All of the following are aspects of affinity seeking strategies except

   a. control
   b. politeness
   c. commonalities
   d. duplicity

10. All of the following statements are true except

    a. we often underestimate how much a new acquaintance is attracted to us
    b. we sometimes hold back from showing attraction for fear of rejection
    c. we often perform a cost/benefit analysis of a potential relationship
    d. relationships based on complementary needs are the strongest

11. All of the following statements about power are true except

    a. failure to self-disclose in a relationship may create a power imbalance
    b. referent power may be used for manipulative purposes
    c. legitimate power depends on charisma to sustain it
    d. mutual claims to expert power may cause heated controversy

Answers

CHAPTER 9

Exercise 9.1

1. (T)
2. (T)
3. (F)
4. (T)
5. (T)
6. (T)
7. (F)
8. (F)
9. (T)
10. (T)
11. (F)
12. (F)
13. (T)
14. (F)
15. (F)
16. (F)
17. (T)
18. (T)
19. (T)

Exercise 9.2

1. Complementary needs
2. Legitimate power
3. Affinity seeking
4. Proximity
5. Reward power/coercive power
6. Trustworthy
7. Similarity
8. Relationships of choice/ relationships of circumstance
9. Interpersonal trust
10. Intimacy
11. interpersonal power/referent power
12. Expert power
13. Self-disclosure
14. Uncertainty reduction
15. Reciprocation of liking
16. Relationship potential
17. Interpersonal attraction/ short-term initial attraction/ physical attraction/long-term maintenance attraction
18. Communicating attraction
19. Social penetration/Johari Window

Exercise 9.3

1. b
2. a
3. c
4. d
5. b
6. d
7. d
8. c
9. d
10. d
11. c

Chapter 10

Developing Interpersonal Relationships

CHAPTER OUTLINE

I. Stages of Interpersonal Relationships

A. Relational development proceeds in discernible stages

B. Interpersonal communication is affected by the stage of the relationship

C. Relational development can be visualized as an elevator that stops at every floor

D. Panel lights in an elevator indicating floors resemble turning points in a relationship associated with positive or negative changes

1. Relational Escalation (the elevator moves up)

   a. Pre-interaction awareness is the first stage or floor

   (1) this stage involves gathering information without direct interaction

   (2) passive observation in this stage forms first impression

   (3) if initial impression is negative, relationship may stop at pre-interaction stage

   b. Initiation is the second stage or floor

   (1) interaction at this stage is routine

   (2) each partner at this stage may respond to many standard questions

   (3) superficial topics and presentation of "public self" dominate this stage

   (4) initiation stage inaugurates an irreversible relational history

   c. Exploration is the third stage or floor

   (1) in this stage more in-depth information begins to be shared

   (2) minimal physical contact in this stage and maintenance of social distance

   (3) time spent together in this stage is limited

   (4) this stage may occur in conjunction with initiation stage

   d. Intensification is the fourth stage or floor

   (1) in this stage dependence upon partner for self-confirmation increases

   (2) in this stage more "risky" self-disclosure begins

   (3) time spent together increases

   (4) the variety of shared activities increases

   (5) physical contact increases

   (6) language becomes personalized

   (7) the relationship itself is often discussed and redefined

   (a) turning point labels may be assigned ("going steady," "best friends")

   (b) decision to date each other exclusively

   (c) become roommates

   (d) spend time with each other's families

   e. Intimacy is the fifth stage or top floor

   (1) in this stage partners turn to each other for confirmation of self-concept

(2) communication becomes highly personalized and synchronized
(3) information and self-disclosure flow freely
(4) commitments are made to maintain relationship
(a) formalized marriage or some other arrangement
(5) partners share understanding of each other's language and nonverbal cues
(6) physical contact becomes frequent
(7) fewer words are necessary to communicate effectively
(8) roles of the relationship are clearly defined
(9) reaching this stage takes time
(a) time to build trust
(b) time to share personal information
(c) time to build commitment and emotional bond

2. Relational De-escalation (the elevator moves down)
   a. Turmoil or stagnation is the first stage or floor in the downward movement
      (1) fault finding and conflict increase in this stage
      (2) definition of the relationship loses clarity
      (3) communication climate becomes tense and exchanges are difficult
      (4) partners become complacent
      (5) communication, physical contact, and time spent together decreases
      (6) established relational routines are substituted for real commitment
      (7) turmoil stage can be maintained or reversed by individuals involved and does not necessarily move to next stage
   b. De-intensification is the second stage or floor in downward movement
      (1) interactions decrease, and physical and emotional distance increase
      (2) definition of relationship may be discussed and assessed
      (3) relationship can still be repaired but it is more difficult to do so
   c. Individualization is third stage or floor in downward movement
      (1) neither partner views the other as significant individual in their life
      (2) "we" and "us" become "me" and "you"
      (3) property ownership becomes "mine" and "yours" not "ours"
      (4) partners turn to others for confirmation of self-concepts
   d. Separation is the fourth stage or floor in downward movement
      (1) partners now make intentional decision to eliminate interpersonal interaction
      (2) property, resources, and friends are divided
      (3) shared activities and child care responsibilities are conducted differently
      (4) previous intimacy may make new superficiality uncomfortable
      (5) time slowly dissolves former intimacy and knowledge of the other
   e. Post-interaction effects stage is last floor in downward movement
      (1) lasting effects of relationship on self and other interactions
      (2) in this stage we may engage in what Steve Duck calls "grave-dressing"
         (a) preparing a public statement to account for the end of the relationship
         (b) dealing with damage done to our sense of self

(3) Some people bypass decline stages by "hopping out" of a relationship
(a) abandoned partners most dislike the "quick exit" without discussion

II. Skills for Starting Relationships

A. Gather information to reduce uncertainty

B. Adopt an other-oriented perspective

1. Use techniques to put your partner at ease (smiling, active listening, etc.)
2. Minimize differences of status and power
3. Don't just react, take initiative to make first interaction pleasant

C. Observe and act on approachability cues

1. Approachability signals indicate openness
   (a) sustained eye contact
   (b) turning toward another person
   (c) animation
   (d) an open body posture
   (e) winking and waving

D. Identify and use conversation starters

1. Use "free information" as a starting point for conversation ("nice day, huh?")
2. Ask an open question ("How do you like . . . ?")

E. Follow initiation norms

1. Most early interactions are scripted
2. Standard topics and responses reduce uncertainty

F. Provide information about yourself

1. Disclosing information about yourself allows others to make informed decision about continuing the relationship
2. Disclosure should not violate cultural expectations embodied in "scripts"
3. Premature or uninvited disclosure may alienate

G. Present yourself in a positive way

1. We tend to find people attractive who have positive self-images
2. It is against our cultural norms to disclose negative information early
3. While remaining genuine be selective about the information you share
4. Remember, the person with whom you interact is also presenting a positive image

H. Ask questions

1. Asking questions serves two purposes
   a. Helps you to acquire information
   b. Shows communication partner you are interested
2. Keep questions open and noninvasive; don't interrogate
   a. Focus on things you have in common
   b. Use the situation as a resource for questions

I. Don't put too much in the initial interaction

1. Initial interactions do not necessarily determine the future of a relationship
2. Scripted nature of initial interactions reduces opportunity for in-depth

understanding

3. Relax and arrange another meeting if you feel the spark of attraction

III. Interpersonal Communication Skills for Escalating and Maintaining Relationships

A. Initial interaction and attraction do not necessarily determine relationship success

B. Many relationships are maintained at lower levels

C. Satisfying relationships can be achieved by interacting with those who have a similar level of interpersonal skill

D. In some instances a partner's strengths can complement the other's weaknesses

E. Intimate relationships require maintenance

F. Skills are need to maintain intimate relationships

1. Monitor your perceptions, listen actively, and respond
    a. Consciously attend to cues, learn how others react to different situations, and shape relationship maintenance behaviours accordingly
    b. Be sensitive to your biases and counterbalance them to avoid overreacting
    c. Checking perceptions may clear up imagined slights and misunderstandings
    d. Listening skills are crucial for developing and maintaining relationships
        (1) Listening demonstrates ongoing interest
        (2) Even in long-term relationships, we do not know all our partner has to say and must listen attentively
    e. Provide confirming responses (Chapter 5)
2. Be open and self-disclose appropriately
    a. The level of self-disclosure needs to be appropriate to the relationship level
    b. Both partners must be sensitive to the timing of disclosures
    c. Restricting amount of self-disclosure can control relationship development
        (1) reducing self-disclosure can help slow the progression of a relationship
    d. Each partner must accept and offer mutual self-disclosure
3. Express emotions
    a. Sharing feelings is one way to escalate relationship development
    b. Sharing the wrong feelings at the wrong time can be detrimental
    c. We share feelings in two ways
        (1) we disclose information about past or current emotional states
        (2) we express emotions directly
    d. As relationships become intimate, we expect more disclosure of emotion
    e. The degree of risk associated with emotional disclosure varies from person to person
    f. We tend to be more reserved in expressing negative emotions
        (1) fear
        (2) disappointment
    g. A constant barrage of negative expressions can alienate a partner
        (1) marital satisfaction rises with number of positive feelings disclosed
        (2) a balance must be achieved between positive and negative emotions

4. Develop and apply communication sensitivity
   a. Communication sensitivity requires an awareness and appreciation of all the dynamics of an interpersonal interaction
   b. Rhetorical sensitivity involves adaptability and perceptiveness
      (1) avoidance of stylized behaviour
      (2) management of strain involved in adapting
      (3) use of placating comments when appropriate
      (4) appreciation of multiple ways ideas and feelings can be communicated
   c. *Noble selves* are inflexible and refuse to adapt
   d. *Rhetorical reflectors* mold themselves to every person and situation
   e. Conversationally sensitive people are usually rhetorically sensitive as well
      (1) they pick up meanings in what people say
      (2) remember what has been said
      (3) compose multiple ways of saying the same thing
      (4) have a desire to listen
      (5) have skill in interpreting levels of liking and power in interactions
      (6) appreciate subtleties
      (7) these skills can be acquired through practice
   f. Nonverbal sensitivity is the ability to interpret nonverbal cues
5. Be tolerant and show restraint
   a. Satisfying relationships minimize disagreement, criticism and negativity
      (1) well-adjusted couples focus their complaints on specific behaviours
      (2) maladjusted couples complain about personal characteristics
   b. Maintaining a relationship requires tolerance
      (1) you must learn to accept partner as is and put up with things you dislike
   c. Be selective in disclosing negative feelings about your partner
6. Manage conflict cooperatively
   a. Management not avoidance is the key to handling conflict effectively
   b. cooperative management of conflict can strengthen relationship
      (1) clarify definition of relationship
      (2) increase exchange of information
      (3) create a cooperative atmosphere
7. Seek compliance
   a. Use persuasive strategies to accomplish personal goals
   b. Compliance-seeking strategies are necessary if you encounter resistance to fulfilling your goals
   c. Seeking compliance raises ethical concerns
      (1) to what degree is it ethical to manipulate others to further self-interest?
      (2) is the ability to gain compliance exploitative?
      (3) is it ever ethical to lie or deceive another to achieve one's own goals?
      (4) are threats and punishment ever ethical ways of achieving compliance?
      (5) seeking compliance involves responsibility not to exploit others

IV. Identifying and Acting upon Trouble Signs in Relationships

A. Women usually sense trouble in a relationship earlier than do men

B. Specific verbal and nonverbal cues signal when a relationship is de-escalating

1. There is a decrease in touching and physical contact
2. Decrease in proximity, eye contact, smiling, tonal variety, and interaction
3. Decrease in amount of time spent together
4. Increase in time between interactions
5. Separation of possessions
6. Interactions become less personal and so does language
7. Couples use fewer intimate terms
8. Use less present and more past tense
9. Make fewer references to the future in their relationship
10. Use more qualified language
11. Make fewer evaluative statements
12. Fight more and disclose less

C. When you pick up signals of relational problems, you have three choices

1. Wait and see what happens
2. Make a decision to end the relationship
3. Try to repair the relationship
    a. Repairing involves all the maintenance skills
    b. Repairing is dependent on willingness of both partners to keep relationship going
    c. Professional counselling might be an important option

D. If you choose to end the relationship, consider your goals

1. Do you want to continue relationship on lower level or terminate?
2. Do you care enough to want to preserve the other's self-esteem?
3. Are you aware of the costs of ending the relationship?

E. How should you react if your friend confirms a desire to end your relationship?

1. Try to have a focussed discussion on what has contributed to the decision
    (1) you might get information needed to repair the relationship
    (2) you might gain information helpful in future relationships

F. When intimate relationships end, we rely on our social networks for support

1. Family and friends

V. De-escalating and Ending Relationships

A. No relationship ever comes to a complete end, because each has a lasting impact

B. De-escalation and termination of a relationship is not inherently bad

C. Termination of a relationship can be a positive and healthy action

1. If the relationship is harmful
2. If it no longer provides confirmation of the self or satisfies interpersonal needs
3. It can open the door to new relationships

D. Sometimes we chose to de-escalate rather than end a relationship

E. Ending intimate relationships is difficult because self-concept is involved

1. The most satisfying breakups confirm rather than degrade both partners' worth

F. The process of breakup differs considerably if one or both parties want out

1. *Bilateral dissolution* involves simple division of possessions and other details
2. *Unilateral dissolution* means the person who wants to end the relationship must use compliance-gaining strategies to get partner to agree to dissolution

VI. How Relationships End

A. A declining relationship usually follows one of several paths

1. The relationship fades away – the two partners drift apart
2. Sudden death – a single precipitating event ends relationship (death, infidelity)
3. Incrementalism – conflicts accumulate to a critical mass leading to breakup
   a. Relationship becomes intolerable
   b. Relationship becomes, from a social exchange perspective, too costly

B. Strategies for Ending Relationships

1. Partners use direct and indirect strategies
   a. Indirect strategies seek to end relationships without explicitly stating a desire to do so
      (1) *withdrawal strategy* reduces interaction without any explanation
         (a) this strategy is most dissatisfying for the other partner
         (b) withdrawal seeks to avoid a confrontational scene to save face
      (2) *pseudo-de-escalation* involves one partner claiming he or she wants to redefine relationship at a lower level of intimacy, but in reality, he or she wants to end the relationship
         (a) both partners may engage in mutual pseudo-de-escalation disguising their move toward disengagement as de-escalation
      (3) *Cost escalation* increases costs associated with relationship to encourage the other person to terminate
         (a) dissatisfied partner may make inordinate demands, pick fights, etc.
   b. Direct strategies seek an explicit end to a relationship
      (1) *negative identity management* is a direct statement of a desire to end a relationship
         (a) it does not take into account the other's feelings, and might include negative criticism
      (2) *justification* is a clear statement of desire to end a relationship accompanied by an honest explanation of the reasons why
      (3) *de-escalation* is an honest statement of a desire to redefine the relationship at a lower level of intimacy or to terminate
         (a) request for trial separation
      (4) *positive tone* is the direct strategy most sensitive to other's sense of self
         (a) this strategy seeks to affirm worth while dissolving relationship

C. Causes of de-escalation and termination

1. Reasons for ending an interpersonal relationship vary widely
2. In general, we end relationships when their costs exceed their benefits

3. Relationships can be compared to savings accounts in a bank
    a. If the relationship is profitable, you deposit excess rewards in an emotional savings account
    b. When emotional costs exceed rewards, you draw from savings account to cover deficit
    c. If savings run out, you may close account – end the relationship
    d. If you foresee future benefits, you might keep overdrawn account open
    e. If alternatives seem dismal, you might decide to "stick it out"
        (1) these relationships often suffer sudden death endings
4. One researcher identifies three main causes of relational breakup
    a. Faults – problems with personality traits that one partner dislikes in other
    b. Unwillingness to compromise – a variety of failings on the part of one or both partners
        (1) failure to put enough effort into relationship
        (2) failure to make concessions for good of relationship
    c. Feeling constrained – one partner's desire to be free of commitments
5. A variety of elements can contribute to romantic and non-romantic breakups
    a. A loss of interest in other person
    b. A desire for independence
    c. Conflicting attitudes about definition of relationship in various areas
        (1) sexual conduct
        (2) marriage
        (3) infidelity

D. A model for ending relationships

1. Researcher Steve Duck developed a model to show stages in ending a relationship
    a. Threshold – one partner arrives at threshold of dissatisfaction prompting thoughts of ending relationship
    b. Intra-psychic phase – evaluation of partner's behaviours often fixing on reasons justifying withdrawal
        (1) you do not intentionally reveal thoughts and evaluations to partner
        (2) termination may be considered but is not enacted
        (3) thoughts may "leak" through emotional displays including hostility, anxiety, stress, or guilt
        (4) confidence of a third party may be sought
    c. Dyadic phase – after passing another threshold, direct confrontation of partner now leads to discussion and assessment of relationship
        (1) you might have to justify thoughts and feelings
        (2) partner may criticize your behaviours
        (3) issues may be raised leading to reevaluation of relationship
        (4) costs of dissolving relationship are assessed
        (5) decision may be made to restore and repair relationship
    d. Social phase – after passing another threshold, mutual decision to end

relationship now leads to making the information public

(1) social networks may be activated to preserve relationship
    (a) family and friends may act as mediators
    (b) friends may reinforce decision to separate

e. Grave-dressing phase – after passing another threshold, one or both partners may attempt "to put flowers" on the grave of their relationship
    (1) a public story is developed to share with others about what happened
        (a) public story often places blame on the other partner
    (2) friends may encourage us to get back into social activities
        (a) we may be "fixed up" with dates
    (3) we go through an internal process working out guilt and blame

CHAPTER REVIEW: SECTION BY SECTION SUMMARY

I. Stages of Interpersonal Relationships

Relational development proceeds in stages, and our interpersonal communication is affected by the stage of a relationship. Your text compares relational development to an elevator moving up and down between floors – each floor represents a relationship stage. Arriving at and leaving the various stages represent **turning points** in a relationship. Turning points are occasions when partners tend to talk about and define the nature of their relationship.

The upward phase of relationships is called **relational escalation**, which has five ascending stages:

(1) **Pre-interaction awareness stage**: in this stage information is gathered through passive observation and initial impressions are formed. If initial impression is negative or circumstances are unfavourable, relationship may not proceed beyond this first stage.

(2) **Initiation stage**: in this stage interaction tends to be routine with both partners presenting a "public self" and answering standard questions about safe and superficial topics. This stage begins a relational history on which partners can continue to build.

(3) **Exploration**: in this stage more in-depth information is shared but physical contact and time spent together remain minimal.

(4) **Intensification stage**: in this stage mutual dependence for self-confirmation increases; "riskier" personal information is shared; physical contact, time spent togther, and variety of activities increase; language becomes personalized; and the relationship is discussed and redefined. Turning point "labels" may be agreed upon ("going steady," "best friends"). Other turning points in this stage may include visiting each other's families, becoming roommates, or dating each other exclusively.

(5) **Intimacy**: this is the top floor of the relationship elevator. In this stage partners turn to each other for confirmation and acceptance of their self-concept; communication is highly personalized and synchronized; information and self-disclosure move freely; partners understand each other's language and nonverbal cues; they have a great deal of physical contact; they use fewer words to communicate effectively; and they have a clear sense of relationship goals. It takes time to reach this stage – time to build trust, share personal information, observe each other in various situations, and establish commitments and emotional bond.

Relational de-escalation also has five stages, but it is important to recognize that these stages are not merely the reverse of the escalation stages. The elevator metaphor is limited in its usefulness because the downward movement in relationships involves different "floors" or stages.

(1) **Turmoil or stagnation phase**: this stage involves increasing conflict; the definition of the relationship loses clarity; mutual acceptance declines; and the communication environment becomes tense. If conflict does not increase, the partners may be in stagnation – a condition in which relational routines are substituted for genuine commitment and feeling. Relationships may remain at this level or be repaired and restored to higher levels.

(2) **De-intensification stage.** Turmoil and stagnation left unaddressed may lead to increased emotional, physical, and psychological distance between partners; the relationship may be questioned and levels of satisfaction assessed. The relationship may be repaired, but it is more difficult at this stage.

(3) **Individualization stage**: in this stage, partners define themselves as separate individuals, and neither views the other as a significant part of their life. The perspective shifts from "we" and "us" to "you" and

"me." Property becomes "mine" and "yours" not "ours." Partners now turn to others for confirmation of self-concept.

(4) **Separation stage**: in this stage individuals make an intentional decision to eliminate further interpersonal interaction; property, resources, and friends are divided; the quality of shared responsibilities (such as child care) changes; and intimacy is replaced with forced superficiality.

(5) **Post-interaction effects stage**: in this stage, the individual partners come to terms with the lasting effects of the relationship upon their self-concept. The relationship may be mourned as if it were a dead loved one. Public statements may be developed to share with others and explain the demise of the relationship.

II. Skills for Starting Relationships

Your text identifies nine relationship starting skills:

(1) **Gather information to reduce uncertainty**: reducing uncertainty involves a variety of skills discussed throughout previous chapters of your text but depends primarily on effective perception and active listening.

(2) **Adopt an other-oriented perspective**: remember the sorts of things people have done to put you at ease in the past when you felt uncomfortable in an initial meeting and do these things yourself: smile, show interest, disclose information about yourself, keep conversation light and friendly. If there is a power and status difference between you and another, seek to minimize it by removing nonverbal signs of power and status: get out from behind a desk, do not insist on formal titles. Be active rather than reactive. Take initiative to make initial interaction positive and pleasant.

(3) **Observe and act upon approachability cues**: look for nonverbal behaviours which signal openness to communication such as eye contact, smiling, animation, open body posture, winking and waving, and pleasant tone of voice. Cues suggestive of inapproachability, such as averted gaze and closed body posture, should be respected.

(4) **Identify and use conversation starters:** use "free" information to start a conversation, such things as the weather, a book someone is carrying which you have read and can talk about, or a shared class or activity. Ask open questions starting with "How" or "What" to invite more than a yes or no response.

(5) **Follow initiation norms:** many of the early interactions in a relationship are ritualistic, or at least scripted. Following conversation scripts helps to reduce uncertainty, but it is also appropriate to expand and develop conversations by listening for details about a person's background that you can inquire about while sharing information about your own interests.

(6) **Provide information about yourself**: disclosing information – without violating scripted and cultural norms – allows the other person to make an informed decision about whether or not to continue the relationship. Excessive or premature disclosure may alienate.

(7) **Present yourself in a positive way:** we tend to find people attractive who have a positive self-image. While being genuine also be selective about the information you share. Both parties in an initial meeting are "putting their best foot forward."

(8) **Ask questions**: questioning accomplishes two goals simultaneously: (1) you learn about the other person and (2) you show interest in them. Keep questions open and nonintrusive; do not interrogate. Focus on things you have in common that are safe.

(9) **Don't put too much in the initial interaction**: the scripted nature of initial interactions restricts opportunities for in-depth understanding. Relax and arrange another meeting if you feel the spark of attraction.

III. Interpersonal Communication Skills for Escalating and Maintaining Relationships

Initial interaction and attraction do not necessarily determine the success of a relationship, and many satisfying relationships remain at lower levels of intimacy. Relationships that have achieved intimacy are not static, and their maintenance requires skill and active effort. Your text identifies seven skills for maintaining intimate relationships.

(1) **Monitor your perceptions, listen actively, and respond**: consciously attend to the cues you receive from others, learn how they react in various situations, and shape your relationship maintenance behaviours accordingly. Be sensitive to biases and work to counterbalance them to avoid overreacting. Listening is crucial at all stages of a relationship. Even in long-term relationships, in which the partners know each other well, there are still new things to be heard and understood. Remember to provide confirming responses as part of your active listening.

(2) **Be open and self-disclose appropriately**: the appropriate level of self-disclosure depends in part on the level of the relationship. Both failure to disclose and disclosing the wrong thing at the wrong time can damage a relationship. Both partners must be open to offering and accepting disclosure while being sensitive to its timing. Restricting the amount of self-disclosure is one way to control the development of a relationship which you may feel is moving too quickly.

(3) **Express emotions:** sharing feelings at appropriate times is one way to escalate a relationship. Sharing the wrong feelings at the wrong times can be detrimental. We share emotions in two ways: (1) either directly or (2) by disclosing information about past or current emotional states. We expect emotional self-disclosure to increase with increases in intimacy. The risks involved in self-disclosure vary from person to person. Most people share negative emotions of fear and disappointment less easily than positive emotions. While a constant barrage of negative expressions can alienate a partner, some expression of negative emotions is necessary and appropriate. A balance must be found. Studies do show that marital satisfaction rises with the number of positive feelings the partners disclose.

(4) **Develop and apply communication sensitivity:** communication sensitivity requires awareness of and appreciation for all the dynamics of an interpersonal interaction. People who have a willingness to adapt in different situations and who have sensitivity and perceptiveness about themselves and others are called **rhetorically sensitive**. They (1) avoid stylized behaviour, (2) have an ability to manage the strains involved in adapting, (3) make placating comments when appropriate, and (4) appreciate the multiple ways ideas and feelings can be communicated. People who tend to be inflexible and who refuse to adapt are called **noble selves**. Noble selves "call it like they see it." People would mold themselves to whatever a situation dictates or to whatever others want are called **rhetorical reflectors.** Noble selves are like rocks; no one can move them. Rhetorical reflectors are like mirrors; you only see yourself in them. In contrast to these two types, **conversationally sensitive** people are able and willing to pick up meanings in what people say, remember what is said, have a desire to listen, are sensitive to levels of liking and power in interactions, and appreciate subtleties. They also know there are many ways to say a thing and that one way may work when another fails. There are many arrows in their quill.

(5) **Be tolerant and show restraint**: most satisfying relationships avoid continual disagreements, criticism, and negative remarks. Well-adjusted couples focus complaints on specific behaviours; maladjusted couples complain about one another's personal characteristics. Maintaining a relationship requires tolerance. Partners must learn to accept each other and live with some things they dislike about each other. Disclosing negative feelings about your partner selectively rather than indiscriminately can contain conflicts.

(6) **Manage conflict cooperatively:** avoidance of conflict altogether is not possible so effective management should be a common goal. Cooperative management can help strengthening relationships by unlocking conflict's potential for clarifying relationship dynamics and increasing information flow.

(7) **Seek compliance**: we use persuasive strategies to accomplish our goals when we want others to comply with our wishes. Seeking compliance from another person involves a responsibility not to exploit others and raises four ethical issues: (1) To what degree is it ethical to manipulate others to further self-interest? (2) Is the ability to gain compliance exploitative? (3) Is it ever ethical to lie or deceive another to achieve one's own goals? (4) Are threats and punishment ever ethical ways of achieving compliance?

IV. Identifying and Acting upon Trouble Signs in Relationships

Women usually sense trouble in a relationship earlier than men. Specific verbal and nonverbal cues indicate relationship de-escalation: (1) *decreases* in touching, physical contact, proximity, eye contact, smiling, tonal variety in voice, ease of interaction, and use of personal language, and (2) *increases* in time between interactions and separation of possessions. Trouble signs for couples also include (1) using fewer intimate terms, (2) using the past tense more often than the present tense, (3) making fewer references to the future in the relationship, (4) using qualified and hedging language ("maybe," "whatever"), (5) making fewer evaluative statements, and (6) spending less time discussing a given topic. These signs accompany a general increase in conflict and concomitant decrease in disclosure.

There are three responses to trouble signs: (1) wait and see what happens, (2) decide to end the relationship, or (3) try to repair the relationship. Repair is only possible if both partners in a relationship desire it. Professional counselling may be part of a repair process.

There are three questions to consider in ending a relationship: (1) Do you want to continue the relationship at a less intimate level or terminate it? (2) Do you care enough about the other person to want to preserve his or her self-esteem? (3) Are you aware of the costs involved in ending the relationship?

When someone has ended a relationship with you, it is best, if possible, to have a focussed discussion about what contributed to his or her decision. By doing this, you may acquire information you need to repair the relationship or that may help you in future relationships.

V. De-escalating and Ending Relationships

No relationship ever comes completely to an end because each has a lasting impact. De-escalation and termination may be beneficial if a relationship is harmful, or if it no longer provides confirmation of self or satisfies interpersonal needs. Breaking up an intimate relationship is hard because self-concepts are involved. The most satisfying breakups are those which confirm both partners' worth rather than degrade it. If both partners agree to dissolve a relationship, the process is **bilateral dissolution** and involves little more than dividing possessions and discussing details. If only one partner wants to dissolve the relationship, the process is **unilateral dissolution** and may require the use of compliance-seeking skills to get the other partner to accept and agree to the termination.

VI. How Relationships End

A declining relationship usually follows one of three paths:

(1) **The relationship fades away** – partners simply drift apart gradually.

(2) The relationship terminates in **sudden death** – some single precipitating evident ends the relationship such as death, desertion, infidelity, major conflict, or other major violation.

(3) The relationship succumbs to **incrementalism** – conflicts and problems accumulate until they achieve critical mass making the relationship intolerable and leading to breakup

There are two major approaches to ending a relationship: (1) **indirect strategies** and (2) **direct strategies**. Which approach is used depends on (1) the level of intimacy in relationship, (2) the level of desire to help the partner save face, (3) the degree of urgency for terminating the relationship, and (4) the person's interpersonal skill.

Indirect strategies seek to end a relationship without explicitly stating a desire to do so and include three distinct varieties: (1) withdrawal, (2) pseudo-de-escalation, and (3) cost escalation. Indirect strategies are used more frequently by men than women.

(1) *Withdrawal* involves reducing the amount of contact and interaction without offering any explanation. This strategy is most dissatisfying for the other partner. Withdrawal represents a desire to avoid a confrontational scene and to save face.

(2) *Pseudo-de-escalation* involves one partner's claim that he or she wants to redefine a relationship at a lower level of intimacy while really wanting to end it. Sometimes both partners may engage in mutual pseudo-de-escalation to hide from themselves and each other a more painful and emotionally demanding termination.

(3) *Cost escalation* involves one partner's attempt to increase the costs associated with a relationship in an effort to force the other partner to terminate. One partner may make inordinate demands, pick fights, criticize excessively, or otherwise violate relational rules in an effort to "price out" the other.

Direct strategies seek an explicit end to relationships and include four distinct varieties: (1) negative identity management, (2) justification, (3) de-escalation, and (4) positive tone.

(1) *Negative identity management* involves a direct statement of a desire to terminate. It does not take into account the feelings of the other and may include criticism.

(2) *Justification* is a clear statement of the desire to end a relationship accompanied by an honest explanation of the reasons. One researcher found that most people on the receiving end like this strategy best.

(3) *De-escalation* is an honest statement of a desire to redefine the relationship at a lower level of intimacy or to move toward termination. This may take the form of a request for a trial separation.

(4) *Positive tone* is the direct strategy most sensitive to the other person's sense of self. This strategy may seem contradictory because it affirms the other while seeking to end a relationship with him or her.

The reasons for ending relationships are as varied as relationships themselves, but most relationships end when their costs exceed their benefits. Your text compares relationships to a savings account at a bank: (1) if the relationship is profitable (emotionally satisfying), we deposit the excess rewards in an emotional savings account, (2) if the costs exceed the rewards, we draw on the account to cover the deficit, (3) if this continues, and the savings run out, we may close the account, (4) if we foresee future benefits, we may leave the account open even when it is overdrawn, and (5) if we have no other options for investment, we may decide to "stick it out." Under the circumstances of (5), relationships often end in sudden death when a better prospect comes along.

One researcher suggests that people attribute breakups to three main causes: (1) faults, (2) unwillingness to compromise, and (3) feeling constrained.

Faults are the number one cause of breakup and are personality traits or behaviours that one partner dislikes in the other.

Unwillingness to compromise represents a variety of failings on the part of one or both partners, including failure to put enough effort into the relationship or failure to make concessions for the good of the relationship.

Feeling constrained reflects one partner's desire to be free from commitments and restraints.

A variety of other factors may contribute to the breakup of both romantic and nonromantic feelings, including loss of interest in the other person, desire for independence, and conflicting attitudes about the definition of the relationship in areas such as sexual conduct, marriage, and infidelity.

Steve Duck has developed a model to show stages in ending a relationship. The model outlines four key stages, each preceded by a transitional threshold: (1) intra-psychic stage, (2) dyadic stage, (3) social phase, and (4) grave-dressing stage.

Intra-psychic stage involves evaluating a partner's behaviours often fixing on reasons to justify withdrawal. Thoughts about terminating a relationship at this stage are not likely to be acted on but may be leaked to a partner through emotional displays of hostility, anxiety, stress, irritability, or guilt. Seeking the confidence of an outside or third party is common at this stage.

Dyadic stage involves openly confronting a partner with a desire to end a relationship. The partner seeking to end the relationship may have to justify his or her thoughts and feelings and may be exposed to criticism from the other partner. Issues may then be raised which lead to a reevaluation of the relationship and the cost of ending it. Repair efforts may be undertaken.

Social stage involves mutual agreement to dissolve relationship and make decision public by informing friends, who may then move to shore up the relationship by acting as mediators or hasten its dissolution by spreading rumours and compounding criticism.

Grave-dressing stage involves management of hurt and pain resulting from termination. Couples may seek to "place flowers on the grave" of their relationship. Each partner needs a public account of the demise of their relationship to share with friends and relations. Such an account often casts blame on the other partner. In this stage, we may be encouraged to resume social activities (e.g., "arranged dates"). Most importantly, we go through a process of letting go of guilt and shame and other feelings of anger and sorrow.

TERMS TO LEARN

Terms
Relational Development
Turning Point
Relational Escalation
Relational De-escalation
Communication Sensitivity
Rhetorical Sensitivity
Noble Self
Rhetorical Reflector
Conversational Sensitivity
Compliance Seeking
Bilateral Dissolution
Unilateral Dissolution
Fading Away
Sudden Death
Incrementalism
Direct Relational Termination Strategies
Indirect Relational Termination Strategies
Intra-psychic Phase
Dyadic Phase
Social Phase
Grave-Dressing Phase

Activity 10.1: Starting Relationships

Objective:
1. To increase your understanding of strategies for starting relationships.

Part 1
Instructions:
1. Reflect on a relationship that you have started recently.
2. Analyze it according to the following categories.

   1. Gathering information to reduce uncertainty.
   2. Adopting an other-oriented perspective.
   3. Observing and acting upon approachability clues.
   4. Identifying and using conversation starters.
   5. Following initiation norms.
   6. Providing information about yourself.
   7. Presenting yourself in a positive way.
   8. Asking questions.
   9. Not putting too much into the initial interaction.

Gathering information to reduce uncertainty:
Adopting an other-oriented perspective:
Observing and acting upon approachability clues:

Identifying and using conversation starters:
Following initiation norms:
Providing information about yourself:
Presenting yourself in a positive way:
Asking questions:
Not putting too much into the initial interaction:

Part 2
Instructions:

1. Roleplay the start of this relationship with a partner.

2. Have an observer give you feedback.

Activity 10.2: Relational Development
Objective: 1. To identify and recognize the dynamics of relationship development.
Instructions: 1. In the examples below explore relational development using the following questions.
Who is more interested in the other?
How equal is the power between the two?
Who discloses the most?
Is the disclosure appropriate?
Are they moving toward or away from intimacy?

1. Marge met Nathan in a communications class at school. They were evening students in their late twenties. They were assigned to the same small group in class. In the first three weeks of the course there were various getting-acquainted exercises so there were opportunities to get to know each other better. Nathan had recently been through a divorce. He was still raw from this experience and feeling quite vulnerable. On the first night that Mary met him in class she was partnered with him for an interview. At that first meeting he poured out his story to Mary, the pain of the divorce, his loneliness. Mary was overwhelmed by this and did not know how to respond. She was not comfortable disclosing as much to Nathan. Each week Nathan seemed to turn to her for support and comfort. He always wanted to talk about his problems. She did feel some sympathy for his problems and somewhat reluctantly agreed to talk to him outside of class. They met a couple of times at a nearby coffee shop. However, Mary's discomfort only increased. She found herself looking for excuses not to have to speak with him. At the end of class she would hurry away with the excuse that she had to meet a friend.

Who is more interested in the other?
How equal is the power between the two?

Who discloses the most?
Is the disclosure appropriate?
Are they moving toward or away from intimacy?

2. Pamela and Jacob, aged 43 and 42 respectively, met at a conference in Vienna in early August. They attended each other's presentations and at the end of the conference spent a day touring the city with a few others. By the end of the day they had wandered off by themselves and spent the evening in a small street café. They shared some of their lives with each other. They had both endured difficult divorces in the last few years and had children who lived apart from them. They parted at 11:00 p.m. for their respective hotels but agreed to get seats together on the plane back to the U.S. the next day. On the plane they sat together for more than eight hours. They disclosed more about themselves. As they parted in the Newark airport, Jacob reached out and clasped Pamela's hand. As he squeezed it, he said, "Keep in touch." Pamela caught her connector flight to Toronto and Jacob headed for his home in Arizona. For the next several weeks they corresponded through e-mail. At first they would write every few days but gradually the messages became more frequent until they were writing twice a day. Jacob invited Pamela to visit him in Arizona. In October she arrived for a five-day weekend.

Who is more interested in the other?
How equal is the power between the two?
Who discloses the most?
Is the disclosure appropriate?
Are they moving toward or away from intimacy?

Activity 10.3: Stages in Relationship

Objective:

1. To understand the different stages in a relationship.

Instructions:

1. Explore what stages the relationships in the following examples have moved through and what stage they are in now. Discuss why. What are your predictions for the next stage the relationship may enter? Discuss why.
2. Use the stages identified in your text: pre-interaction awareness, initiation, exploration, intensification, intimacy, turmoil, stagnation, de-intensification, individualization, separation, post-interaction effects stage.

Example:

1. *Joan, a colleague at work, confides in you about a personal problem. Until now your encounters have been purely professional. You work well together and have a good rapport with each other. She discloses to you that her twin brother has terminal cancer. You lost a sister to cancer five years ago and can empathize with her situation. You suggest that you both meet for lunch one day and talk about it further. Over the next few weeks you begin meeting for lunch twice a week.*

   Stages: *The relationship has moved through the first two stages -- pre-interaction awareness and initiation -- and is in the stage of exploration . We are sharing more in-depth information about ourselves but are confining our interactions at this point to work and lunch. It may soon move into the stage of intensification. We share a common bond and through personal disclosure we are deepening our bond. There is a natural inclination to want to spend more time together.*

1. Mike and Jack have been dating for one year. They spend weekends together, usually at Jack's apartment. Lately, they have begun to talk about moving in together. Mike has two cats. Jack is severely allergic to cats and they both realize that if they are to live together the cats will have to go. Mike says he will put an ad up at work to try to find them a new home but he keeps forgetting. When he finally does advertise, he is never satisfied with prospective owners. Three months have gone by when Jack finally explodes with, "I think you like your cats more than me!" Mike responds with, "I think we just need to move more slowly. Perhaps it is too soon to live together. Maybe we should try spending a few weekends apart to see if we really miss each other." Jack says, "Sounds to me like you are moving away or are you just scared?"

Mike replies, "I guess I'm just scared. You know, I've never lived with anyone before. But I really do love you. So let's give it a shot. Oh, and by the way, Mary down the hall from me says she'll take the cats. I think she'll give them a good home."

Stages:

2. Eileen, aged 38, and Trevor, aged 36, met ten months ago. They have been dating steadily since then. At Christmas they went on a holiday together to the Caribbean. Eileen is a psychologist and Trevor is a lawyer. They are both committed to their careers; however, Eileen has also realized that having children is an important goal in her life. The biological clock is ticking, and she knows she needs to act on this soon. When she broaches the subject with Carl he is evasive: "I like the idea of children. I just don't know if I have what it takes to raise them. I can't make that kind of commitment now." Eileen loves Carl but knows that the issue of children is an important one to her. She suggests that they spend less time together and consider dating others.

Stages:

3. Ashvin and Sandy were married for ten years. Two years ago they were divorced. Sandy had been dissatisfied in the marriage for several years. Ashvin had a career that entailed considerable travelling. He was rarely home. Alone most of the time with two young children, Sandy felt lonely and neglected. Three years ago she met a teacher, John, at her son's school. They began a friendship which gradually became more intimate. This contributed to the end of her marriage. She and John were married within a few months of her divorce. Ashvin and Sandy have shared custody of their children and speak weekly about childcare issues. Ashvin still harbours a deep sense of betrayal and hurt and these discussions are often heated.

Stages:

4. Kamal and Kathy have been living together for two years. When they finish their graduate degrees they plan to get married. Two months ago Kamal's best friend at work, Ian, went through a very difficult divorce. His wife left him and retained custody of their two children. Ian is living alone in a one bedroom apartment struggling with his pain and loneliness. In the last month Kamal has been spending more and more time with Ian to offer him support. It started with drinks after work, turned into dinners, and then late nights. Some nights Kamal doesn't make it home at all. This week he announced to Kathy that he and Ian were going away on a skiing trip for the weekend. Kathy burst into tears at this announcement.

Stages:

Activity 10.4: Escalating and Maintaining Relationships

Objective:
1. To help you explore strategies for escalating and maintaining relationships.

Part 1
Instructions:
1. Consider how would you escalate and maintain the relationships described in the following examples.

Example:

You and Irene are teachers who have been working on organizing a large international conference on education together. You are co-chairs of the planning committee. You meet at biweekly meetings for almost two years. On occasion, the two of you meet for dinner meetings at a local restaurant. Here the conversation sometimes turns to more personal matters. You find you share many common understandings and life experiences. You are both mothers who have experienced divorce. You have each studied relaxation and visualization techniques and have integrated this into your classroom practice.

Escalating: *We could escalate the relationship by disclosing more about ourselves. I can also express how much I value our connection. Irene's insights have lent a greater perspective to my own understandings. I can tell her how much I appreciate her empathic responses. At times when conference planning becomes hectic we need to be tolerant of each other's frustrations.*

Maintaining: *When the conference is over I would like to continue our dinner meetings. I am going to suggest this. We are both going to need some support after the conference because it has been such an intense and positive experience. It will be hard to lose this. We will need to listen to each other as we let go of this. No one else can really understand what this has been like for us. We also need to recognize that we may need to give more attention to other areas of our life and respect each other's boundaries. If we see less of each other it will be important not to take it personally. Perhaps we can explore new projects that we might do together.*

1. You met Joan in a class you share at school. You have bumped into each other a few times in the library. Last week you were absent from class. On your return Joan offered to share her lecture notes with you. You would like to get to know her better.

Escalating:
Maintaining:

2. You have recently begun a rigorous exercise program at your local gym. You had several sessions with a trainer, Bill, when you started your program. These ended about two months ago. You frequently bump into him at the gym and he always asks how you are doing. Recently, he suggested you meet for coffee sometime to discuss your progress. You are attracted to him and would like to get to know him better.

Escalating:
Maintaining:

3. A casual friend, Frank, whom you have known for several years and who has recently been divorced, begins to ask you out for coffee. You were divorced several years ago and can empathize with his situation. Soon coffee leads to dinner. Over dinner one evening he discloses to you that he is very attracted to you and would like to begin dating. You feel awkward about this because you value his friendship but don't feel what you would need to feel to take the relationship to a romantic level. You have also

recently begun a long-distance relationship which seems to have a potential to develop into a long-term relationship. You tell Frank about this new relationship while stressing the importance of the friendship that you and he share. He respects your honesty and stresses that even if he can't consider a romantic relationship he wants to continue the friendship and have dinner occasionally.

Escalating:
Maintaining:

4. While completing your masters degree at university you have developed a professional relationship with one of your professors. You are both women. She has been intrigued by your research and has helped you in the writing of your thesis. After you finish your degree, she suggests you meet for breakfast to discuss your work. The conversation eventually moves from professional talk to a greater degree of disclosure on a personal level. You discuss relationship issues with regard to your respective partners. You appreciate her confidences. At the same time you know that you are contemplating further graduate work and would like her continued professional support. You begin to meet every couple of weeks for breakfast or lunch. On a few occasions she invites you to her home. You never invite her to yours.

Escalating:
Maintaining:

Part 2

Instructions:

1. Give an example of a relationship in your own life and discuss strategies that you might use to escalate and maintain the relationship.

Relationship:
Escalating:
Maintaining:

DIFFICULT POSITION 10

Sheena and Richard are both employees of a large insurance agency. Richard is a manager of assessors and Sheena works in accounting. Two years ago they met at an agency party. They gravitated toward one another immediately. Richard is a good listener, and Sheena had recently gone through some difficult personal problems. Her younger brother had died after a lingering illness, and she had felt drained and exhausted with grief. She needed someone to talk to. Over the course of a year their relationship deepened. Richard was always running upstairs to Sheena's desk with coffee and a donut or just to talk. They had lunch together most days, and Richard began driving Sheena home. One day Sheena's manager approached her and expressed her concern that the relationship with Richard was interfering with the work she needed to do. She noted that the staff had begun to talk about the relationship and had complained that neither Sheena nor Richard were available to their co-workers when they should be. This was a wake-up call for Sheena. She and Richard were both married, and while the relationship was platonic, she had begun to suspect that Richard's increasing attentions spoke to something more than friendship. While she felt attracted to Richard and grateful to him, she realized that she might need to distance herself for the sake of her job and marriage.

INSTRUCTIONS

1. Take this scenario and imagine an ending for it. Write out seven different versions using each of the *direct* and *indirect relational termination strategies*: (1) withdrawal, (2) pseudo-de-escalation, (3) cost escalation, (4) negative identity management, (5) justification, (6) de-escalation, and (7) positive tone. Be sure to imagine the sorts of things that could happen in each case and what both Sheena and Richard might feel and say. What advantages and disadvantages are part of each approach? If, as is reasonable to assume, Richard wants to maintain the relationship, what communication strategies might you use to do so?

2. What would you do in Sheena's situation? Would you choose to de-escalate or terminate? Explain your reasons.

Exercise 10.1: Learning Objective: General Review (**TRUE/FALSE**)

Instructions: Identify the following statements as either true or false.

1. Relationships escalate and de-escalate through the same series of stages. ( )

2. The most sensitive and adaptive communicators are called noble selves. ( )

3. Women favour indirect strategies to end relationships more than men. ( )

4. Both partners in a relationship can and may engage in pseudo-de-escalation. ( )

5. The initiation stage of relationship escalation begins the relational history. ( )

6. One of the best ways to start a conversation with a stranger is to come up with some clever deviation from scripted or ritual conversation formulas. ( )

7. A person's income and marital status are "free information" to use as conversation starters. ( )

8. Initial interactions determine the future of a relationship. ( )

9. Two people with weak emotional communication skills might establish a satisfying relationship. ( )

10. Expressing negative feelings is a number one problem of romantic couples. ( )

11. Abrupt endings to relationships are commonly motivated by a desire to spare the feelings of those who are being left behind. ( )

12. Three out of the four stages of Steve Duck's model of relationship termination are preceded by a transitional threshold. ( )

13. The intra-psychic phase of ending a relationship has no outward manifestations. ( )

14. In the grave-dressing phase of relationship ending, friends act as mediators trying to preserve a relationship. ( )

15. "Positive tone" as a direct strategy for ending relationships may seem contradictory to those on the receiving end. ( )

16. Incrementalism is the technical name for relational fading. ( )

Exercise 10.2: Learning Objective: General Review (**FILL-IN-THE-BLANKS**)

Instructions: Fill in the blanks using the appropriate term or terms from the following list.

relationship development	rhetorical sensitivity	fading away	indirect relational termination strategies
turning point	conversational sensitivity	sudden death	
relational escalation	compliance seeking	incrementalism	direct relational termination strategies
relational de-escalation	bilateral dissolution	noble self	
communication sensitivity	unilateral dissolution	rhetorical reflector	grave-dressing phase
	dyadic phase	social phase	intra-psychic phase

1. "That's just the way I see it," he said over and over again. There's just no getting through to him. He's a real ________________ and inflexible as granite.

2. Romeo and Juliet agreed to end their relationship which had caused their families so much distress. Instead of getting married secretly, they decided on________________ and met at Friar Lawrence's cell to divide up their things.

3. "Whatever you say," he kept saying. I thought he was being sarcastic, but I realize now that if I asked him to jump out a window, he might do it. He is the most extreme example of ________________ I have ever seen, a real chameleon.

4. ________________ is an awareness and appreciation of all the dynamics of an interpersonal interaction, and ________________ is the ability and willingness to adapt to those dynamics and the sensitivity to understand yourself and others in various interaction situations.

5. When Hamlet told Ophelia to go to a nunnery and never trouble him again, and when he left her distracted and in tears without listening to her pleas, it was clearly a ________________ of their relationship.

6. Moving from *initiation* to *exploration* is one step in________________.

7. Moving from *separation* to *post-interaction effects* is one step in________________.

8. Moving from *initiation* to *exploration* and from *separation* to *post-interaction effects* are collectively steps in the overall process of ________________.

9. Moving from an *exploration* to an *intensification* stage marked a ________________ in their relationship that they talked about for weeks.

10. He kept telling me how much better I would be without him and how much he would respect and appreciate me for letting him out of his promise. I knew he was really ________________with a vengeance, and I guess it worked because I let him off.

11. Mary told me the whole story of her unhappy marriage and divorce, and she made it clear that Brad was the cause of their problems. This is her public story anyway, and I recognize that it's part of the ______________________ described by Steve Duck.

12. After years of marriage and three children born, raised, and now moved away, Tom and Sylvia started to go their separate ways, and after awhile they hardly spent a day together. Their relationship was _________________ before their eyes, but neither made a move to stop it.

13. When King Arthur was confronted with the undeniable fact of Queen Guinevere's adulterous love for Sir Lancelot, he consented to her being burned alive at the stake. Her infidelity caused a ____________ ending to the royal relationship.

14. We admitted to our friends that we were breaking up, and right away, they started taking sides and spreading stories about it. I think we both secretly hoped that in this _____________ of our relationship our friends would act as mediators and help us stay together.

15. Paul Simon's famous song called *Fifty Ways to Leave Your Lover* describes men running away from relationships without offering any explanation. The fifty ways are really only one way – abrupt withdrawal. Simon's fifty ways are just examples of the most basic of the ____.

16. Wendy told Trevor he was a great sport, a fine father, a good citizen, and a noble friend, but she didn't want to see him anymore. Trevor was confused, he felt flattered but wondered what could possibly make Wendy want to break off their relationship if he were really such a wonderful fellow as she said. Unfortunately Trevor had not read *Interpersonal Communication* and did not recognize this as a "positive tone" example of______________________________.

17. Brian spent hours and hours in the ___________________________ thinking to himself about all that Marian did that justified his wanting out. Later, in the difficult _________________ , when she confronted him with his own failings, he started to reconsider whether ending things with Marian was worth the cost of going it alone yet again. It was true, he never had much _______________________ as Marian said. He never understood the subtle meanings of what people were trying to say and forgot most of what was said anyway. What was worse, he could never think of but one way to say anything even if it seemed insulting or hurtful to others. Maybe he was lucky Marian put up with him at all.

Exercise 10.3: Learning Objective: General Review (**MULTIPLE CHOICE**)

Instructions: Choose the best answer for each question below.

1. Persons who adapt everything they say to the desire of others are called

   a. compliance seekers
   b. noble selves
   c. rhetorically sensitive
   d. rhetorical reflectors

2. The technical term for relationships ending as a result of accumulated conflicts and difficulties is

   a. incrementalism
   b. unilateral dissolution
   c. relational de-escalation
   d. cost escalation

3. When someone deliberately increases his or her demands on a relationship partner in an effort to drive that partner out of a relationship, we have an instance of

   a. compliance seeking
   b. bilateral dissolution
   c. stagnation
   d. cost escalation

4. Preparing a public story to share with friends and relations about the end of a relationship is a part of

   a. the social phase
   b. the grave-dressing phase
   c. the pseudo-de-escalation stage
   d. negative identity management

5. The relationship stage in which friends may act as mediators to bolster a troubled relationship is known as

   a. the dyadic phase
   b. intra-psychic phase
   c. social phase
   d. window-dressing phase

6. Using persuasive means to obtain one's own end against resistance is an instance of

   a. rhetorical reflection
   b. pseudo-de-escalation
   c. negative identity management
   d. compliance seeking

7. All of the following are trouble signs in relationships except

   a. couples use fewer intimate terms
   b. couples use the past tense in conversation more than the present tense
   c. couples use more qualified language
   d. couples use immediacy cues to express dissatisfaction

8. All of the following statements are true except

   a. intimate relationships require less maintenance
   b. the intra-psychic phase may be "leaked" despite an individual's wish to hide it
   c. negative identity management is used to handle expression of negative emotions
   d. people often find it easier to self-disclose positive feelings than negative ones

9. All of the following are stages in relational de-escalation except

   a. turmoil
   b. separation
   c. de-intensification
   d. post-stress

10. All of the following statements about relationships are true except

    a. bilateral dissolution requires mutual use of compliance seeking to achieve
    b. we continue in a relationship simply because we have no better prospect
    c. feeling constrained is often cited as one cause for ending a relationship
    d. pseudo-de-escalation can be a unilateral or bilateral process

11. All of the following statements about direct relational termination strategies are true except

    a. evidence suggests that the justification strategy is most preferred by those on the receiving end
    b. the positive tone strategy is the most considerate of the other person's feelings
    c. negative identity management does not take account of the other person's feelings
    d. de-escalation disguises a wish to terminate a relationship completely

Answers

CHAPTER 10

Exercise 10.1

1. (F)
2. (F)
3. (F)
4. (T)
5. (T)
6. (F)
7. (F)
8. (F)
9. (T)
10. (T)
11. (F)
12. (F)
13. (F)
14. (F)
15. (T)
16. (F)
17. (F)

Exercise 10.2

1. Noble self
2. Bilateral dissolution
3. Rhetorical reflector
4. Communication sensitivity/ rhetorical sensitivity
5. Unilateral dissolution
6. Relational escalation
7. Relational de-escalation
8. Relationship development
9. Turning point
10. Compliance seeking
11. Grave-dressing phase
12. Fading away
13. Sudden death
14. Social phase
15. Indirect relational termination strategies
16. Direct relational termination termination strategies
17. Intra-psychic stage/dyadic stage/conversational sensitivity

Exercise 10.3

1. d
2. a
3. d
4. b
5. c
6. d
7. d
8. c
9. d
10. a
11. d

Chapter 11

Relating to Family, Friends, and Colleagues

CHAPTER OUTLINE

I. Relating to Family

A. Families have changed since the 1950s

1. Divorce has dramatically increased
2. People are now waiting until later in life to marry
3. Common-law relationships have increased
4. Women's roles are changing
5. Family teamwork has given place to greater autonomy for family members
6. Increased mobility affects communication patterns

B. Family is a self-defined unit of individuals sharing a common living space who are often, although not always, united by marriage and kinship

C. Researcher Virginia Satir has identified four types of families

1. **Natural** – mother, father, and biological children
2. **Blended** – two adult parents and children of divorce, separation or adoption
3. **Single-Parent** – mostly women
4. **Extended** – aunts, uncles, cousins, grandparents and surrogate family members

D. Family of origin is the family in which you are raised no matter what type it is

E. A model for family interaction: **Circumplex Model of Family Interaction**

1. The model has three basic dimensions
   a. **Adaptability** is the family's ability to modify and respond to changes in its own power structure and roles – (ranges from chaotic to rigid)
   b. **Cohesion** is emotional bonding and feelings of togetherness – (ranges from enmeshed to disengaged)
   c. **Communication** is key to a family's ability to adapt to change

F. Improving Family Communication

1. Virginia Satir found several characteristics of healthy families
   a. members' sense of self-worth is high
   b. communication is direct, clear, specific, and honest
   c. rules are flexible, humane, and subject to change
   d. family's links to society are open and hopeful
   e. members listen actively (they look *at* not *through* each other)
   f. members treat children as people
   g. members touch one another affectionately regardless of age
   h. openly discuss negative (e.g., anger and fear) as well as positive feelings
2. Judy Pearson's book *Lasting Love: What Keeps Couples Together* identifies eight factors of marital satisfaction and stability

a. lowered expectations (realistic understanding of what marriage means)
b. unconditional acceptance of each other
c. seeing others in a positive way
d. viewing themselves as a united team
e. remaining separate
f. mutually satisfying sexual relations
g. skills to manage conflict
h. persistence

F. Take time to talk about relationships and feelings

1. Researcher Navaran found married couples who are satisfied take time to talk
    a. Talk over pleasant things that happened during the day
    b. Feel understood by spouse
    c. Discuss shared interests
    d. Avoid pouting and breaking off communication
    e. Talk with each other about personal problems
    f. Use words that have a private meaning for them
    g. Talk over most important things
    h. Are sensitive to each other's feelings and make adjustments to suit them
    i. Discuss issues without restraint or embarrassment
    j. Tell what type of day they had without being asked
    k. Intentionally communicate nonverbally
2. Active listening is vital (Chapter 4)
    a. Stop, look, listen, ask questions, reflect content and feelings, check perceptions

G. Support and encourage one another

1. Healthy families nurture one another
2. Parents have a special obligation to disclose responsibly to children
    a. Excessive negative and controlling feedback can cause damage
    b. Supportive messages lead to higher self-esteem
3. Researcher Jane Howard identifies ten aspects of "good" families
    a. They have a chief, heroine, or founder
    b. They have a switchboard operator
    c. They maintain strong bonds within the family
    d. They are hospitable
    e. They deal directly with stress and tragedy
    f. They cherish family rituals and traditions
    g. They express affection in a meaningful way to other members
    h. They have a sense of place
    i. They find some way to connect with future generations
    j. They honour elders
4. Use productive strategies for managing conflict, stress, and change
    a. Too often parents resort to violence
    b. Managing conflict with siblings is a challenge

(1) sibling conflicts have a special intensity
   (a) we drop our guard in the privacy and security of a family
   (b) we often communicate with family members when we are tired and stressed, so emotions are less controlled

c. John Gottman identifies four warning signs of communication behaviour
   (1) criticism: attacking personality
   (2) contempt: intentional insult, verbal and nonverbal
   (3) defensiveness: denying responsibility and making excuses
   (4) stonewalling: withdrawing, not responding, being minimally engaged

d. Gottman recommends ten ways for managing couple conflict
   (1) pick your battles
   (2) schedule discussions
   (3) structure your conflicts
   (4) acknowledge partner's viewpoint
   (5) moderate your emotions
   (6) trust your partner and communicate nondefensively
   (7) soothe your partner
   (8) take stock in partnership
   (9) find the glory in your story as a couple
   (10) know when to get help or when to give up

II. Relating to Friends

A. Friendship is a relationship of choice

1. There are several ideals involved in friendship
   a. A friend will see you through after others see you are through
   b. A friend will tell you what you should know even if it offends momentarily
   c. A friend thinks of you when all others are thinking of themselves
   d. A friend stays with you even if he or she knows you well (warts and all)
   e. A friend lets you make a fool of yourself without thinking you a fool
2. Reasons for friendship
   a. Have an intimate talk
   b. Have a friend ask you to do something for him or her
   c. Go out to dinner in a restaurant
   d. Ask your friend to do something for you
   e. Have a meal together at home or at your friend's home
   f. Go to a movie, play, or concert
   g. Go drinking together
   h. Shop together
   i. Participate in sports
   j. Watch a sporting event
3. Friends help us in many ways
   a. Coping with stress – bolster self-esteem
   b. Physical needs – provide material help

c. Develop personality
d. Shape attitudes and beliefs
4. How many friends do we need?
a. Typically, people have five close friends, fifteen other friends, twenty or more members in a social network
5. Three factors determine the kind of love relationship we have with another
a. Intimacy (trust, caring, honesty, supportiveness, understanding, openness)
b. Commitment (loyalty, devotion, putting others first, needing one another)
c. Passion (romantic excitement, sexual passion, butterflies in the stomach)
6. Six categories classify types of love
a. **Eros** – sexual love based upon the pursuit of beauty and pleasure
b. **Ludis** – love as a game, something to pursue to pass the time
c. **Storge** – the love common to most friendships and between relatives
d. **Mania** – a relationship that swings wildly between extreme highs and lows
e. **Pragma** – practical relationships based on compatibility and interests
f. **Agape** – a spiritual ideal of love
7. Friendships at different stages of life
a. W. J. Dickens and D. Perlman examine friendship in four stages of life
(1) childhood friendships have five, sometimes overlapping, stages
(a) momentary playmates – ages three to seven
(b) one-way assistance – ages four to nine
(c) fair-weather friend – ages six to twelve
(d) mutual intimacy – ages nine to fifteen
(e) independence – ages twelve through adulthood
(2) adolescent friendships
(a) greater intimacy with our peers
(i) boys may join either socially acceptable or unacceptable gangs
(ii) girls begin to develop intimate relationships
(3) adult friendships
(a) among our most valued relationships
(b) adult friendships may dissolve for four reasons
(i) physical separation
(ii) new friends replace old
(iii) we dislike something our friend did
(iv) mate selection changes friendship
(4) the elderly and friendship
(a) the elderly make new friends but value old ones most
(b) there is more negative self-disclosure between elderly friends
(c) retired couples have fewer marital problems than younger couples
(d) the elderly express negative attitudes in conflicts less than younger individuals, unless issue is important; then they are more heated
b. Making friends
(1) encourage others to be your friend using conversation starters

(a) volunteer name and information about yourself
(b) make a comment or ask a question about the other person
(c) talk about where you are, the weather, something you both observe
(2) encourage others to be your friend by keeping a conversation going
(a) adapt to your listener
(b) remember what you talk about
(c) take turns initiating and responding
(d) don't talk excessively about yourself
(e) don't say anything to make the other devalue him or herself
(f) reveal information about yourself so the other can get to know you

c. Understand how friendships develop and grow
(1) Agyle and Henderson list five areas of conversation among friends
(a) social talk about events, jokes, mutual enjoyment of company
(b) gossip about others
(c) common interests
(d) sharing information and solving problems
(e) support and encouragement in times of stress

d. Losing friends
(1) Argyle and Henderson list ten friend-losing behaviours
(a) acting jealous or being critical of relationship
(b) discussing with others what your friend said in confidence
(c) not volunteering help in time of need
(d) not trusting or confiding in your friend
(e) criticizing your friend in public
(f) not showing positive regard for your friend
(g) not standing up for your friend in his or her absence
(h) not being tolerant of your friend's other friends
(i) not showing emotional support
(j) nagging your friend

III. Relating to Colleagues

A. One researcher estimates 98 percent of work problems are people problems

B. The number one skill in job performance is ability to communicate effectively
1. Speaking
2. Listening

C. Charles Redding recommends six minimum competencies for managers
1. Be an effective speaker and listener
2. Possess the ability to be an empathic listener and effective reader
3. Have an understanding of how corporate decisions are made
4. Identify the communication roles of both superiors and subordinates
5. Understand organization communication policies and programs
6. Develop a knowledge of how to communicate in various media and methods

D. There are three principal levels of workplace communication

1. **Upward communication** – communication from subordinates to superiors
    a. May be impeded by subordinates' apprehensions
    b. Lack of upward communication can damage an organization
    c. Subordinates often have most direct knowledge of products and customers
2. **Downward communication** - from superiors to subordinates
    a. Good managers develop and send other-oriented, ethical messages
    b. Bad managers indulge in egocentric abuse of legitimate power
    c. Sexual harassment may involve an abuse of power
        (1) encounters must be unsolicited and unwelcome to complainant
        (2) behaviour continues despite the complainant's protests and involves punitive actions against complainants
        (3) cooperation of complainant results from employment-related threats and promises
3. **Horizontal communication** – among co-workers at same level of organization
    a. Share plans and information, solve problems, manage conflicts, etc.
    b. Grapevine messages
    c. Quality circles discuss issues
        (1) services and products
        (2) ways to reduce mistakes and costs
        (3) ways to improve safety and work cooperation

E. Outward communication: Talking with customers
1. Successful organizations are other-oriented; they focus on customer needs

F. Enhancing leadership skills
1. The essence of leadership is the ability to influence others
2. First qualification of leadership is knowledge about the task at hand
3. Managers also require ability to motivate, inspire, and instruct
4. Author Stephen Covey lists *Seven Habits of Highly Effective People*
    a. Be proactive: Don't wait until situation becomes a problem
    b. Begin with the end in mind: Effective people envision goals
    c. Put first things first: Manage your time so you can manage your life
    d. Think win/win: Don't assume someone must lose and someone win
    e. Seek first to understand, then to be understood: Listen effectively
    f. Synergize: Working together may be more creative than working alone
    g. Sharpen the saw: periodically enhance skills
5. Most effective leaders combine task and relationship orientation
6. There are eight task functions
    a. *Initiate* new ideas and approaches to achieving the task
    b. *Provide information*, such as facts, examples, statistics
    c. *Seek information* by asking for facts and data that can help do the job
    d. *Seek opinions* and ask for clarification of opinions expressed by others
    e. *Offer opinions* about issues and ideas under consideration
    f. *Elaborate* and amplify the ideas of others

g. *Evaluate* advantages and disadvantages of issues, ideas, solutions
h. *Energize* and motivate the group to take action and be productive

7. There are four relationship functions
   a. *Encourage* others and offer praise and acceptance of others' ideas
   b. *Harmonize* and mediate disagreements and conflict
   c. *Compromise* and seek ways of finding common ground among group members
   d. *Be a gatekeeper* by encouraging less talkative members to participate and limiting orations from big talkers

G. Enhancing followership skills
1. Seek opportunities to provide input and suggestions
2. Listen well
3. Provide appropriate feedback
4. Support suggestions with evidence
5. Don't abandon ethical principles

H. Technology and workplace communication
1. Our homes are increasingly also our workplaces
2. The pace at which we use technology to help us work will quicken
3. Some workers are reluctant to embrace new technologies ("cyberphobic")
4. Women tend to fear technology more than men
5. Computers and modems have had most effect on workplace communication
6. We tend to use electronic media selectively for workplace communication
   a. The more positive the message, the more immediate the media we use
   b. We prefer mediated communication (e-mail) when we need to communicate data and content-rich messages
   c. Mediated messages work best if a task is highly structured or involves many steps
   d. Groups who use video conferences and e-mail messages are more likely to have polarized opinions than those who meet face to face
   e. Groups and individuals will be more productive if they have tech support and training
   f. Use of sophisticated technology does not necessarily result in improved quality
   g. In future, people will still solve complex issues and problems face to face

CHAPTER REVIEW: SECTION BY SECTION SUMMARY

I. Relating to Family

Chapter 11 of your text differs significantly from preceding chapters. New information is provided but much of the chapter is review and application of principles outlined in earlier chapters, notably Chapters 4, 5 and 6. The new information is presented in a series of lists, and this summary will compress and highlight these lists.

Families have changed dramatically over the last half century. Divorce, postponed marriage, common-law relationships, and single parenting have all increased. The family as a survival unit focussed on production, like the farm families of the past, has been replaced by consumer families allowing considerable autonomy to family members. Family members are often separated by distance.

The definition of "family" has consequently changed. Your text suggests that "a family is a family if it thinks it is a family." Virginia Satir identifies four types of family: (1) natural, (2) blended, (3) single-parent, and (4) extended.

VIRGINA SATIR'S FOUR FAMILY TYPES

1. Natural families – a mother and father and their biological children – less common now -- sometimes called an idealized natural family.
2. Blended families -- two parents with children – because of divorce, separation, death, or adoption, the children may be the product of other biological parents.
3. Single-parent families – mostly women – sometimes voluntary but not often.
4. Extended family – a family with several generations together – aunts, uncles, cousins, grandparents, and surrogate members not related by marriage or kinship.

Family of origin is the family you are raised in no matter what type it is.

The Circumplex Model of Family Interaction is a graph with three basic dimensions: (1) adaptability, (2) cohesion, and (3) communication.

THE CIRCUMPLEX MODEL'S THREE DIMENSIONS OF FAMILY INTERACTION

1. Adaptability is a family's ability to modify and respond to changes in its own power structure and roles. Adaptability ranges from chaotic to rigid.
2. Cohesion refers to the emotional bonding and feeling of togetherness in a family. Cohesion ranges from enmeshed to disengaged.
3. Communication is the key to successful adaptation and strong cohesion.

Families with balanced levels of cohesion and adaptability function better across entire family life cycle.

VIRGINIA SATIR'S EIGHT CHARACTERISTICS OF HEALTHY FAMILIES

1. members' sense of self-worth is high
2. communication is direct, clear, specific, and honest
3. rules are flexible, humane, and subject to change
4. family's links to society are open and hopeful
5. members listen actively (they look *at* not *through* each other)
6. members treat children as people
7. members touch one another affectionately regardless of age
8. openly discuss negative (e.g., anger and fear) as well as positive feelings

JUDY PEARSON'S EIGHT FACTORS OF MARITAL SATISFACTION AND STABILITY FROM *LASTING LOVE: WHAT KEEPS COUPLES TOGETHER*

1. lowered expectations (realistic understanding of what marriage means)
2. unconditional acceptance of each other
3. seeing others in a positive way
4. viewing themselves as a united team
5. remaining separate
6. mutually satisfying sexual relations
7. skills to manage conflict
8. persistence

Effective listening is as important as effective talking. Review your listening skills outlined in Chapter 4.

FOUR BASIC ELEMENTS OF EFFECTIVE LISTENING

1. Stop, look, listen
2. ask questions
3. reflect content and feelings
4. check perceptions

RESEARCHER NAVARAN'S ELEVEN ASPECTS OF "TALK" IN HAPPY MARRIAGES

1. Talk over pleasant things that happened during the day
2. Feel understood by spouse
3. Discuss shared interests
4. Avoid pouting and breaking off communication
5. Talk with each other about personal problems
6. Use words that have a private meaning for them
7. Talk over most important things
8. Are sensitive to each other's feelings and make adjustments to suit them
9. Discuss issues without restraint or embarrassment
10. Tell what type of day they had without being asked
11. Intentionally communicate nonverbally

Healthy families are nurturing families. Parents especially have an obligation to disclose responsibly to their children. Too much negative and controlling feedback can cause permanent damage. Supportive messages can lead to higher self-esteem, more conformity to the wishes of parents, higher moral standards, and less aggressive and antisocial behaviour.

RESEARCHER JANE HOWARD'S TEN ASPECTS OF "GOOD" FAMILIES

1. They have a chief, heroine, or founder – someone around whom others cluster
2. They have a switchboard operator – someone who keeps track of who is doing what
3. They maintain strong bonds within the family, but have other group associations
4. They are hospitable
5. They deal directly with stress and tragedy
6. They cherish family rituals and traditions
7. They express affection in a meaningful way to other members
8. They have a sense of place
9. They find some way to connect with future generations
10. They honour elders

In family relationships, as in all relationships, it is important to manage stress, conflict and change. Parents too often resort to violence, as statistics indicate. Conflict with siblings can be challenging. Sibling conflicts have a special intensity, perhaps because we are unguarded in our home environments and frequently tired and stressed. Emotions may be less controlled in the home environment.

JOHN GOTTMAN'S FOUR WARNING SIGNS OF COMMUNICATION TROUBLE

1. criticism: attacking personality
2. contempt: intentional insult, verbal and nonverbal
3. defensiveness: denying responsibility and making excuses
4. stonewalling: withdrawing, not responding, being minimally engaged

GOTTMAN'S TEN RECOMMENDATIONS FOR MANAGING COUPLE CONFLICT

1. pick your battles
2. schedule discussions
3. structure your conflicts
4. acknowledge your partner's viewpoint
5. moderate your emotions
6. trust your partner and communicate nondefensively
7. Soothe your partner
8. take stock in partnership
9. find the glory in your story as a couple
10. know when to get help or when to give up

II. Relating to Friends and Lovers

FIVE IDEALS OF FRIENDSHIP

1. A friend will see you through after others see you are through
2. A friend will tell you what you should know even if it offends momentarily
3. A friend thinks of you when all others are thinking of themselves
4. A friend stays with you even though he or she knows you well (warts and all)
5. A friend lets you make a fool of yourself without thinking you a fool

PSYCHOLOGY TODAY'S TEN REASONS FOR FRIENDSHIP

1. Have an intimate talk
2. Have a friend ask you to do something for him or her
3. Go out to dinner in a restaurant
4. Ask your friend to do something for you
5. Have a meal together at home or at your friend's home
6. Go to a movie, play, or concert
7. Go drinking together
8. Shop together
9. Participate in sports
10. Watch a sporting event

Liking is different from love, of course. While friendships meet a wide range of physical and emotional needs, our most intimate relationships are commonly romantic ones.

THREE FACTORS OF LOVE RELATIONSHIPS

1. Intimacy (trust, caring, honesty, supportiveness, understanding, openness)
2. Commitment (loyalty, devotion, putting others first, needing one another)
3. Passion (romantic excitement, sexual passion, butterflies in the stomach)

SIX TYPES OF LOVE

1. Eros – sexual love based upon the pursuit of beauty and pleasure
2. Ludis – love as a game, something to pursue to pass the time
3. Storge – the love common to most friendships and between relatives
4. Mania – a relationship that swings wildly between extreme highs and lows
5. Pragma – practical relationships based on compatibility and interests
6. Agape – a spiritual ideal of love

The nature and number of our friendships differ at different times of life. Researchers W. J. Dickens and D. Perlman have examined differences among friendships at four stages in life: (1) childhood, (2) adolescence, (3) adulthood, and (4) old age.

CHILDHOOD FRIENDSHIPS

FIVE STAGES OF CHILDHOOD FRIENDSHIPS

1. momentary playmates – ages three to seven – interaction with those in immediate environment
2. one-way assistance – ages four to nine – viewing friendships from a "take" perspective
3. fair-weather friend – six to twelve – reciprocity occurs if things are going well but not otherwise
4. mutual intimacy – ages nine to fifteen – developing possessiveness
5. independence – twelve through adulthood – interdependence and independence balanced

ADOLESCENT FRIENDSHIPS

In adolescent friendships, we move away from relationships with our parents and other adults, to greater intimacy with our peers. In this stage, boys may join either socially acceptable or unacceptable gangs and girls begin to develop intimate relationships.

ADULT FRIENDSHIPS

FOUR REASONS WHY VALUED ADULT FRIENDSHIPS MAY DISSOLVE

1. physical separation
2. new friends replace old
3. we dislike something our friend did
4. mate selection changes friendship

ELDERLY FRIENDSHIPS

FOUR ASPECTS OF FRIENDSHIP AMONG THE ELDERLY

1. the elderly make new friends but value old ones most
2. there is more negative self-disclosure between elderly friends
3. retired couples have fewer marital problems than younger couples
4. the elderly express negative attitudes in conflicts less than younger individuals, unless issue is important; then they are heated and intense

To have friends we must make them. Making friends is a matter of using "friendship opportunities" available in our everyday activities. To develop a friendship with another person, you must show him or her something that will encourage interaction. One of the chief friendship builders is conversation.

NINE TIPS FOR CONVERSATION

1. volunteer name and information about yourself
2. make a comment or ask a question about the other person
3. talk about where you are, the weather, something you both observe
4. adapt to your listener
5. remember what you talk about
6. take turns initiating and responding
7. don't talk excessively about yourself
8. don't say anything to make the other devalue him or herself
9. reveal information about yourself so the other can get to know you

ARGYLE AND AYERS' FIVE MAJOR AREAS OF CONVERSATION

1. social talk about events, jokes,
2. gossip about others
3. common interests
4. sharing information and solving problems
5. support and encouragement in times of stress

If we can make friends by our own efforts, we can also lose them by neglect, indifference, or offensive behaviours.

ARGYLE AND AYERS' LIST OF TEN FRIENDSHIP-LOSING BEHAVIOURS

1. acting jealous or being critical of relationship
2. discussing with others what your friend said in confidence
3. not volunteering help in time of need
4. not trusting or confiding in your friend
5. criticizing your friend in public
6. not showing positive regard for your friend
7. not standing up for your friend in his or her absence
8. not being tolerant of your friend's other friends
9. not showing emotional support
10. nagging your friend

III. Relating to Colleagues

Researchers suggest that the most important skills in the workplace are communication skills: (1) good speaking and (2) effective listening.

CHARLES REDDING'S SIX MINIMUM COMPETENCIES FOR MANAGERS

1. Be an effective speaker and listener
2. Possess the ability to be an empathic listener and effective reader
3. Have an understanding of how corporate decisions are made
4. Identify the communication roles of both superiors and subordinates
5. Understand organization communication policies and programs
6. Develop a knowledge of how to communicate in various media and methods

Organizational communication flow has three distinct directions: (1) upward, (2) downward, (3) horizontal.

UPWARD COMMUNICATION

From subordinates up to superiors
May be impeded by subordinates' apprehensions
Lack of upward communication can damage an organization
Subordinates often have most direct knowledge of products and customers
DOWNWARD COMMUNICATION

From superiors to subordinates
Good managers develop and send other-oriented, ethical messages
Bad managers indulge in egocentric abuse of legitimate power
Sexual harassment may involve an abuse of power
HORIZONTAL COMMUNICATION
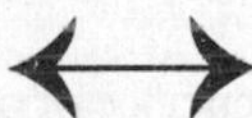
Among co-workers at same level organization
Share plans and information, solve problems, manage conflicts, etc.
Grapevine messages
Quality circles discuss issues
services and products
ways to reduce mistakes and costs
ways to improve safety and work cooperation
OUTWARD COMMUNICATION
Talking to and with customers about their needs and interests

AUTHOR STEPHEN COVEY'S *SEVEN HABITS OF HIGHLY EFFECTIVE PEOPLE*

1. Be proactive: Don't wait until situation becomes a problem
2. Begin with the end in mind: Effective people envision goals
3. Put first things first: Manage your time so you can manage your life
4. Think win/win: Don't assume someone must lose and someone win
5. Seek first to understand, then to be understood: Listen effectively
6. Synergize: Working together may be more creative than working alone
7. Sharpen the saw: periodically enhance skills

EIGHT TASK FUNCTIONS OF MANAGERS

1. Initiate new ideas and approaches to achieving the task
2. Provide information, such as facts, examples, statistics
3. Seek information by asking for facts and data that can help do the job
4. Seek opinions and ask for clarification of opinions expressed by others
5. Offer opinions about issues and ideas under consideration
6. Elaborate and amplify the ideas of others
7. Evaluate advantages and disadvantages of issues, ideas, solutions
8. Energize and motivate the group to take action and be productive

FOUR RELATIONSHIP FUNCTIONS OF MANAGERS

1. Encourage others and offer praise and acceptance of others' ideas
2. Harmonize and mediate disagreements and conflict
3. Compromise and seek ways of finding common ground among group members
4. Be a gatekeeper by encouraging less talkative members to participate

FIVE WAYS TO ENHANCE FOLLOWERSHIP SKILLS

1. Seek opportunities to provide input and suggestions
2. Listen well
3. Provide appropriate feedback
4. Support suggestions with evidence
5. Don't abandon ethical principles

Technology in the workplace has made tremendous changes, but many people are still reluctant to embrace the new technologies. These people are "cyberphobic." Women are more likely to be cyperphobic than men. The new technologies make it increasingly possible for us to work "at home" at our computers.

SEVEN ASPECTS OF NEW TECHNOLOGIES IN WORKPLACE COMMUNICATION

1. The more positive the message, the more immediate the media we use
2. We prefer mediated communication (e-mail) for communicating data and content-rich messages
3. Mediated messages work best if a task is highly structured or involves many steps
4. Groups who use video conferences and e-mail messages are more likely to have polarized opinions than those who meet face to face.
5. Groups and individuals will be more productive if they have tech support and training
6. Use of sophisticated technology does not necessarily result in improved quality
7. In future, people will still solve complex issues and problems face to face

TERMS TO LEARN

Family
Natural Family
Blended Family
Single-Parent Family
Extended Family
Family of Origin
Circumplex Model of Family Interaction
Family Adaptability
Family Cohesion
Family Communication
Eros
Ludis
Storge
Mania
Pragma
Agape
Upward Communication
Downward Communication
Sexual Harassment
Horizontal Communication
Outward Communication
Leadership
Electronic Message

Activity 11.1: Improving Family Communication

Objective:
1. To help you improve family communication.

Instructions:
1. In the next week practise the following skills in your family communication.

   take time to talk about the relationship and feelings
   listen actively and clarify meaning of message
   support and encourage
   use productive strategies for managing conflict, stress, and change

2. Record examples of interactions where you engaged in these behaviours on the chart below.

3. Answer the questions at the end of the exercise.

Interaction	Skills Used	Effect

What skills were most effective in your family interactions?

How did using these skills help your family communication?

What did you learn from this experience?

Activity 11.2: Communication Between Couples

Objective:

1. To help you understand the elements of satisfying communication behaviour between couples.

Part 1

Instructions:

1. In the following situations identify examples of unsatisfying communication between couples referring to the list on p. 382 of your textbook.
2. Discuss how this communication could be more satisfying.

Example:

Adrian returns home from work. As Marion, who has also just arrived home after a busy day at the office, greets him at the door, he says, "I can't believe the rotten day I had. I missed my bus and had to walk five blocks to the subway. You wouldn't believe how crowded the subway platform was. It took fifteen minutes to even squeeze on a train. I got to work half an hour late. The boss chews me out and gives that new account to Jan, because I wasn't around, or so he says. You know Jan -- the perky little miss goody two shoes that you met at the Christmas party -- the one with a smile glued on her face. If that isn't enough, when I call to get tickets for the symphony they are already sold out, and now I come home and we haven't enough food in the house to make dinner."

Unsatisfying Communication:

Adrian is talking about all the bad things that happened to him.

Satisfying Communication:

Adrian should not dump so much of his bad day on Marion. He could talk about something good that did happen, ask her about her day, and maybe suggest they go out for dinner because they are both tired and there is not much food in the house.

1. Bethany says to Michael, "I try to talk to you about what it is like for me to be alone here all week while you are away on business but you never want to listen. Your life is so fast-paced you just can't understand how lonely I feel sometimes."

Satisfying Communication:
Unsatisfying Communication:

2. Marg is a freelance writer. She is very irritable today because she is working to meet a magazine deadline. Her husband, Andreas, asks about having dinner together. He offers to cook. She explodes, "Can't you see I'm busy and I'm not hungry!" Andreas storms out to the local bar for dinner.

Satisfying Communication:
Unsatisfying Communication:

3. Nancy has just returned from a visit to her doctor. She has received the results of some medical tests that indicate she may need more invasive tests for possible cancer. Her husband, returning home from work, asks how her day was. She says, "Fine."

Satisfying Communication:
Unsatisfying Communication:

4. Larry has been married to Shauna for a year. Their relationship has been rocky and riddled with arguments. A few months ago he began calling his ex-girlfriend long distance. Shauna discovers these calls on their phone bill and confronts Larry. She feels upset that he is rekindling this old relationship rather than trying to work through their difficulties. Larry agrees that he will not call his old girlfriend again and that he will make a commitment to work on his relationship with Shauna. However, when the next phone bill arrives, there are several more calls to his old girlfriend.

Satisfying Communication:
Unsatisfying Communication:

5. Mary Lee arrives home from work early. She has just been informed that day that her company is downsizing and her job will be eliminated within two months. She has been offered a small severance package. She has held this position for twelve years. When she gets home she is more quiet and reserved than usual. Her husband Brad doesn't seem to notice this and says, "So when are you going to have dinner ready? I want to watch that baseball game."

Satisfying Communication:
Unsatisfying Communication:

6. Anne and Jim have been married for four years. They are both avid classical music lovers. When they were first married they enjoyed going to concerts together. Afterwards they would go out for a drink and talk for a couple of hours about the performance. This is how they spent many of their weekends. Gradually they began to spend less and less time doing this. They were each busy with their jobs and friends. They didn't have time for lengthy conversations about their love of music.

Satisfying Communication:
Unsatisfying Communication:

7. Joseph and Sue have been saving to buy a house for three years. They anticipate being able to afford this in about one year. They have a joint savings account to which they both contribute. One night Joseph arrives home. "Have I got news," he says. "I saw this new car today. You know how ours is starting to rust a little. Well, I got a real deal on this baby. You won't believe it. It was a steal. Now, I realize that this means we will have to postpone our plans for that house next year but we really did need a new car. I know you are going to love it."

Satisfying Communication:
Unsatisfying Communication:

Part 2:

Instructions:

1. Give two examples of unsatisfying communication in your own relationship with your significant other or in the relationship of another couple that you know.
2. How could this communication be improved?

1.
2.

Activity 11.3: The Nature of Friendship

Objective:

1. To encourage you to apply the definitions of friendship to your own experience.

Instructions:

1. Reflect on three friendships:

   - one that was significant to you in your childhood
   - one that was significant to you in your adolescence
   - one that is significant to you now in adulthood

1. Answer the questions following the exercise.

Childhood Friendship:

Adolescent Friendship:

Adult Friendship:

What was most significant about each of these relationships?

What did you learn about yourself in these friendships?

How are these relationships similar?

How are these relationships different?

Activity 11.4: Relating to Colleagues

Objective:
1. To give you practice in relating effectively to colleagues.

Instructions:
1. In the following examples, what would you say?

1. Situation:

A new computer system has just been introduced in your organization. Unfortunately, this change has been implemented before employees have had adequate training. It is frustrating for staff and customers to wait while people try to get up to speed with the new system. Imagine that you area department manager in this organization. You approach the following people to discuss the problems with the new system. What might you say?

Talking to Boss:
Talking to Subordinate:
Talking to Colleagues:
Talking to Customers:

2. Situation:

A new product that was scheduled to hit the market just before Christmas has had production delays. You have just received this information today and you must relay it to the following people. What would you say?

Talking to Boss:
Talking to Subordinate:
Talking to Colleagues:
Talking to Customers:

3. Situation:

You are the manager of a local bank branch. Early this morning the computer network crashed and you have not been able to get on-line all day. It is mid-afternoon and the stress is rising. Bank tellers are unable to access their computers. Customers are irate because they cannot get their necessary financial information. As you try to deal with the situation what would you say to the following people?

Talking to Boss:
Talking to Subordinate:

Talking to Colleagues:
Talking to Customers:

4. Situation:

You manage the service department in a large car dealership. Lately customers have been complaining about delays in getting their cars serviced. Customer service is touted as the highest priority in the dealership and yet you are getting mixed messages from your boss, the president of the company. He has a pet project that has been taking priority over customer needs. When he needs something, everything else has to be put on hold. Cars that were to be serviced in one hour are still waiting after four hours. In approaching the following people what would you say?

Talking to Boss:
Talking to Subordinate:
Talking to Colleagues:
Talking to Customers:

Activity 11.5: Enhancing Leadership Skills

Objective:
1. To help you identify the skills and qualities of effective leaders.

Instructions:
1. Think of three leaders that you admire.
2. For each leader list the qualities, characteristics, or skills that make them good leaders.
3. Answer the questions at the end of the exercise.

Leader 1

Leader 2

Leader 3

1. What can you learn from these leaders to be a more effective leader yourself?

2. What skills or behaviours might you practise to enhance your own leadership capabilities?

3. Imagine a situation in the present or future where you might be in a leadership role. What would be the three most important qualities or skills you would like to bring to that role? Why?

Activity 11.6: Observing Task and Relationship Functions

Objectives:

1. To identify task and maintenance roles in group discussions.

Instructions:

1. Choose a hot topic to discuss from the following list or select a topic of your own choosing.

   Abortion

   Capital Punishment

   Legalization of Marijuana

   Separation of Quebec from Canada

   Cloning or Reproduction Technologies

1. Select six students to debate this topic in a fishbowl setting (sitting in a circle in the middle of the room) for 10-15 minutes.
2. Be sure your debate involves proposals for actions relative to the issue.
3. The rest of the class will act as observers attending to different roles played by group members -- task and relationship.
4. Observers should record their observations on the Observer sheet (being as specific as possible about who said what and what was said) and be prepared to give verbal feedback at the end of the activity.

Observer Guide

NAME:						
Task Roles						
Institute new ideas						
Provide information						
Seek information						
Seek opinions						
Offer opinions						
Elaborate						
Evaluate						
Energize						
Relationship Roles						
Encourage						
Harmonize						
Compromise						
Be a gatekeeper						

DIFFICULT POSITION 11

Daniel is the adopted son of Wendy and Carl. He grew up thinking he was the natural son of his parents who told him of his adoption only when he was sixteen years old. Almost immediately Daniel began to wonder about his biological parents. Wendy and Carl knew Daniel's biological father, but had always told Daniel they didn't know about his parents. The lie concerned them deeply, but they knew Daniel's father was a troubled man who had spent time in prison, and they were afraid to tell Daniel about him, fearing he might go looking for him. Daniel suspected his adopted parents knew, and they knew he suspected. Wendy was hurt that Daniel seemed resentful of them. She loved him just as much as she did her natural children and wanted to shield him from the pain of knowing his real father. She was afraid of what he might feel knowing his father had a criminal record. Daniel felt entitled to know, but he didn't want to hurt his adopted parents. After two years of this, the strain began to be more than Wendy could take. She couldn't decide what to do, and Carl didn't know either. For some reason, Daniel no longer looked up to Carl as he once had now that he knew he was not his biological son. Wendy was hurt, afraid, and ashamed of having lied. Daniel was alternately resentful and ashamed. They had always been so close, but now they seemed to be pulling apart.

INSTRUCTIONS

What should Wendy do? What would you do? How would you communicate your feelings in this situation? What challenges is the family facing in terms of the three dimensions of adaptability, cohesion, and communication?

Discuss the situation in small groups and record your discussion.

Exercise 11.1: Learning Objective: General Review (**TRUE/FALSE**)

Instructions: Identify the following statements as either true or false.

1. Common-law relationships are as stable on average as traditional marriages. ( )

2. A *blended family* is one with parents of differing ethnic backgrounds. ( )

3. The higher the degree of *enmeshment* in families, the happier they are. ( )

4. In the friendships of the elderly, negative self-disclosure tends to decrease. ( )

5. Fear of technology is as common among men as among women. ( )

6. Projections for the future suggest that with continuing advances in technology face-to-face communication will become unnecessary. ( )

7. Synergy is the combination of male and female characteristics in management. ( )

8. Grapevine messages in the workplace are commonly highly inaccurate. ( )

9. Childhood attachments formed between the ages of four and nine are the least selfish and self-centred. ( )

10. All forms of gang membership in adolescence are socially unacceptable. ( )

11. According to John Gottman, *contempt* in a relationship is the best predictor of divorce. ( )

12. The first qualification for leadership is a capacity for empathy. ( )

13. The chief cause of friendships ending in adulthood is political disagreements. ( )

14. Over half of all white-collar workers are seriously cyberphobic. ( )

15. *Family of origin* refers to the imaginary ancestral family of all human beings. ( )

16. An extended family may include as members individuals with no kinship or marriage ties within the family. ( )

17. *Natural family* refers to common-law couples with children. ( )

18. Sibling conflict can often be the most intense we experience. ( )

Exercise 11.2: Learning Objective: General Review (**FILL-IN-THE-BLANKS**)

Instructions: Fill in the blanks using the appropriate term or terms from the following list.

natural family	family cohesion	agape	outward communication
blended family	family communication	upward communication	leadership
single-parent family	eros	downward communication	sexual harassment
extended family	ludis		
family of origin	storge	horizontal communication	
family adaptability	mania		

1. My brothers and I all had our peculiarities I admit, but they didn't seem especially strange to us because that's how things were in our______________________. If you knew our parents and how we lived, it would all make perfect sense to you.

2. In our company __________________ just wasn't safe because the supervisors didn't trust or respect the rank-and-file workers. All we could do was gripe about things during our breaks. At least we had our ______________________ among ourselves. It made some of the insulting____________________________of orders easier to take.

3. Trina was Bruce's daughter by his second wife Melissa who was now married to Bruce's former supervisor, Frederick, whose son, William, was dating Trina. Trina liked her new mother, Marian, her father's third wife, but she sometimes missed Theresa, her own mother, her father's first wife. She didn't get along with Melissa at all because she disapproved of her seeing William, and she sometimes fought with Marian's children, Timothy and Ethan, by her first husband, Henry, who was teaching Trina's sociology course at the university. On the phone that night, Trina told Theresa, her biological mother, that living in a __________________ could sometimes be a little confusing.

4. Paula was aware that Tom was dating one of his former students who was still attending classes at the college. She disapproved of romantic relationships with students, and seeing the two of them together made her uncomfortable. She thought the college's____________________ policy should have some kind of language suggesting disapproval of such relationships, but the personnel officer said that it was not a matter of law if it was consensual.

5. Homer came in from the barn and sat at the kitchen table. His wife Mary was getting some coffee ready and they talked while they were waiting for the boys to get in from harvesting. They all lived and worked together miles from anyone else. They were all a sort of prototype of a ____________________.

6. I used to call Mike "tio" or "uncle," but the truth is he was no relation to me. He was my father's old army buddy. Mike meant as much to me as any relative. He was a part of our ____________________ along with grandma and my father's three sisters.

7. We always had good_________________________ and talked freely about our feelings and needs. We managed to roll with the punches over the years and make changes because we had enough________________________ to accept challenges. We stuck together and stayed in touch even after we moved away to find work. My family had quite a bit of ________________________.

8. Going to school all day and working all night left little time for Belinda to spend with the children. In her _____________________ it was all she could do to earn enough to keep them fed and in a good preschool program.

9. ______ is sexual love based on the pursuit of beauty and pleasure. There is an element of it in __________ love, of course, which looks upon love as a game, but there is also an element of it in __________, which swings between contrary intensities and is often quite serious. Even down-to-earth__________, which is concerned mostly with compatibility and shared interests, has some of it. The love one has for old friends called______________ is different, there's not much physical desire in it, and sacrificial and selfless love like __________ would appear to be the opposite. But who knows? Love is not easy to label.

10. I think a lack of _______________ caused us to lose confidence and motivation, and without someone to provide guidance, the________________ we needed with our clients was never all it should have been. We needed to learn from those we served, but we spent too much time fighting among ourselves and lost our market.

Exercise 11.3: Learning Objective: General Review (**MULTIPLE CHOICE**)

Instructions: Choose the best answer for each question below.

1. The three basic dimensions of the circumplex model of family interaction are

   a. attitudes, beliefs, values
   b. adaptability, cohesion, communication
   c. chaotic, rigid, flexible
   d. interdependent, dependent, autonomous

2. The stage of childhood friendship characterized by conditional reciprocity is

   a. momentary playmates
   b. one-way assistance
   c. fair-weather friend
   d. mutual intimacy

3. Polls suggest the most common anxiety about technology in the workplace is

   a. information overload
   b. being forced to constantly learn new skills
   c. diminished face-to-face contact
   d. loss of privacy

4. The informal communication of information among peers in an organization are

   a. quality circles
   b. gatekeeper messages
   c. grapevine messages
   d. downward communications

5. The most typical method of handling sibling conflict is

   a. minor physical violence
   b. verbal abuse
   c. withdrawal
   d. manipulation

6. Communicating a complaint about a colleague to his or her supervisor would be an instance of

   a. upward communication
   b. downward communication
   c. grapevine message
   d. enhanced followership

7. All of the following statements are true except

   a. single-parent families are now most commonly a lifestyle choice
   b. single-parent families are headed overwhelmingly by women
   c. common-law relationships are much less stable than traditional marriages
   d. the highest rate of marital violence is in couples between the ages of 18 and 24

8. All of the following statements are true except

   a. one of the chief causes of ending adult friendships is physical separation
   b. studies suggest that "people problems" are the most common workplace problem
   c. Quebec has the highest per capita level of common-law relationships in Canada
   d. over half of all Canadian children are cared for in the homes of non-relatives

9. All of the following are communication warning signs identified by John Gottam except

   a. criticism
   b. contempt
   c. distracting
   d. defensiveness

10. All of the following may be considered instances of sexual harassment except

   a. sexist jokes frequently repeated to someone who objects to them
   b. an offer to promote a coworker in return for sexual favours
   c. the display of nude pictures in an office cubicle
   d. a consensual relationship between two coworkers in a supervisory capacity

11. All of the following statements about workplace technology are true except

   a. new technologies can blur the old distinction between "home" and "office"
   b. video-conferencing may polarize opinions more often than face-to-face meetings
   c. training can be as important as hardware when introducing new technologies
   d. new technologies ensure the production of superior goods and services